Advising the Rulers

Advising the Rulers

Edited by
William Plowden

Basil Blackwell

Copyright © Royal Institute of Public Administration 1987

First published 1987

Basil Blackwell Ltd
108 Cowley Road, Oxford, OX4 1JF, UK

Basil Blackwell Inc.
432 Park Avenue South, Suite 1503
New York, NY 10016, USA

British Library Cataloguing in Publication Data

Advising the rulers.
1. Policy sciences
I. Plowden, William
351.007'2   H97

ISBN 0–631–14675–X

Library of Congress Cataloging in Publication Data

Advising the rulers.
Includes index.
1. Political consultants.   2. Comparative government.
I. Plowden, William.
JF331.A38   1987   351.009'3   86–32671
ISBN 0–631–14675–X

Typeset in 10/12pt Ehrhardt
by Cambrian Typesetters, Frimley, Camberley, Surrey
Printed in Great Britain by T. J. Press Ltd, Padstow

Contents

Preface

In the concluding chapter of this volume, Professor Yehezkel Dror argues, as he has done elsewhere, that in the modern world the importance of 'rulers' – that is, those at the head of governments – is so great that one of the most effective ways of improving the capability of governments is to improve the ways in which rulers are advised and supported. The papers in this volume consider the arrangements for advising and supporting rulers in six countries in particular – Australia, Canada, France, West Germany, the United Kingdom and the United States. They thus encompass presidential and prime ministerial systems, federal and unitary states, European and non-European experience, countries sharing the Anglo-Saxon tradition and those quite distant from it.

The papers were presented at a conference which brought together participants from these six countries and also from Israel, Portugal, Spain and the Organization for Economic Cooperation and Development. The Conference was held on 22–5 November 1984 at Wiston House, the Wilton Park Conference Centre at Steyning, Sussex. It was jointly organized by the European Centre for Political Studies at the Policy Studies Institute and the Royal Institute of Public Administration.

The main aim of the conference was to pool, compare and, if possible, learn from the several experiences discussed. The organizers were looking both for descriptions of current practice in each country and also for analyses of trends, problems and possible future developments. The structure of this book derives from the structure of the conference. Each of the six countries was discussed in turn, with the discussion opened by the presentation of a paper given in all cases except that of France by an academic. These presentations were followed by a commentary from a 'practitioner' from the country in question in all cases except Australia, for which no practitioner was available. These presentations form Part I of this book.

The main contributions at the conference were thus designed to balance the theoretical insights and in-depth knowledge of academics with the practical, first-hand experience of people who had worked in the governmental systems studied. Not surprisingly, the practitioners often had something to add to the picture drawn by the academic, and did not always agree with the emphasis of the latter. (Reciprocally, the academics felt that the practitioners' very closeness to events sometimes hampered their full understanding of the processes in which they were involved.) The rest of the participants were similarly divided between academics and practitioners, and their views were correspondingly varied.

After discussing each of the six countries in turn, the conference moved on to a group of common issues – the different types of advice which rulers might need or be offered, the significance of advice on matters of economic or foreign policy, the balance of advantage between institutionalized and informal advisory systems, working relationships between advisers and others. A final session was introduced with some general comments by Professor Dror.

These five cross-cutting discussions are reflected by Part II of this book, but this does not claim to be a precise record of these discussions. The five chapters rather use the conference proceedings as a starting point for more wide-ranging comments. In his contribution Professor Dror has also drawn on his own extensive work on policy-making and advice-giving in government.

It is clear from the papers, as it was clear during the conference, that the subject of advice to rulers is one where transnational comparisons are both feasible and, probably, useful – at least within the relatively limited range of countries in question. How advisers should handle the major specialized fields of foreign and economic policy (by inference, how they should relate to the specialized bureaucracies in departments of foreign affairs and of finance), how they should deal with the permanent bureaucracy in general, how far and in what way their activities should be structured and institutionalized, were topics on which representatives of every country had something relevant to contribute. Whatever the difficulties of making useful comparisons between whole systems of government, the personal requirements of rulers seem to be sufficiently similar for exchanges of experience to be both meaningful and instructive. In fact, precisely because it may often be assumed that arrangements for helping rulers are in some sense too personal to be thought about and developed systematically, comparisons are probably all the more useful. Comparing and sharing experiences can show that this assumption is mistaken: it is possible to infer some general principles about the kinds of arrangements which work or do not work, or about the conditions that must be satisfied if advisers are to be genuinely effective.

The papers presented at the conference naturally drew on past experience and arrangements in place up to November 1984. They have not been revised to take account of developments since then.

The costs of the conference were met by grants from the European Cultural Foundation and the Economic and Social Research Council, to whom the organizers are grateful. They are also particularly grateful to Virginia Crowe, then working at the RIPA, who virtually single-handed managed the organization of the conference from start to finish.

PREFACE

ix

Participants at the conference were: Yossi Beilin (Secretary to the Cabinet, Israel); Dr Tessa Blackstone (Deputy Education Officer, Inner London Education Authority); Professor Colin Campbell SJ (Georgetown University, Washington, DC); Brian Cartledge CMG (Cabinet Office, London); Virginia Crowe (RIPA); Professor Yehezkel Dror (Professor of Political Science, The Hebrew University of Jerusalem); David Hancock (Permanent Secretary, Department of Education and Science, London); The Rt Hon. Lord Hunt of Tanworth GCB (Secretary of the Cabinet, 1973–9); Nevil Johnson (Nuffield College, Oxford); Professor George Jones (London School of Economics and Political Science); Dr Rolf Kaiser (Bundeskanzleramt, Bonn); Marie-Ange Laumonier (Bureau du Premier Ministre, Paris); Dr Howard Machin (London School of Economics and Political Science); Professor Renate Mayntz (University of Köln, West Germany); Professor Roger Morgan (European Centre for Political Studies, Policy Studies Institute, London); Jean-Pierre Mounier (Institut International d'Administration Publique, Paris); Peter Mountfield (Under-Secretary, HM Treasury, London); Ravi Kapil (Organization for Economic Cooperation and Development, Paris); Dr Yanni Papanicolaou (Director, Prime Minister's Office, Athens); David Pascall (BP Group of Companies); The Hon. Michael Pitfield QC (The Senate, Ottawa); Dr William Plowden (Director-General RIPA); Dr Roger Porter (Director, Office of Policy Development, The White House, Washington, DC); Pedro Salgado (Chef du Cabinet du Secretaire d'Etat à la Presidence du Conseil des Ministres, Lisbon); Dr Dietmar Seiler (Bundesakademie für Offenliche Verwaltung im Bundesministerium des Innern, Bonn); Professor Colin Seymour-Ure (University of Kent at Canterbury); Professor Stephen J. Wayne (The George Washington University, Washington, DC); Dr Patrick Weller (Griffith University, Australia).

Roger Morgan
William Plowden

PART I

Academic and
Practitioner Views

1

West Germany

Renate Mayntz

Discussions about policy advice often start implicitly from a normatively biased conception of the political decision process, which assumes that it is the prime function of the top executive to make policy decisions. Descriptively, of course, this is not so. Crisis management, the building of political support or the resolution of conflicts between dissenting factions are all strong contenders for the title of 'prime function' – not to mention the more expressive tasks of political representation and management of a public image. For all these tasks the top executive may be in need of advice, but not, strictly speaking, of policy advice alone. The importance of policy advice in particular, and the arrangements made for its generation and delivery, will vary according to how centralized policy-making functions are at the top level of government. An evaluation of the existing arrangements for policy-making within a government should accordingly be prefaced by a realistic assessment of the needs for such advice.

Top Executive Involvement in Policy-making and the Need for Policy Advice

Policy advice should not only be distinguished from other kinds of advice, but also from two other types of communication which, though analytically distinct, tend to merge with it at the boundary. Advice, which essentially contains recommendations for action, is distinct from mere information – which, incidentally, does not mean that information is less important than advice; the contrary is often true. Data banks, reports from lower level agencies, statistical records etc. provide the essential raw material out of which advice is fashioned. On the other hand, advice is distinct from a request because, although a recommendation for action, advice is supposedly in the interests of the receiver rather than the giver. The real-life boundaries between these analytically distinct categories are, of course, fluid. Requests sometimes come clothed as advice, advice is not always free from self-interest and mere information can constitute a direct call to action. Since, moreover, policy cannot be separated from politics, decisions often have multiple functions – and so does the advice upon which they are based. It is, therefore, anything but self-evident that policy advice is a distinct entity, or that it plays a focal role for the top political executive and that organizationally and procedurally distinct arrangements for its provision can and should be made. The existence of such specialized advisory units might equally be seen as a mere institutionalized reflection of a legitimating ideology – the ideology of the rational political actor as public welfare maximizer.

With these cautionary remarks in mind, let us first try to assess briefly the nature and extent of top executive involvement in policy-making in West Germany.[1] In this it will not be sufficient to consider the chancellor alone, since leadership functions are constitutionally accorded not to one, but to three major political actors: the chancellor, the ministers heading the operative departments and the cabinet as a group. The chancellor enjoys the constitutional power to formulate general policy guidelines, though he may not make decisions in matters which belong to the domain of any of the ministries.[2] Every minister is personally and fully responsible for the activities of his department; within his sphere of jurisdiction, no minister can be given specific orders. As for the cabinet, all proposals submitted by the federal government to parliament must first obtain cabinet approval.

Of the three constitutional principles – the principle of leadership by the chancellor (*Kanzlerprinzip*), by the cabinet (*Kabinettsprinzip*) and by the departmental ministers (*Ressortprinzip*)[3] – none is so fully realized and jealously guarded as the third. The bulk of policy development, the substantive work of initiating, drafting, refining and building consensus for a policy decision, is performed by the federal departments. Since the German constitution assigns most legislative functions to the federal level, while policy implementation lies largely in the hands of the individual states, and since most subsequently enacted legislation is developed, even if not necessarily always initiated, by the federal bureaucracy, the ministries are organizations with rather specialized functions. In fact, the operative units of the ministries are officially responsible for the development of policy proposals within their respective substantive domains. Even in terms of working time, policy-making and programme development are their major concerns.[4] There are some programmes which the federal departments administer directly, mainly financial incentive and subvention programmes, but programme management and implementation have never been their predominant tasks. To overstate the case slightly, the federal departments function as large policy staffs under the leadership of the ministers.

Chancellors tend to use their authority to formulate policy guidelines quite selectively, at least with respect to designating a decision formally as a 'policy guideline' according to paragraph 65 of the constitution. As decision-maker, the chancellor is most actively involved in crisis management. Most routine decisions are of a sectoral nature and belong to the domain of a particular minister. Only where sectoral problems become so acute as to produce a threat to the system in general must the chancellor become personally involved. The chancellor's most important function is not to make substantive policy decisions himself, but to manage the decision-making process and to see to it that the often diffuse and fragmented opinions form in time into a concrete decision.

The cabinet is expected to function as a collective decision-making body. Ministers are held to abide by cabinet decisions and not to oppose them publicly even if they were themselves outvoted. However, the function of the cabinet is limited by the chancellor's right to formulate general policy guidelines on the one hand, and by the independent jurisdictions of the departmental ministers on the other. In many cases, the formal requirement of obtaining cabinet approval is fulfilled by circulating a proposal in written form to the ministers and the chancellor who, normally acting upon the advice of their officials, sign it as requested. In these cases, informal agreement among all concerned has been reached beforehand, so that cabinet approval is a mere formality. Matters which actually get on to the cabinet agenda are those of greater importance or greater urgency. Even here, however, informal consensus has in many cases been achieved beforehand. Most cabinet decisions should, therefore, be described as decisions approved, rather than made, by government collectively. The chancellor as cabinet chairman must manage especially those relatively few, but important decisions which reach the cabinet without being already fully agreed upon.

This discussion has established then that in West Germany the ministers heading the major departments must be included in a consideration of top level policy-makers. However, they are not *primarily* policy-makers. Their role in the process of policy development is a limited and very specific one, with a focus on giving selective political impulses and selectively supporting proposals developed by the ministerial bureaucracy. The chancellor's involvement in policy-making is even more selective and this reflects upon his and the ministers' need for information and advice. Detailed substantive information, the 'facts and figures' behind a policy proposal, is only called for where a decision is politically sensitive or remains controversial as it reaches cabinet. Advice in this context should emphasize the political costs and consequences of adopting specific courses of action; it should be a kind of advice that presupposes 'strategic' information about the preferences and action dispositions of major participants in the policy process. It is against the background of such requirements that arrangements for providing policy advice must be evaluated.

Turning now to the organizational and procedural arrangements designed to meet the needs of ministers and the chancellor for policy advice, one general feature stands out. In West Germany there are hardly any advisory staffs *outside* the regular ministerial bureaucracy which serve the top executive *directly*. The chancellor is supported in all of his tasks by the Chancellor's Office (*Bundeskanzleramt*, BK), an administrative unit with a long tradition. He does not command the help of any special units for policy analysis or of official advisers in a staff capacity outside the BK. Staff help at the top of the federal departments is also very limited. An institution like the French ministerial *cabinet* is unknown in German ministries, nor do we find here counterparts of that large and ill-defined circle of personal advisers typical of the American system. Whether or not it is an expression of the German inclination to work through *existing* (line) agencies rather than creating new ones as new tasks come up, this institutional set-up has important consequences both for the givers and the receivers of policy advice.

Sources of Policy Advice for Ministers

Leadership at the departmental level includes the minister and two or more state secretaries. One of them, the parliamentary state secretary, as he is known, serves specifically to assist the minister with his genuinely political tasks and in his relations to parliament and party. The minister has at his disposal a personal assistant, usually a younger civil servant, a press and public relations assistant and a small office (or an official) for cabinet and parliamentary matters. There is also a ministerial bureau which takes care of the more routine clerical tasks. Over time, the number of persons serving ministers directly in a staff capacity has tended to increase,[5] but it is still very small. Special assistance and advisory functions for the departmental leadership and advisory functions for the departmental leadership are sometimes rendered by a traditional line unit dealing with *Grundsatzfragen* (leading decisions). Besides, since the middle of the 1960s, a number of new units have been created which directly assist ministers in their decision-taking functions.[6] Such units, again normally rather small, are sometimes, but by no means universally, organized as top level staffs. Others are embedded in the line organization, that is, formally subordinate to the divisional leadership, but in fact working directly for the top executive. Such units fulfil supportive functions of a primarily political nature; they can be used as a task force to monitor critical decision processes, to collect information in preparation for an anticipated controversy in cabinet or parliament, and even to develop initiatives that might bolster the popularity of the minister.

One example of such top level staff can be found in the Foreign Office. This unit, designated as a planning staff, is attached to the minister directly. With its ten members it is unusually large. Its members are exclusively career civil servants and civil service rules prevent the temporary recruitment of outsiders, even though this would seem desirable. The planning staff prepares expert analyses, action proposals and short evaluations for the minister on a variety of topics, partly upon his request, but occasionally on their own initiative. The staff does not have at its disposal sufficient funds to commission contract research or employ costly outside experts, though outsiders are invited for discussion. Under these conditions, the staff's advisory capacity is obviously quite limited. Nor are there any other special arrangements for obtaining policy advice in the foreign policy field. The Foreign Office does not make much use of advisory boards, nor of the work of existing research institutes such as that which the German Association for Foreign Policy (*Deutsche Gesellschaft für Auswärtige Politik e.V*) maintains in Bonn.[7] Outside information and policy advice seem to come mainly from persons and organizations with which the department maintains operative relations.

Other departments often have smaller top level staffs, but make more intensive use of advisory councils and scientific expertise. In fact, the present system of councils and scientific advice is so extensive as to provoke critical queries and comments both in the press and in parliament.[8] Gerd Rauhaus mentions that in 1970, 264 advisory councils were counted;[9] in 1976, the federal government identified nearly 100 more.[10] In 1980, some 1,500 expert reports are said to have been commissioned by the government.[11] These figures sound impressive. They reflect the fact that the federal ministries are the most important policy-makers in the German political system, and it is therefore they who collect and process most of the information relevant to policy decisions. But Germany also has a long tradition of advisory bodies established to provide expert advice on specific policy matters to the bureaucracy, dating back to the beginning of the nineteenth century.[12] These advisory bodies are composed of representatives of special interests as well as independent scientists. They may provide some scientific information, but their main purpose is to articulate the demands and wishes of special groups and to supply situational information relevant to the development of policy proposals.

There is, then, a plethora of advisory bodies and scientific consultants, but by and large they do not address the head of the ministry directly. A few advisory councils are immediately attached to the departmental executive – such as the scientific advisory boards of the ministries of finance and of economic affairs – but most of them report to a division, sub-division or even section. Even where, as sometimes happens, the minister formally heads such as commission, he is rarely a direct discussion partner. This lower level organizational location is an indicator of the function attributed to these bodies: they are not intended to give political advice, but stand in a service relationship to senior civil servants. Most of the advice which reaches the departmental executive from these councils and other forms of scientific expertise has therefore normally passed through departmental filters which screen and condense the material to draw conclusions for policy decisions.

The bulk of the policy advice received by federal ministers comes from the senior civil servants and the line organization of their department who also assist them in their other tasks. This does not necessarily spell a shortcoming. If senior civil servants possess sufficient expertise in their field of work and if, in addition, outside contacts make them sensitive to existing contextual constraints, coalition chances etc., they will be able to advise their ministers not only on the substantive aspects of specific policy proposals, but also on their more political implications, such as their potential for generating conflict, for meeting with support or with resistance. In fact, German senior civil servants do possess these qualities to a significant degree.[13] Moreover, the politicization that has taken place, especially among the higher ranks of the federal bureaucracy, effectively prevents their being too professional in outlook to appreciate the more political aspects of the decisions the minister has to take. But for all this, it is normally only a relatively small circle, even among senior officials, whose advice a minister seeks over and beyond the matters they must routinely bring to his attention. In particular, and for all their politicization, he will rarely find among his officials an adviser on party politics.

The dependence of the federal ministers on the ministerial bureaucracy for advice and for other kinds of support and assistance requires a relation of trust, which may be hard to establish where the advisers cannot be freely chosen. This problem is mitigated by the institution of 'political civil servants', a special group of civil servants defined by rank and position who can be temporarily retired by the minister at any time.[14] This legal possibility is mainly used when there is a change in government, especially if this also involves a change in the majority party or coalition.[15] No minister is therefore forced to work with state secretaries or a divisional leadership whom he cannot trust. But while he has absolute freedom of dismissal as regards these ranks, his freedom of recruitment is much less, since normal civil service criterial apply to the selection and appointment of political civil servants. Similar restrictions hold for the appointment of personal assistants, bureau chiefs and even secretaries, though the criteria to be met for appointment are less stringent in the case of salaried employees.

Institutionalized Sources of Policy Advice for the Chancellor and Government

While the ministers receive policy advice individually from their departments, the cabinet as such is not served by any special office or unit. Necessary secretarial and administrative tasks connected with the preparation and conduct of cabinet meetings are fulfilled by the Chancellor's Office. There are some advisory bodies and policy research institutes which serve the government collectively, but the influence of these bodies on government policy is mostly rather indirect and it would be difficult to trace specific policy decisions to their advice. The – temporary – Commission for Economic and Social Change, for instance, has produced numerous reports based on scientific investigations involving mainly problems of domestic policy.[16] The government-financed Research Institute for International and Security Policy, with an interdisciplinary staff of more than 100 specialists, produces analyses which provide valuable background knowledge, but do not make recommendations for action in specific situations. The institute has access to confidential government documents and most of its reports remain confidential in turn, but the choice of topics is determined by a board on which representatives of the federal government are only a minority.[17] Yet another example is provided by the – permanent – Economic Advisory Council, an independent group consisting of five well-known economists. This council must report once a year to the government on its evaluation of present and future economic developments, but though of obvious policy relevance, the council may not formally derive specific recommendations from its evaluation.[18]

Since economic and fiscal policy are those areas which in many countries became the first objects of systematic planning efforts, it is worth emphasizing that even here the West German system has relatively little by way of a specialized infrastructure for policy analysis and advice. There is the Economic Advisory Council just referred to, and there is also a joint federal–state financial planning council. This council makes budgetary recommendations to the cabinet, but its voice does not appear to carry much weight. The federal budget is prepared in an essentially bottom-up procedure in which the Ministry of Finance plays the role of coordinator and ensures that projected expenditures are balanced as far as possible by anticipated revenues. The draft budget is discussed in cabinet, which must vote on it before presenting it to parliament. The budget is a classical line-item budget in which programme categories are hardly visible. There also exists, it is true, a system of functional categories to which line-item expenditures are related, but this functional budget is included for informational purposes only and is not the object of explicit budget decisions. Since 1967, the federal budget has been supplemented by a middle-range financial plan; it extends three years beyond the year of the next budget and is updated and extended annually.[19] The main function of this financial plan is indicative rather than prescriptive, and it has not been integrated, either procedurally or substantively, with policy planning. This, as well as the fact that programme budgeting has never been introduced in West Germany, may have lowered the need for special analytical capacity and advice, but the main reason for its weak development seems to be the traditional strength of the bureaucratic line organization.

The most important institutionalized source of policy advice for the head of government is undoubtedly the Chancellor's Office (BK). From the time of the monarchy German chancellors have been served by a special office, and since the years of the Weimar Republic this office has been more than a mere secretariat. Even under Hitler, the *Reichskanzlei* had two divisions and was formally expected, among other things, to supply information and policy advice.[20] Today's BK has departmental rank. In addition to its service functions it has some specific jurisdictions; thus it is responsible for the Federal Intelligence Service. The BK is directly subordinate to the chancellor. The chief of the BK is normally a state secretary and in three cases – Westrick under Erhard, Ehmke under Brandt and now Schäuble under Kohl – he has been given the rank and title of a federal minister. In addition, one or more ministers of state, charged with special tasks or liaison functions, may be attached to the office. In 1960, the BK had some 300 members, civil servants, salaried employees and workers altogether. Its size increased sharply with the advent of the Social–Liberal government in 1969, rising to 477 in 1980 and remaining virtually unchanged since then.[21] However, only 126 (as of 1984) of these are higher civil servants; the group of potential advisers in the BK thus does not number more than 50 or 60.

At the time of writing, the office has the following six divisions:

1 legal and administrative matters;
2 foreign policy and international relations;
3 domestic policy, social policy and planning;
4 economic and fiscal policy;
5 social and political analyses and communication;
6 intelligence.

As can be seen, the internal organization of the office replicates the structure of the government, with the sections in divisions 2 – 4 covering the domains of the various ministries; they are therefore called 'mirror-image sections'. Owing to this mirror-image structure, the office can provide the chancellor with expert knowledge and advice on all major policy problems, making him independent of the expertise concentrated in the federal departments. In this function the BK enjoys a monopoly, at least formally, since the chancellor has no other institutionalized sources of policy advice. However, two things should be emphasized at the outset: first, that the BK has more than just this advisory function, and there can be shifts in the relative importance of its various tasks; and secondly, the extent to which the BK's advisory capacity is used can change with the situational needs and leadership style of an individual chancellor.

The office has traditionally fulfilled general assistance functions and served as a secretariat of the cabinet. General assistance tasks include the drafting of speeches and answers to letters for the chancellor, commenting on news items which have caught his attention, issuing invitations to people and setting up meetings for him, or collecting information on specific points or issues. The search for information which the chancellor may need or has asked for is often the dominant – and most time-consuming – concern of BK officials. Attempts are made to keep information clearly distinct from advice. Thus, in briefs for the chancellor, information and evaluation/advice are to be treated in separate sections.

As the secretariat of the cabinet, the BK organizes the input of proposals subject to cabinet action, circulates proposals that need no discussion and prepares the agenda for cabinet meetings. Obviously all this can be performed as an administrative routine, but it may also be the starting point for the development of advisory functions and even for more ambitious attempts to guide the policy-making process.

An advisory function that grows directly out of these tasks is the customary preparation of evaluations of proposals coming up for cabinet decision, whether by way of routine circulation or direct treatment at the weekly meeting. These comments do not treat substantive matters at length, nor are the likely long-range and side effects of a policy or the effectiveness of a proposed measure highlighted in these evaluations. Considerable attention is paid instead to the political implications of a specific proposal: who might be hurt if it is accepted, where resistance is likely to arise, how the decision will 'look' to the general public. Given his particular role in managing the policy process, this is in fact the kind of advice *the chancellor* needs with respect to policy proposals coming from the departments. It would be a misunderstanding of his particular role if, with the help of his office and the professional expertise it can muster, the chancellor attempted to style himself as the master policy-maker. On the other hand, each chancellor normally has one or a few policy areas in which he is particularly interested and/or professionally competent. At the very least, he has his own pet projects, issues, or measures with which he identifies personally, and in these areas at least he may ask for detailed information and substantive policy advice.

The formal task of organizing the decision-making process, which culminates in cabinet meetings, can easily be extended to a more encompassing substantive coordination, and to attempts at government-wide policy planning. It was the Social–Liberal coalition which tried to develop this potential of the Chancellor's Office after it took power in 1969. So-called 'planning commissioners' were appointed in all federal departments and a reporting system was developed which obliged them to inform the Chancellor's Office routinely and in a standardized form of all projects which at some later time would come up for cabinet and/or *Bundesrat* approval.[22] The system was meant to help maintain a balance between the departments and aid the early detection of areas of conflict or redundant projects. Such a watchdog function is indeed crucial to a system where policy is largely developed within departments that guard their autonomy jealously and where the chancellor and his office cannot therefore aspire to a fully-fledged and systematic control of the policy-making process. A side effect of this reporting system, which soon became its most important function, was to enable the BK to coordinate departmental projects and fit them into a timetable of government activities over the whole legislative period. Coupled with the agenda setting function for cabinet meetings, the information thus gained could not only be used to urge the departments to keep to planned deadlines, but also provided the opportunity to establish priorities, a genuine function of the chancellor as manager of the policy-making process.

During the first years of the Social–Liberal coalition, the intervention opportunities offered by this coordination procedure were fully used, but this soon provoked resistance and increasingly even hostility on the part of the ministries who saw their autonomy threatened. The interventionist stance of the BK was curbed after a few years when Willy Brandt returned as chancellor for the second time, but those functions of the new reporting system which are of a more advisory nature have been retained. The information provided routinely by the departments is computerized; today the data bank contains information on several thousand projects. This stored information is used to put together a selection of some hundred projects which constitute the working programme of the government for the legislative period. Of course this listing is, *per se*, only an element of indicative planning, and one that might need frequent revisions, but it can, if the chancellor so wishes, be used to alert him to future decision needs. Under Helmut Schmidt this 'need for decision' had already become formalized, turning the erstwhile coordination procedure into yet another instrument of policy advice for the head of government. Today efforts are being made to integrate this instrument with the routine agenda setting for the cabinet to ensure that action is taken.

Aside from its various advisory functions, the Chancellor's Office can also serve to carry the chancellor's point of view into the departments – a use to which Adenauer had already put the office quite successfully. Such attempts to exert influence stem from the routine participation of officials from the Chancellor's Office in the preparation of major proposals to be put before the cabinet by one or more of the ministries. The representative from the Chancellor's Office, usually coming from the appropriate 'mirror-image section' and hence well qualified in the matter under discussion, normally plays an observer's role, evaluating specific political aspects of the decisions which gradually take shape, with respect to the conflicts they might produce if formally adopted and put into effect, for example. But obviously this observer's role can be used in the early stages of departmental policy development to push for a decision that would be in line with the chancellor's preferences. The chances of exerting such influence rest on the possibility of mobilizing the head of the BK who may raise the issue with a recalcitrant official's superior. One opportunity for this is the Monday morning meeting of all state secretaries with the head of BK. Thus, a higher degree of centralization in policy-making can result than the principle of departmental autonomy and the chancellor's limitation to the formulation of guidelines would seem to permit. Departmental officials, of course, are wary of such attempts and tend to reject them as soon as they believe that the chancellor's personal authority no longer stands behind the BK's representatives. The BK's chances of influencing negotiation and exerting informal pressure are thus a direct function of the extent to which the chancellor is ready to use the office and involve it in his own decision-taking.

A last function of the Chancellor's Office, to be mentioned at least briefly, is policy planning. In reaction to the problems arising with the end of the 'economic miracle' and the period of peaceful domestic reconstruction, the Social–Liberal coalition tried to institutionalize policy planning after it assumed office in 1969.[23] The small planning staff which already existed within the BK at the time of the Grand Coalition was developed into a fully fledged division. This division not only attempted to use the new reporting system in order to draw up a prescriptive list of policy priorities, it also set up a number of working groups for forward planning. These groups, covering all major policy areas, were intended to develop substantive inputs for policy-making on the basis of forecasts. The departments were asked to delegate members to these project groups, but they cooperated only reluctantly, and the task itself soon proved more difficult than expected. First the original planning groups were replaced by a joint federal–state venture addressing comprehensive problem analysis and operating at a reduced level of aspiration, but even this was discontinued after the 1972 election. The planning division survived as such until Helmut Kohl dissolved it after taking office, but its function had changed long before, serving more as the chancellor's special task force than engaging in any substantive planning.

Horst Ehmke's attempt as chief of the BK to develop the Chancellor's Office into an organ of government-wide, future-orientated policy planning did not founder on the rocks of departmental autonomy alone. It also proved to be quite unrealistic in view of the reduced scope for governmental action in a time of increasing domestic and international tension and mounting economic difficulties. The aspiration behind the planning system – that it would enable the head of government to direct the development of society on the basis of rational problem analyses and the intervention needs derived from them – was then, and is probably always, based on an erroneous rationalistic perception of the nature of political leadership.

However, this is not to deny that the Chancellor's Office is potentially quite powerful, even if its major functions lie less in the field of policy development than in the coordination of government policy and the management of conflict between the departments, and especially between the partners in a coalition government. To fulfil these functions, the chief of the BK must be able to balance seemingly contradictory demands in playing his difficult role: as the chancellor's trusted top servant, he should work quietly behind the scenes and refrain from personal political ambitions – yet he should be strong enough to serve his coordinative and conflict management functions effectively. Ehmke was too ambitious and emphasized the power aspect of his role too much; Waldemar Schreckenberger, Helmut Kohl's first chief of the BK, apparently over-emphasized the opposite part of his role. If one believes extensive press comments, he was too tolerant of the chancellor's special leadership style and suffered him repeatedly to make policy decisions without involving the BK chief and staff.[24] By the later summer of 1984, this had contributed to a number of much publicized decision 'mistakes' and finally led to Schreckenberger's replacement as office chief by Wolfgang Schäuble.

The Chancellor's Advisory Needs and the Role of his Office

The Chancellor's Office is too big, and has too many diverse functions to fulfil to be able to operate only as a specialized advisory unit. It is also not a staff of the chancellor's own choosing, with the exception of that minority of positions which every new head of government may fill after temporarily retiring their incumbents or shifting them to other jobs (as is the case with a handful of persons in the chancellor's bureau who are often salaried employees and can be disposed of more easily). For an incoming chancellor who is of the former opposition party this means that he must rely for policy advice on a relatively large body which is not easy to manage and which may be mainly staffed by partisans, if not formal members of what has now become the parliamentary opposition party. This difficulty is one of the obvious drawbacks of this type of institutional arrangement for rendering policy advice to the head of government. A new chancellor faced with this problem may either circumvent it by expanding the size of the office in order to bring in enough persons of his own choice, or he may turn elsewhere for advice in politically sensitive matters.

Even if the chancellor is not distrustful of the BK staff, its character as a permanent, multi-purpose administrative organ restricts the advisory functions it can perform, so that the chancellor may wish to tap other sources of advice. The most obvious candidate for an alternative source of policy advice is the chancellor's own political party. All major German parties maintain sizeable central offices in Bonn where their leadership meets, the party's general secretary resides and specialized staff is available. A chancellor's position within his own political party is his most important power base so he normally maintains close relations with it. Though the offices of chancellor and party chairman are separate in principle, no constitutional norm forbids them being united in one person and most chancellors have in fact also been party chairmen – with Helmut Schmidt the most notable exception to this rule. The present chancellor, Helmut Kohl, has led his party in many years of parliamentary opposition and has in this time established particularly close links with the party organization. It is not surprising, then, that he seems to place great importance on counsel from these quarters and is said to consult regularly with the other members of the CDU's executive organ before major decisions.[25] In addition, Chancellor Kohl maintains regular contact with the leader of his party's parliamentary group and, in a coalition government, with the party chiefs of the other government parties.

Another important source of advice is the press office and its chief, who also serves as official spokesman of the government. The press office closely observes the media, which reflects public opinion, and is tied into the national and international information network. The press office chief often belongs to the small inner circle of the chancellor's closest advisers, as in the case of Helmut Schmidt and his famous 'clover leaf', whose core consisted of the chiefs of the press office and the BK, and a state minister attached to the latter. The chancellor's closest advisers are normally persons with whom he maintains regular working contacts; in the West German case this means that they will mostly occupy leading positions in the bureaucracy.

By virtue of his elevated position, a chancellor also has the opportunity to ask other members of the Republic's variegated functional elite for advice – bankers and church leaders, the heads of industrial and labour organizations and so on. The extent to which he avails himself of this opportunity varies with the chancellor's personal leadership style. If one believes press comments, the present chancellor has a pronounced tendency to talk over policy problems on the telephone with prominent experts.[26] In fact, the more a chancellor sees his role in terms of conflict management and consensus building, the more important to him will be that kind of strategic information about the views and intentions of other major actors in the political game which the civil servants in his office are not optimally situated to provide, and the more he will rely on his own contacts in the world of party politics, banking, industry etc.

In the case of the present chancellor, several of the reasons mentioned here as arguing for a less intense reliance on the Chancellor's Office as source of policy advice seem to come together. Helmut Kohl had been for many years the leader of the major opposition party, which he also chaired, and has therefore taken over an office staffed to a considerable degree by persons recruited in the period of SPD government. Moreover, Helmut Kohl apparently also does not aspire to become the master policy-maker, but emphasizes instead the consensus building functions of his role. His leadership style is quite different from that of his predecessor, and so is his pattern of seeking advice, where he seems to rely more on the various outside sources mentioned than on the civil servants in the Chancellor's Office, with the exception of a few trusted collaborators whom he brought to the BK when he assumed the chancellorship.[27] Since the BK's authority is a derived one and depends directly on the use which the chancellor makes of this instrument, the fact that Helmut Kohl tends to operate quite independently of his office cannot but impair the latter's function.[28] As soon as other decision-makers perceive that the BK officials are not the first to know of the chancellor's plans, nor the crucial gatekeepers controlling the flow of information, their influence wanes and they become successively crowded out of the decision-making process. As one journalist has put it: 'Nichts funktioniert, wenn er diesen Apparat nicht vollständig an den eigenen Informationsfluß anschließt' ('Nothing works unless he [the chancellor] links the office fully to his own information flow').[29]

The contrast between Helmut Schmidt, who used the potential of the Chancellor's Office fully, and Helmut Kohl, who would probably have been more content had he been permitted to select a circle of personal advisers in a less formal staff capacity, serves to highlight the advantages and disadvantages of the German model of providing policy advice to the head of government. A permanent unit of the line organization type may have certain advantages: a high 'productive capacity'; its members are experienced; the 'institutionalized memory' is assured and their status as civil servants removes the pressures of personal dependence from them. This arrangement also fits an administrative culture where the tenured civil service has traditionally played an important role in policy-making.[30] However, it is also a very inflexible kind of arrangement that cannot easily be adapted to new demands and a different, non-bureaucratic kind of leadership style. The chancellor is constrained by this arrangement in the choice of his advisers (he must largely work with persons selected by his predecessor) and in the formal role he may assign to them (they must occupy line positions in a permanent administrative unit). Civil service rules make for a generally low rate of turnover among the BK officials, especially at the echelons below the replaceable political civil servant. The consequences of this, such as large differences in the workload of officials and the development of a closed, 'in' culture, are felt especially when lack of personnel expansion prevents a sizeable influx of new blood by way of growth. Finally, and perhaps most importantly, all permanent units tend to lose their purely instrumental character and become autonomous power centres. The BK's effective power depends on the use the chancellor makes of it, but the office continues to exist, to offer its services and to want to fulfil its functions, even if a chancellor does not want to make full use of its potential. The ensuing frustration of its officials is a symptom of the discrepancy between supply and demand which, in a more flexible, staff-type arrangement, could not arise.

Notes

1 For a more detailed analysis of the respective roles of the chancellor, the individual ministers and the cabinet in the policy process, see Renate Mayntz, 'Executive leadership in Germany: dispersion of power or "Kanzlerdemokratie"?', in R. Rose and E. Suleiman (eds) *Presidents and Prime Ministers* (AEI, Washington, DC, 1980).

2 'Ministry' and 'department' will be used synonymously; the German term is *Ministerium*.

3 For these three principles, see Hartmut H. Brauswetter, *Kanzlerprinzip, Ressortprinzip und Kabinettsprinzip in der ersten Regierung Brandt 1969–1972* (Eichholz Verlag, Bonn, 1976).

4 Renate Mayntz and Fritz W. Scharpf, *Policy-Making in the German Federal Bureaucracy* (Elsevier, Amsterdam, 1975).

5 Dieter Schimanke, 'Assistenzeinheiten der politischen Leitung in Ministerien', *Verwaltungsarchiv* 73 (1982), p. 216.

6 Mayntz and Scharpf, *Policy-making*, pp. 107–9.

7 Gerhard W. Wittkämper, 'Außenpolitikberatung durch Berichte – Oder was?', *Liberal* 23 (1981), pp. 257–63.

8 See the question 8/3846 entered by the CDU/CSU parliamentary party which asked for the number, topics and costs of scientific expert reports which the federal ministries had commissioned in the course of the 7th and 8th legislative periods – a question that the government was not able to answer precisely since no central listing existed.

9 Gerd Rauhaus, 'Geheime Räterepublik: Wissenschaftler entwerfen Bonner Politik', *Frankfurter Neue Presse*, 26 August 1982.

10 Holger Bonus, 'Die sanfte Diktatur der Experten', *Rheinischer Merkur*, 2 October 1981.

11 Ibid.

12 Hannes Friedrich, *Staatliche Verwaltung und Wissenschaft: Die wissenschaftliche Beratung der Politik aus der Sicht der Ministerialbürokratie* (Europäische Verlagsanstalt, Frankfurt/M, 1970), p. 48.

13 For this, see Renate Mayntz, 'German federal bureaucrats: a functional elite between politics and administration', in Ezra N. Suleiman (ed.) *The Role of Higher Civil Servants in Central Government* (Holmes & Meyer, New York, 1984).

14 Dieter Kugele, *Der politische Beamte: Eine Studie über Genesis, Motiv, Bewährung und Reform einer politisch-administrativen Institution* (tuduv Verlagsgesellschaft, Munich, 1976).

15 For an extensive review of the practice of temporary retirement, see Renate Mayntz, 'The political role of the higher civil servants in the German Federal Government', in Bruce L. R. Smith (ed.) *The Higher Civil Service in Europe: Lessons for the US* (The Brookings Institution, Washington, DC, 1984); Hans-Ulrich Derlien, *The Politicization of the Civil Service in the Federal Republic of Germany: Facts and Fables* (Verwaltungswissenschaftliche Beiträge No. 15, University of Bamberg, 1984).

16 *Schriften der Kommission für wirtschaftlichen und sozialen Wandel* (Otto Schwartz, Göttingen, 1973 ff), vols. 1–115.

17 Horst Zimmermann, 'Schon 20 Jahre lang läßt Bonn in Bayern denken: 109 Experten sehen für die Regierung in die politische Zukunft', *Bonner Rundschau*, 29 July 1982.

18 Hans K. Schneider, 'Der Sachverständigenrat zur Begutachtung der gesamtwirtschaftlichen Entwicklung: Auftrag, Arbeitsweise, Konzeption.' Lecture given on 27 March 1984 and published by Beiräte der Gelsenwasser-Gruppe.

19 A detailed description of this system of financial planning and its development can be found in Heribert Schatz, 'Auf der Suche nach neuen Problemlösungsstrategien: Die Entwicklung der politischen Planung auf Bundesebene', in R. Mayntz and F. W. Scharpf (eds), *Planungsorganisation: Die Diskussion um die Reform von Regierung und Verwaltung des Bundes* (Piper, Munich, 1973), especially pp. 21–6, 34–7.

20 Klaus Seemann, 'Moderne Regierungstechnik: Richtlinienkompetenz, wissenschaftliche Staatsführung und Bundeskanzleramt', *Soziale Welt* 18 (1967), p. 160.

21 Bundeshaushaltsplan für das Haushaltsjahr 1984, p. 2.

22 This is also described at length in Schatz, 'Auf der Suche nach neuen Problemlösungsstrategien'.

23 For the development and subsequent changes in the planning system, see Klaus Seemann, *Entzaubertes Bundeskanzleramt*, (Verlag Politisches Archiv, Landshut, 1975); and Hartmut Bebermeyer, 'Idee und Wirklichkeit einer politischen Planung des Staates', *VOP – Verwaltungserfahrung, Organisation, Personalwesen*, no. 6, vol. 2, 1984, pp. 51–9.

24 See, for instance, Gunter Hofmann, 'Helmut Kohl ist und bleibt Kanzler', *Die Zeit*, 17 August 1984; Robert Leicht, 'In Kohls Kanzlei', *Süddeutsche Zeitung* 192/1984 (21 August), p. 4.

25 See Gunter Hofmann, 'Eine Insel der Harmonie', *Die Zeit*, 9 December 1983.

26 This has, for instance, been commented on by Jörg Sottorf, 'Die heißen Drähte des Kanzlers zur Wirtschafts- und Finanzwelt', *Handelsblatt*, 9 March 1984.

27 See, for instance, the partly sympathetic, partly very critical description of Kohl's leadership style by Carl-Christian Kaiser, 'Kohl auf dem Kutschbock', *Die Zeit*, 12 November 1982, and the title story 'Kohl: Die lange Schonzeit ist zu Ende', *Der Spiegel*, 40/1983.

28 See the analysis by Hermann Rudolph, 'Der Musterschüler als Sündenbock', *Die Zeit*, 24 August 1984.

29 Kurt Becker, 'Späte Einsicht', *Die Zeit*, 16 November 1984.

30 This historical tradition is described in more detail in Mayntz, 'The political role of the higher civil servants'.

Rolf Kaiser

I am now in my eleventh year at the Chancellor's Office in Bonn and am in my fifth posting, which is characteristic for someone working there. I have worked for about two years as private secretary to four consecutive heads of the office (the BK) during the historically interesting time of transition from Helmut

Schmidt to Helmut Kohl. Professor Mayntz has given a faithful representation of what is happening in West Germany and I would like first to reflect on one aspect of what she discussed – that is, the dichotomy between advice and information.

In my practical experience, a chancellor does not take political decisions all the time; in fact, I should say less than 50 per cent of his time is devoted to political decisions. A great deal of attention is devoted to various types of crisis management, and as Professor Mayntz has said, to building a power base and to the resolution of conflict. One might describe this as performing a 'damage control' function in central government. It would be a mistake to treat policy advice as the first-class merchandise and consign information to a minor role. Very often for days on end – sometimes even for a week – no *policy* advice is needed, because the chancellor is not required to take policy decisions, but during crisis management times, a great deal depends on information.

What is needed, then, is a clear distinction between the two categories. We have in the Chancellor's Office a standing order to differentiate the labelling of the two. When we write a position paper, an opinion paper or other document for the chancellor, we are required to make a clear distinction between the 'news' and the 'editorial' content, between the information on the one hand and comment or political advice on the other. Certainly, in terms of volume, information still constitutes by far the biggest chunk of the work – at least in the German case.

The German system is quite different from most others in Europe and in the United States. Germany is not only a federal state but its government is quite decentralized. Once a minister is sworn in in Germany, usually for the full four-year legislative period, he runs his department independently within the policy guidelines of the chancellor. It is usually quite difficult for political scientists and historians to find out what a chancellor's 'policy guideline' is. Apart from the general 'government statement' (*Regierungserklärung*) at the beginning of each term, they are rarely written down during a legislative period. They may be only general guidelines, such as those on economic policy to signal expansion or to signal contraction and braking. So each minister runs his department independently, which means of course that policy is drafted within the ministries first. The ministries come up with policy through their ministers, who then present it to the cabinet. The chancellor himself is *constitutionally* relatively weak in Germany, because he has no power to control the ministries on a day-to-day basis. Consequently, the chancellor's men and women, the civil servants who work in the Chancellor's Office, cannot pick up a telephone and phone a ministry or a department with the result that everybody stands still to hear what the voice from the top has to say. This great independence of ministries is probably the governing principle of – and also the major difference between – the German system and other systems in Europe and the United

States. This, of course, has a bearing on how the Chancellor's Office operates, because if the chancellor cannot control his ministers on a day-to-day basis, his advisers, his civil servants, cannot control them either. Their function is therefore much more that of being the chancellor's 'watchdogs', so to speak, his early warning system, finding out what is happening in the system, what is in the pipeline and, of course, giving him political advice. Precisely because of this relative constitutional weakness *vis-à-vis* the ministries, the Chancellor's Office, in the German case, must be quite highly developed in terms of manpower and in terms of differentiation between policy fields. As Professor Mayntz stated, there is now a staff of about 450, of whom I should say only between 50 and 60 higher civil servants – assistant secretary and above – could be termed the real 'political operators' in the Chancellor's Office. The rest are support and technical staff.

As regards structure, Professor Mayntz described the 'mirror system', i.e. when there are, say, 16 ministries, there will be at least one unit in the Chancellor's Office for each ministry. For the larger ministries, such as foreign affairs, economics or the interior, there is more than one unit in the Chancellor's Office, but it is true to say that each policy field, from defence to culture, is represented or reflected within the Office in a specialized unit – a very small unit usually comprising one assistant secretary in the British sense plus his deputy with an academic training and then people at executive level.

That these units are quite small is very important. Professor Dror has coined the phrase 'islands of excellence' for situations where smallness is an important feature, and these units do not comprise more than two or maybe three people with an academic training. People in a unit like this, which is called a *Referat* in German, stay in that post for at least two to three years. If they wish, they may stay there longer; this happens quite often. They try to establish a very close contact base in 'their' ministry to find out what is happening there in order to report back to the chancellor or to the head of the BK. It is quite important for them to stay in post for a longer period because, as already said, they have no outright prerogative to 'control' the ministries and their position is, in fact, fairly delicate. They have to try to extract the maximum amount of information from a ministry and yet have no constitutional power *vis-à-vis* that ministry, no legal power. Their power is entirely pragmatic. They must convince the people in the ministries they cover that, within the Chancellor's Office, it is through their hands that everything that happens within that field – say research and technology – passes. They must persuade the ministries that it is they who will finally write the comments or opinion for the chancellor when a measure gets into cabinet. Ultimately it is the men in these units who have to persuade the ministries that in certain circumstances this could make life difficult for them. What happens ideally, therefore, is that when a unit's contacts in 'its' ministry – let us continue our example of research and technology – draw up a new project, very early on they will contact the unit and sound out its opinion. Sometimes the unit is even looked on as an arbiter in inter-ministerial squabbles in the early stages.

This leads me to one last observation on a point which, in my experience, is essential as regards the quality of work within a prime minister's office; that is, the question of *feedback*. This is one dimension we have not yet discussed. Until now it seems we have been talking about something of a 'one-way street', with information and policy advice moving from the bottom up to where those at the top, somehow, make use of it. I think the question of feedback should be introduced here. Let us go back to the case of an assistant secretary for research and technology in his unit within the Chancellor's Office. He maintains his power by persuading his colleagues in the ministry that he knows and sees everything that happens in that field, including letters that come directly on to the chancellor's desk. He must convince them that letters like that, from the ministries or from the major lobby groups, will find their way, within a day or two, on to his (the specialist's) desk so that he can grasp the whole situation in his policy field. Moreover, in Germany cabinet minutes are secret, but importantly each assistant secretary in the Chancellor's Office has a right to see them. That is one essential aspect of feedback, to know what has happened in cabinet; there are others. In the German system if the people in the ministries find out that they can 'get around' the specialist in the Chancellor's Office, for example, by letting their minister write a letter to the chancellor which the specialist never sees, then he is out of a job. The ministries have to know that whatever happens in their field passes over the specialist's desk very rapidly. Also, the question of feedback has a decisive effect on morale; in a prime minister's office it is very important that staff eventually get back the things they sent 'up', with some notes or just a simple check mark by one of the top people.

2

Australia

Patrick Weller

The Australian system of government is a variant of the British parliamentary model. The language is the same and many of the conventions have been adopted, particularly in relation to the position of prime minister. The prime minister is not recognized in the constitution, but he is the leader of the party or coalition of parties that can maintain a majority in the House of Representatives. He acts as chairman of cabinet, is the main spokesman of the government and is the centre of media attention during elections. Yet, as in Britain, the process of government remains collective. However dominant the prime minister may appear, he usually has to work with and through his cabinet. Decisions are formally made by cabinet, not by the prime minister as an individual. The practice of collective responsibility ensures that cabinet members stand together in public, while ministerial responsibility means that ministers, not the prime minister, are responsible to parliament for their department. At least that is the illusion created by the adopted 'principles' of the Canberra model, however hard those principles may be to define in particular cases. The prime minister is notionally the head of a team, dependent for survival on the continuous support of ministerial and backbench colleagues.

There are also considerable differences within the Australian system that have an important impact on the way that prime ministers do their job. First, the prime minister must work within the confines of a written and often rigid constitution. That constitution prevents a federal government from using many of the weapons of economic management, such as wages and price control, because it has no legal authority in those areas. Prime ministers are limited to those solutions that lie within their power; those restrictions may not be as great as at first sight they appear, but they demand constant attention. Further, the federal system creates multiple centres of power and state premiers who are jealous of their prerogatives and conscious of their status. Some of them may belong to the prime minister's own party; all of them are conscious of the particular interests of their own state. They must be treated with some care – and that normally requires the prime minister's attention. Federalism both creates work for, and restricts, the prime minister.

Second, in Australia Parliament can be obstructive. Although, by definition, prime ministers must be able to maintain the support of the lower house, they are often faced by a Senate that is either controlled by their opponents or in which a third party holds the balance of power. It seems likely that in the next decade neither the Labor Party nor the Liberal–National (formerly Country) Party coalition will gain a majority there. Yet the Senate has almost co-equal powers with the House of Representatives. It can amend or reject all legislation except the supply bills; and those it can defer or reject, as it did in 1974 and 1975 – in both cases forcing an election.

Third, prime ministers are vulnerable to revolt from their Parliamentary party and need to depend directly on their supports. They are elected by the Parliamentary party; they can be (and have been) sacked by the party.[1] The Parliamentary party expect and receive prior notice of the legislation to be introduced; they may then require alterations to be made. A Liberal prime minister chooses the ministers from his own party, but has to take account of federal and bicameral factors in that selection; he must also work with the ministers chosen by the leader of the National Party. Labor ministers are elected by caucus; the prime minister only distributes the portfolios. Further, the Labor Party's platform, determined at the five-day national conference held every second year, is meant to be binding on the Parliamentary party. As a consequence, a Labor prime minister must attend all sessions of these conferences, must participate actively and regularly and must ensure that the adopted policy as far as possible suits his preferences. Australian prime ministers can never stand above their party.

Parliament, the parties and the federal system all have important, if different, impacts on the prime minister's activities. To some extent the advisory structures are designed to meet these needs as well as the more routine functions of advisory agencies.

Structures for Support and Advice

The prime minister is supported by a group of organizations, most of which are staffed by career public servants. The most important bodies are the Department of Prime Minister and Cabinet (PMC) and the Prime Minister's Office (PMO); the staff of the former are public servants, those of the latter are partisan.

There are other important bodies that also lie in the prime minister's bailiwick. The Public Service Board is responsible for the control of staff numbers (although it is soon to lose that function to the Department of Finance); it also deals with pay and conditions, industrial relations in the public service, efficiency, recruitment and training. It will soon become responsible for senior staff planning when the Senior Executive Service is established. The

Board has a statutory independence in some of its functions. On some matters, such as the allocation of staff ceilings, it deals directly with the prime minister. In other areas of ministerial involvement it usually works with the minister assisting the prime minister in public service matters. The Office of National Assessments, created in 1977, is responsible for the analysis of (but not the gathering of) intelligence. It reports directly to the prime minister.

The Department of Prime Minister and Cabinet (PMC)

PMC is a flexible organization. It is in part designed to meet the needs of the prime minister and can be adjusted as those needs change. In 1981, for instance, it consisted of eight divisions: the Cabinet Office, Parliamentary and General, Operations, Economic, International, Communications, Trade and Industries and Welfare. By 1984, after the election of the Labor Government, there were some significant changes. The first five divisions remained, at least in name; new divisions of Security and the Office of the Status of Women had been created, and others had been changed to Industries, Social Policy and Community Development. Functions were redistributed around the department. The new divisions, particularly women's affairs, were indications of the importance that the new government gave to those areas of policy.

The staff of PMC, about 400 in number, are almost exclusively career public servants, although one or two consultants may occasionally be attached on a short-term basis. Recruitment to the department, as elsewhere in the service, is primarily a matter of individual choice. There is as yet no career planning for high-flyers. Sometimes senior officers will deliberately try to recruit talented individuals from elsewhere in the service, but often senior officials themselves have spent almost their entire career in the one department. The Secretary, Sir Geoffrey Yeend, has been in the department for 30 years. Some of the younger and brighter do not want to work anywhere else. Indeed in 1982, 74 per cent of the second division officers had been recruited from within the department.

The staff structure of PMC is usually top-heavy. In 1980, one in 16 of the staff (35 out of 544) were senior executives (second division); in June 1983 it was 31 out of 522. On each occasion only one second division officer was a woman. Further, almost all the department (97 per cent) were located in Canberra, a most unusual phenomenon in a federal state. Its staff are young and well-qualified. For instance, in May 1982, 75 per cent of its senior executives were under 50, compared to 52 per cent in the public service as a whole. Some 55 per cent of them had honours or higher degrees and 90 per cent had degrees of some sort; the service-wide figures were 31 and 75 per cent respectively. Service in PMC is regarded as a useful, if hectic, route to top positions in the public service. In 1984 a quarter of the permanent heads had worked in PMC at a senior level.

PMC fulfils two main functions, described by one senior official as serving the prime minister's two main roles:[2] as team leader and as initiator of government policy. In the former role, the Cabinet Office provides a service to all members of the government. It ensures that the cabinet is running smoothly as an organization. It receives submissions; it checks that they have met the requirements set out in the *Cabinet Handbook* (1983) and that all the relevant departments have been consulted. It keeps the minutes for meetings of cabinet and its committees and circulates its decisions. The Cabinet Office's responsibility is to hold the ring, to see that all the information is available, that the points of dispute are clearly indicated and that everyone knows what has happened. The Parliamentary and General division supports the government in its dealings with Parliament. PMC is also responsible for maintaining an overview of federal–state relations and for the regular correspondence between the prime minister and state premiers.

The other divisions are functionally organized to cover all areas of government activity. These divisions contain between 17 and 33 people each. They provide the prime minister with a brief on any item that may be coming to cabinet, or on any other question that is of interest to him. That task is substantial: in 1980–1 alone, 1,664 submissions or memoranda were submitted to cabinet. Members of PMC have also played a leading role in coordinating policy and acting as chairmen of major task forces. In 1975 a member of PMC was chairman of the official committee that provided data for the expenditure review committee in its efforts to slow the expansion of public expenditure under the then Labor government. In 1981 another member was chairman of the officials' committee that supported the massive review of Commonwealth functions. The permanent head of the department chaired four of the official committees that for a time provided backing to the standing committees of cabinet.

For a long time the facilitating role was PMC's main function. The growth in the policy capacity of PMC has been comparatively recent. Throughout the 1950s and the 1960s the department filled a role similar to that of the Cabinet Office in Britain. It serviced cabinet and its committees, circulated the minutes and was primarily a post-box. Then for a time the two main functions were separated. From 1968 to 1971 the Cabinet Office had a separate existence from the department of the prime minister. The reasons were political, not organizational. The incoming prime minister, John Gorton, wanted his own policy adviser and chose the abrasive Lenox Hewitt to lead the department; but he also had to find a position for the then secretary of PMC, Sir John Bunting, who had been head of department since 1958. Therefore the cabinet-servicing function was divided from that of advising the prime minister. The split did not work well, partly because of the personalities involved, but primarily because the prime minister's principal adviser was not in cabinet and therefore less able to understand all that was going on, while the secretary to the cabinet did not have a large advisory role. The two halves were reunited under Bunting after Gorton's fall.

Later, under Gough Whitlam and even more under Malcolm Fraser, the department developed a greater policy capacity. In 1974 Whitlam replaced Bunting with John Menadue, once Whitlam's private secretary and more recently an executive in the Murdoch newspaper empire. Whitlam wanted an active department that could give him policy advice on a wide range of issues. As a result, the department increased its ability to advise on particular functional problems, particularly in the economic arena, because both Whitlam and Fraser were suspicious of the Treasury and argued that they needed a second opinion on economic questions.

Fraser was an interventionist prime minister who chose to become involved in all areas of policy. He therefore replaced Menadue with Alan Carmody, a departmental secretary who espoused a 'can–do' philosophy. Under Carmody's aggressive leadership, and in trying to serve Fraser's onerous demands, PMC was for a time unpopular, even arrogant. When Carmody died, he was replaced by Geoffrey Yeend whose approach was more conciliatory and quiet. But, as Fraser demanded briefing on a wide variety of issues, PMC still had to provide that assistance. Although its officers generally preferred to act in cooperation with the relevant department, the pressures of time did not always make it possible.

Policy advisers were not intended to indicate alternative solutions, or to provide unexpected information with which the prime minister could gain the upper hand in cabinet: 'It is not our business to have ministers surprised in the Cabinet Room with questions they have not anticipated, or be faced in the Cabinet Room with propositions they have not considered', said a secretary of the department.[3] But if the prime minister chose to surprise his ministers, that was his prerogative. Nevertheless, on a range of issues PMC is far more than a simple coordinator of government initiatives. It played an active role and was prepared to acknowledge it: 'We do not feel inhibited in what some might interpret as the role of second opinion. Our branches have built up an understanding of policy issues and an expertise in coordination; our officers are sought out for their advice and assistance. We have scope for probing and proposing.'[4] He also argued: 'A Prime Minister's Department is a tool of government that can be used in a very direct and telling way in ensuring that government policies are got under way, that changes in direction are made, that there is a responsiveness by the public service as a whole to new instructions and changes of style.'[5] He acknowledged that these powers had to be used sensitively to ensure the department's coordinating capacity was not threatened, but saw no contradiction between the two functions.

How active PMC is in policy areas depends on how much policy advice the prime minister wants. Fraser wanted to be kept informed about everything that went on, at least in part so that he could maintain a check on his ministers' proposals. PMC's activities reflected those demands. Hawke's style is very different. He likes predictability and routine. He does not like to be surprised or to take his ministers by surprise. He is much more prepared to leave his ministers alone – until they get into trouble when he will intervene, usually supportively. This style has its impact on the way that PMC works. It still briefs the prime minister on every submission to cabinet and cabinet committees, and the prime minister devours and understands those briefs, but because his policy interests are primarily those core issues, such as foreign affairs, economic issues and the ALP-trade union accord, that are central to the government's success and re-election, PMC is not required to range so widely in its policy advice. If details are uncertain in cabinet, then it is likely that the decision will be delayed.

PMC has a third main function that is related to its policy capacity: it acts as a trouble-shooter. It may detach senior officers to work with a task force, whether it is concerned with the organization of the 1981 Commonwealth Heads of Government Meeting in Melbourne, or with expenditure review exercises. When the Fraser government tried to reduce expenditure on several occasions, the officials' committee supporting the exercise was chaired by a PMC officer. On occasion PMC has filled a gap which a department ought to have filled. When the Department of National Resources failed to produce a green paper on energy quickly enough, PMC largely wrote it. At other times they provided recommendations on economic management, taxation and health care that were adopted in preference to the Treasury's when the government was under pressure.

Prime ministers often choose to roam widely across the affairs of the government; PMC has developed the capacity to help them in that task. The extent to which it is used will depend on political circumstances and on the personal style of the prime minister.[6]

The Prime Minister's Office (PMO)

The prime minister receives further support from a private office. One or two of its members are liaison officers on secondment from PMC. The others are political appointments; even those who are public servants on secondment to the office are chosen by the prime minister and are retained at his pleasure. The growth of the office has substantially occurred in the past decade. When Whitlam gained office in 1972, he relied at first on his personal staff for alternative advice to that provided by the public service; it was made particularly necessary by the limited capacity of PMC. The office was highly partisan, concerned to ensure that the party's platform was implemented and that the

Labor government had a good chance of being re-elected. The involvement was varied and hectic, although the office remained small. At times members of the office had a considerable impact on details of policy, even though those policies were not always successful. Gradually, however, the importance of the office declined as the role of PMC expanded under John Menadue. By November 1975 when Whitlam was dismissed by the governor-general, its policy impact had lessened; its leading figures had moved on.

Under Fraser the private office went through several forms. Several people headed it, the most notable being David Kemp, a professor of political science. By 1981, it consisted of about 30 people, some eight of whom were senior policy advisers. In part it was responsible for ministering to the prime minister's needs, making appointments and so on. It included the press office. It has also developed the capacity to provide advice on policy questions. After the 1980 election it included four senior academics on secondment, with ready access to a fifth who was nominally attached to the Department of Foreign Affairs. Its influence reached its height under Kemp, whose position in Fraser's confidence was secure enough for his comments to be regarded as authoritative. When he left, the leading members of the office lacked his weight and the office declined in importance.

Fraser's PMO was in part staffed by generalists, with specialist advisers on foreign and economic affairs serving part-time or being on call. The business of the private office was the business of the prime minister. It included everything that went across his desk – foreign affairs, economics and any particular interest of the moment. The purpose of the PMO was to aid the prime minister and the cabinet (in that order) to maintain coherence; to help integrate the philosophy and policy of the government; to assist the prime minister by adding an alternative voice to that of the bureaucrats; to keep other links with the parties. The office was responsible for the 'political input', a role that it could play far more readily than PMC, even if it was difficult to define precisely. David Kemp has described the role in the following terms:

> There has been a tendency in the past to view politics negatively, as disruptive of government, and to downplay its significance by loading the whole of the political role on one man, the prime minister or minister.
>
> In essence the political job is a leadership function. It identifies the identification of philosophy and values underlying decision-making, the establishment of priorities, definition of task and the integration of information and ideas from many sources 'into a coherent function'.
>
> Political judgement is a major part of a prime minister's role and one which, it is now acknowledged, requires assistance; with the increasing complexity of government it would require a superhuman effort of one man to do it without staff support.[7]

At the highest level, the PMO can assist in the broad objectives of government. By asking the right questions it can ensure that all the political implications of proposals have been worked out.

Hawke's private office is organized differently. It contains three streams. The administrative managerial group is headed by Graham Evans, a career public servant on secondment from the Treasury, who is in charge of the office; it includes liaison officers with cabinet, PMC and the electorate. The policy advisory group contains two party experts (one a former successful state secretary), two economic specialists (one an academic), a diplomat on secondment from Foreign Affairs, and one full-time and one part-time speech-writer. The third stream is the press office.

Two or three times a week, the senior members of the PMO will meet with the prime minister to discuss topical problems. Those meetings may include senior officials from PMC, other ministers (particularly the Treasurer) and their staff, depending on the topic and the circumstances. In these meetings the advisers, selected because they have specialist knowledge of a high calibre, might present options that are later filled out by officials and later adopted. They have an opportunity at those meetings to influence policy; access is easy too at other times.

When the prime minister is briefed for an overseas trip, that briefing is the responsibility of PMO and PMC. Although information will be obtained from the Ministry of Foreign Affairs, it does not necessarily follow that a Foreign Affairs officer will be present at the briefing. Before cabinet and question time, PMO and PMC officials will be present, although the prime minister prefers to master the briefs on paper rather than orally.

Members of PMO may sit in on official committees to infom themselves or to suggest factors that need consideration, but they do not often have the time; they are more likely to talk to the PMC delegate. They will then brief the prime minister as required; those briefings are totally confidential – for the prime minister alone. No member of any PMO has complained that they were denied access to information or found it hard to obtain.

The staff of PMO are also concerned with political fire-fighting. It keeps open links with the party and the other sections of the community. One of Fraser's closest advisers was the federal director of the Liberal Party, Tony Eggleton, who was in daily contact with him before Parliamentary question time, but Eggleton was not actually part of PMO. By contrast, Hawke's office contains directly political, rather than policy, support. One principal adviser keeps him in contact with his principal factional support while another, a former very successful state secretary of the Victorian branch, is his link to all the other sections of the party. When the prime minister attended the national conference of the party in July 1984, his political supports were responsible for liaising with faction leaders to obtain the numbers, while the policy specialists assisted in writing drafts of his speeches for the occasions when he chose to intervene. Those members of the PMO who are public servants are consciously somewhat withdrawn when the more detailed number-gathering is required.

Relationships between the Supporting Agencies

A Canadian observer has commented that the Canadian Privy Council Office is 'non-partisan, operationally active and politically sensitive' while the PMO is 'partisan, politically active and operationally sensitive'.[8] Similar comments could be made with regard to Australia.

As Kemp has commented,[9] the existence of a smooth and well-functioning partisan office can help preserve the apolitical nature of the public service. It means that many of the political assessments can be made by the political office, including most of the speech-writing. Indeed, there is a belief that PMO can help get the best out of PMC. However, there is a need to be careful about overstating the apolitical nature of PMC. Canadian officers who have been involved in the exchange scheme between the Canadian Privy Council Office and the PMC have commented that the decisions they are required to make in PMC have a much greater partisan content than was true in the PCO. In Australia senior PMC officers will talk of maintaining some check on the winners and losers in the community; they see their role as part of maintaining the strategy of the government and its consistency. PMC officials are likely to be more aware of political implications than public servants elsewhere. But there is a distinction, particularly at election time, when PMO takes over the central stage.

PMC and PMO usually act closely together. PMO may try out some of its policy ideas on PMC. Both unite to brief the prime minister before Parliamentary question time. When the prime minister wants details, PMO will work through the relevant PMC division head rather than contact operating departments directly. However, when it comes to immediate and constant access, PMO has some distinct advantages. The main one is geographical. The prime minister works in a suite of offices in Parliament House; the suite includes the cabinet room. The PMO staff is all around him. His ministers all work in adjoining offices; the press gallery is directly above him; the chamber of the House of Representatives is ten yards down the corridor. Access for all ministers, party members and PMO officers is comparatively easy. By contrast, the PMC is some 300 yards down the road in a separate building. This is not to suggest that PMC's senior officials find access difficult, but rather that access is inevitably less immediate for some than for others.

Relationships between Supporting Agencies and Other Departments

The growing policy capacity of PMC and PMO has not been achieved without problems. Some departments have criticized the process by which the central agencies try to force agreement on the 'facts' before the remaining matters of dispute are presented to ministers for settlement. They believe that that process is likely to 'squeeze the life out of proposals' and thus reduce options. There is also a belief that an overactive prime minister, served by an activist policy department, may confuse lines of responsibility. When the prime minister, occasionally directly in Fraser's case but more often working through his department, asks for information or advice – usually required immediately – then the permanent head may indeed wonder whom he is serving. At times there has been criticism of the department for pre-empting proper discussion. But one prime minister, Malcolm Frazer, responded to the criticism by arguing the case for a policy capacity in the centre: 'Specialist departments are not always right; they may have an axe to grind in a particular area and there is nothing wrong with that; but to have people with knowledge on a subject to ask questions – just to make sure everything comes out in cabinet – is very useful.'

PMC's unpopularity perhaps reached its height under Carmody; as it has pulled back from that more aggressive stance, so relations with other departments have improved. Hawke's determination to give his ministers greater independence (as long as they stay out of trouble) has meant that PMC makes less urgent demands on departments. Whether PMC is regarded as intrusive or necessary becomes finally a matter of perspective, depending on what functions are regarded as proper.

Ministerial advisers, and particularly those attached to the PMO, have never been accepted in many parts of the bureaucracy. In particular the Treasury has never become comfortable with the existence of distinguished economists providing advice direct to the prime minister. In 1974 they considered that ministerial advisers were mainly responsible for the ignoring of their advice.[10] During the Fraser government the Treasury went in and out of favour; in 1976 it was suddenly split into two departments. By 1982 the Secretary to the Treasury was very scathing about the performance of the economics professors on the prime minister's and the Treasurer's staff. In a letter to the editor of a business review that was widely circulated and, not surprisingly, leaked, he wrote: 'Public servants – perhaps because they have a continuing responsibility to provide advice and stay on to live with its consequences – have longer memories than the more meretricious players who flit across the private ministerial advisory stage.'

He warned of the dire consequences that befell governments who stopped listening to Treasury.[11] The strong terms of the letter showed the depth of the antagonisms that occasionally surfaced. Public servants sometimes objected to the fact that advisers had the last word to which they were then unable to respond.

The Supporting Agencies and Ministers

At times ministers regarded PMC with some suspicion. Some argued explicitly that a prime minister's main advisers should be his ministers. One claimed that PMC

> is not as well equipped with advice as the operative department and it tends to give the prime minister superficial advice rather than advice with the knowledge and experience of the department concerned. If the prime minister did not listen to his ministers that would be a dangerous aspect of government. If the prime minister listens to his ministers, who are advised by their department, he ought to be able to be convinced that some of the advice he gets from his own department is just not accurate.

Others questioned the department's very role and its pervasive influence:

> PMC is very much the department through which one goes if one wants to be a permanent head and that, I think, is devastating. I think it is the most serious administrative problem facing the government structure. I find it quite unconscionable to think that in that department in all policy areas there's some cell of public servants allegedly second-guessing, but they're doing it from a fairly high academic background, not necessarily any experience in the area whatsoever ... The minister in turn is being intimidated by it ... There is a whole series of people just sitting there censoring and putting alternative advice to the prime minister. I just find that extraordinary.[12]

But they did not necessarily argue that they could not get sufficient access to the prime minister, or that the existence of supporting agencies necessarily pre-empted full cabinet discussion. Some ministers also appreciated the need for prime ministers to be well informed. 'Prime ministers tend to be super-heated people and they can't leave things alone; at least not things they are interested in and their tastes tend to be fairly eclectic', said one minister.[13]

The officers of PMO are always conscious of the need to maintain careful links with ministers and their staff. They realize that they have regular access to the prime minister, an access of which some ministers may be jealous; and that their activities have to be seen to be constructive. In Hawke's cabinet his political staff are acknowledged to be political heavyweights in their own right and they will deal with ministers as faction leaders and with the officials of state branches. But the staff as a whole are conscious of the dangers of abusing their position by pretending to speak for the prime minister when they do not know what he thinks; and they claim to be scrupulous not to over-extend their influence. Ministers do not appear to have any problems of access as a result of PMO's activities. In particular, Hawke's ministers are conscious of their responsibilities and their rights. As long as everything is going well for the government, and Hawke's consensual style is retained, clashes are likely to be rare.

Planning and Setting Priorities

There has seldom been any attempt to introduce planning in Australia. In part it was ideological; when the Vernan committee of inquiry into the economic system recommended in 1965 the establishment of a planning council, it was rejected by the Liberal government as being incompatible with Australia's free enterprise system. In part it is a consequence of the federal system which limits the weapons of economic management available to government. Control of inflation and unemployment have been the immediate objectives, while forward planning has never been considered more than one year ahead. A Treasury officer's comment, 'I've never come across a politician interested in planning',[14] summarized the general attitude. As a consequence there has been no planning machinery available for the prime minister or his government.

In 1973 Whitlam created the Priorities Review Staff (PRS), based on Britain's Central Policy Review Staff (CPRS), to advise on strategy and provide collective advice. However, after one strategy paper, it became almost entirely involved in areas of policy analysis. The PRS was abolished when Fraser won office. Under the Liberal government a series of *ad hoc* task forces, usually headed by senior ministers, examined possible areas for spending cuts; these committees were supported by task forces of senior officials, but they had no permanent existence.

In part that changed when the Hawke government created the Economic Planning Advisory Committee (EPAC). EPAC emerged out of the economic summit that Hawke convened directly after his electoral victory in March 1983. It was to be representative of many sections of society (unions, business, state and federal governments predominated) and its secretariat was to take responsibility for medium-term planning. Its existence and frequent meetings were intended to maintain the spirit of cooperation and consensus that was to be the hallmark of the Labor administration. However, whatever its stated purposes, EPAC has become more of a public relations exercise than a serious forum for determining economic policy. It has evolved into an arena useful more for an exchange of views than for any indicative planning proposals.

Decisions remain exclusively in the government's hands, and they are based primarily on the Labor–trade union accord that was reached before the last election.[15]

Assessment

There is little value in asking whether the support provided by PMC and PMO is constitutionally valid in a parliamentary system or compatible with concepts of ministerial responsibility. Obviously it is both, because the structures exist and work well in Australia. Besides, such queries are concerned with normative assumptions about what the prime ministers ought to do, rather than asking operational questions about how well the system works and how it might be improved. The latter are both more useful and more practicable, since prime ministers are unlikely to be limited by any theoretical propositions of what is proper, rather than what is possible.

The conclusion in Australia must be that over the past decade PMC has developed into a very efficient department for providing support to any mixture of prime ministerial demands. The 'team support' operation, epitomized by the Cabinet Office, is now generally smoothly run and sophisticated, so that cabinet procedures and cabinet committees are now more predictable. The policy sections of the department are flexible, usually sensitive and aware of the political implications of proposals. Whether a prime minister is demanding, as Fraser was, or in policy terms more consensual, like Hawke, the department can adapt to those challenges. PMC invariably reflects the style of the prime minister; that indeed is its skill. PMO is now large enough to move directly political issues out of officials' hands without being so large that it has become unmanageable.

Obviously there is potential for tension in the system, a tension that depends in part on the observer's perspective. But two important conclusions can be drawn. First, the development of these supports for the prime minister is bi-partisan; it is unlikely to be dismantled in the future. Second, given the pressures of government, the important question is now not whether the prime minister needs support, but whether any of them could do without PMC and PMO. Given their important procedural, policy and political roles, it seems unlikely.

Notes

1 Patrick Weller, 'The vulnerability of prime ministers', *Parliamentary Affairs*, Winter, 36(i), 1983, pp. 96–117.
2 P. H. Bailey 'The Department of Prime Minister and Cabinet: an inevitable case of

schizophrenia', Seminar Paper, Australian National University, 1974.

3 G. J. Yeend 'The Department of Prime Minister and Cabinet in perspective', *Australian Journal of Public Administration*, 38 (1979), p. 143.

4 Ibid.

5 Ibid., p. 146.

6 For further details of PMC, see Yeend, 'The Department of Prime Minister and Cabinet'; Geoffrey Hawker, R. F. I. Smith and Patrick Weller, *Politics and Policy in Australia* (University of Queensland Press, St Lucia, 1979); F. A. Mediansky and J. A. Nockels, 'The prime minister's bureaucracy', *Public Administration* (*Sydney*), 34 (1975); Mediansky and Nockels, 'Malcolm Fraser's bureaucracy', *Australian Quarterly*, 53 (1981); Patrick Weller, 'Do prime minister's departments really create problems?', *Public Administration*, 61 (1983); Weller, *First Among Equals: Prime Ministers in Westminster Systems* (Allen & Unwin, Sydney, 1985); Patrick Weller and Michelle Grattan, *Can Ministers Cope? Australian Federal Ministers at Work* (Hutchinson, Melbourne, 1981).

7 D. A. Kemp, 'PM's private office supports "political" role', *Monash Reporter*, 6 August 1983.

8 Marc Lalonde 'The changing role of the Prime Minister's Office', *Canadian Public Administration*, 14, 4 (1971).

9 Kemp, 'PM's private office'.

10 Hawker et al., *Politics and Policy*.

11 John Stone's letter was reproduced in *The Age*, 25 November 1982.

12 Quoted in Weller and Grattan, *Can Ministers Cope?*

13 Quoted in Weller and Grattan, *Can Ministers Cope?*

14 Quoted in Patrick Weller and James Cutt, *Treasury Control in Australia* (Novak, Sydney, 1976).

15 See Gwynneth Singleton (1984), 'The National Economic Summit and the Economic Planning Advisory Council: the limits to consensus', BA Hons Thesis, Department of Political Science, The Faculties, Australian National University.

3

The United Kingdom

G. W. Jones

Britain has no Prime Minister's Department. There is a loose network of advisers and secretaries who work for the prime minister at No. 10 Downing Street and who constitute the 'Prime Minister's Office', a title used in official parlance only since 1976. From time to time the suggestion is made that a Prime Minister's Department should be established, but it provokes such a furore that the proposal is dropped. The questions this paper addresses are: why has Britain no Prime Minister's Department, and should it have one? The method is to explain the evolution of the present arrangements from the start of the modern system of 'democratic' government in the 1860s, and thus to illuminate the pressures that have shaped the very core of central government and still determine the structure of its organization. The task is to show how the two private secretaries who served the prime minister in 1867–8 at a cost of £600 a year have been transformed into around 90 aides in 1983–4 costing £1,123,000. Another objective is to assess whether this provision is appropriate for the needs of the prime minister, the requirements of the British constitution and for the good governance of the country.

This paper divides into five parts. The first is an examination of how the processes of specialization, fragmentation and hiving-off have shaped the evolution of the aides of prime ministers. The second outlines the history of the aides of prime ministers from 1868 to 1976. The third presents the arrangements for James Callaghan, 1976–9, while the fourth shows the arrangements for Margaret Thatcher, 1979–84. Thus the paper reveals the current system in the context not only of the one immediately preceding it, but also of historical trends from the 1860s. The fifth and final part makes the case why Britain does not need a Prime Minister's Department.

The Evolution of Prime Ministers' Aides

Although the size of the prime minister's staff has grown considerably over the past century and a half, the number of those at the core of the personnel has remained fairly small and constant. These private secretaries who form the 'private office' have risen in number from two to only six. In the eighteenth century a prime minister like the Duke of Newcastle had only one private secretary, a personal adherent paid from his private purse and not from public funds, who would assist him both in government and out. It was an easy transition to move from serving the patron in his private capacity to helping him perform his governmental roles. He was a personal, political and administrative aide, engaged in a variety of tasks, some humdrum and trivial but essential to smooth the master's daily life, and some of critical importance for the conduct of government.

The first time a salary was provided from public funds for a private secretary to the prime minister was in 1806, when £300 was allocated for one secretary for Lord Grenville. In 1812 Lord Liverpool was empowered to have two paid from public money. The number rose to three in 1875 for Disraeli, to five in 1965 for Harold Wilson and to six for James Callaghan in 1976. At times the number of private secretaries was higher than these figures, for instance in war time and when the prime minister held other portfolios which entitled him to extra assistance, and sometimes there have been private secretaries receiving no public remuneration, acting without pay or financed by the prime minister personally or by his political party.

The reason for only a small increase in the private office over the period is that many of the functions once carried out by the initial two private secretaries have been hived off to other aides or units within No. 10 Downing Street or else to institutions not serving the prime minister directly. Over time the jumble of activities that the private secretaries performed individually became specialized, fragmented and hived-off, leaving to the private secretaries the key jobs of providing a channel of communication between the prime minister and the official machine in Whitehall, of ensuring that the prime minister has all that is necessary for him or her to take decisions, and generally of overseeing all that the prime minister does.

Crown Appointments

One of the earliest areas of activity to be detached from the private secretaries was that of handling the appointment of bishops and other ecclesiastical appointments that the Crown made on the advice of the prime minister. During the Second World War Winston Chuchill left this work to one of the private secretaries, Anthony Bevir, who revelled in the preliminary processes of consultation. He was responsible also for preparing submissions to the prime minister on other Crown appointments, such as regius professorships or the Poet Laureate, for advice on those deserving aid from charitable funds in the gift of the prime minister, for the fabric and upkeep of No. 10 and for managing the more junior staff at Downing Street. Bevir developed this role into a full-time position, which in 1947 became known as the 'Secretary for Appointments'. The holder of this office usually stayed in it longer than the other private secretaries in theirs. On appointment he was often coming towards the end of his civil service career, unlike the others who had been picked out as younger high-flyers.

Press Liaison

Handling the press was a function once performed by the private secretaries. In 1931 the first press officer, George Steward, was appointed at No. 10 to deal with the economic crisis. He remained there throughout the thirties, providing a channel between the prime minister and the press. Churchill was suspicious of him and reverted to using the private secretaries as press links. But since Clement Attlee appointed Francis Williams as his public relations adviser there has always been a press and information officer at No. 10, responsible for advising the prime minister about the presentation of information, and for managing the relations between the prime minister and the media. Some have come from the ranks of the Government Information Service and were civil servants, while others have been former journalists politically sympathetic to the prime minister.

Policy Advice

Giving the prime minister policy advice was once a function of the private secretaries, especially of the most senior and closest to the prime minister. At times prime ministers sought policy advice from people brought to No. 10 specifically as policy advisers. Chamberlain relied on the civil servant Horace Wilson; Attlee had Douglas Jay, a former civil servant and aspirant MP; while Churchill depended on Lindemann, later Lord Cherwell, an academic, who built up a team of assistants in his Statistical Unit to serve the prime minister. This group in the Second World War was similar to the secretariat set up by Lloyd George in the First World War. Headed at the outset by the academic W. G. S. Adams, it consisted of a group of experts who gave policy appraisals only to the prime minister. So numerous were they that huts to accommodate them had to be constructed in the garden of No. 10, thus giving them their nickname of the 'garden suburb'.

A major innovation in the arrangements for giving policy advice to the prime minister was instituted by Harold Wilson in 1974, when he set up the Policy Unit at No. 10 Downing Street. Although in his governments of the 1960s Mr Wilson had the Oxford don Thomas Balogh to provide policy advice, especially on economic matters, Balogh and his assistants were not located in No. 10 but in the Cabinet Office building, and he was called an economic adviser to the cabinet, not to the prime minister alone. In 1974 Mr Wilson appointed as his senior policy adviser the London School of Economics academic Dr Bernard Donoughue, who was supported by around seven to eight assistants, who had their offices in No. 10. He also drew on the help of part-timers and outsiders when required. They were all experts in a particular policy area, usually had some experience of government, and were politically sympathetic to the government party.

When James Callaghan became prime minister in 1976 he continued to rely on the Policy Unit, even retaining the same personnel. On the change of government in 1979, Mrs Thatcher introduced her own staff into a slimmed-down version headed by John Hoskyns, but after his departure in 1982 she increased its size and brought to No. 10 a number of individual policy advisers for specific issues.

Support Staff

Another development has reduced the range of work once carried out by the private secretaries: the emergence of supporting staff within No. 10, performing personal, clerical and middle-rank executive duties, which once fell to the private secretaries. The clerical staff, who keep the office running smoothly, open the correspondence, file, type and generally handle routine business. They are organized into five sections under assistant private secretaries, covering honours, appointments, correspondence, records and confidential filing. These permanent staff provide continuity at No. 10. They now number around 70. At the turn of the century the three private secretaries would have had to carry out these chores themselves, although they were aided by a typist and shorthand writer in the 1890s. By the 1920s such supporting staff had risen to around 20, by 1952 to 52, by 1964 to 59 and by 1974 to 77.

Cabinet Office

Other tasks once performed by the private secretaries have been transferred out of No. 10, above all to the Cabinet Office. Set up in 1916 by Lloyd George, it took over from the private secretaries such functions as preparing the agenda for cabinet, calling ministers to attend, noting its decisions for the prime minister and circulating them to the other ministers, and generally helping the prime minister to ensure that ministers carried out cabinet decisions. Although the main role of the Cabinet Office is to serve the cabinet as a whole, and to secure collective government, it has come to perform functions primarily for the prime minister, which in some other countries might be located in a separate Prime Minister's Department. Even giving policy advice to the prime minister has become an important task of the Cabinet Secretary and his staff; he provides policy advice to the prime minister in his capacity as chairman of the cabinet.

For a time, between 1970 and 1983, there was a special unit in the Cabinet Office, the Central Policy Review Staff, which conducted analyses of policy issues, formally for the cabinet as a whole but in practice chiefly for the prime minister. This was a group of around 18, a mixture of seconded civil servants and outside experts, headed at first by Lord Rothschild and then by Sir Kenneth Berrill, Sir Robin Ibbs and finally by Sir John Sparrow, until in 1983 Mrs Thatcher decided it no longer met her needs.

The Cabinet Office has also been the place where prime ministers have put other aides with particular responsibilities, such as Mr Wilson's economic adviser, Thomas Balogh, or Mrs Thatcher's first adviser on efficiency in government, Derek Rayner, whose team to promote savings and value for money in the civil service was headed in 1983 by Sir Robin Ibbs. When Edward Heath had wanted to encourage business practices in government in 1970 he placed a group of businessmen under Richard Mejyes in the Civil Service Department, but Mrs Thatcher had abolished that department in 1981.

Thus the reason why the private office of the prime minister has been able to remain so small and so constant in size is because many of the functions it once performed at the end of the century have been re-allocated to other parts of the Prime Minister's Office or to other units outside No. 10. In a similar way to the process by which, in the middle ages, the household offices of the monarch were transformed into governmental institutions by a process of specialization and fragmentation, so for the prime minister the personal functions and services once carried out by the private secretaries became specialized and hived-off to distinct entities. Through this process there evolved not a Prime Minister's Department, but a loose network of assistants, which could be easily shaped to meet the particular needs of different prime ministers.

The History of Prime Ministers' Aides 1868–1976

The history of the network of aides to prime ministers is difficult to analyse into periods because each prime minister shapes the system to suit his or her purposes, and often wants to differentiate his style from that of his predecessor. So instead of a clear progression or evolution, there is a frequent sharp break as a new prime minister dispenses with some innovation of the former prime minister and introduces some new feature of his own. Prime ministers differ also in their modes of working. Some like many assistants and sources of advice; others prefer to rely more on their ministers and civil servants, and not to be surrounded with aides at No. 10. They differ too in their conceptions of the role of prime minister. Some want to be assertive, dominating their governments and imposing their own policy ideas; others act more as facilitators, helping their ministerial colleagues to achieve their objectives. Since there is no formally structured Prime Minister's Department the loose network of advisers and aides can easily be moulded to meet the distinctive needs of the individual prime ministers.

However, there are some trends and continuities, as has been shown in the previous section. It is also possible to divide the years from the 1860s into significant periods, and distinguish changes that were sustained from those that were peculiar to a particular prime minister.

1860s to 1900s

In this period the prime minister was helped by a mixture of personal, political and official aides. Some were relatives and close friends, or the relatives of close friends and political allies to whom the prime minister could dispense favours. They were often young men with political ambitions, who welcomed the chance to see politics from the top and to make useful contacts to further their political careers. Even the civil servants, invariably from the Treasury, were often known political supporters of the prime minister's party and owed their appointment at No. 10 to his political patronage and personal selection.

All stayed on the staff of the prime minister for only as long as the prime minister was in office. They departed when he left. There was no continuity at No. 10 from one prime minister to another. Although there was provision from the 1870s to pay three private secretaries from public funds, there were sometimes more serving the prime minister, financed privately. If a private secretary was an MP, then he would receive no salary. His role was like that of a Parliamentary private secretary (PPS) today, keeping the prime minister in touch with his party in Parliament. The rough division of work at No. 10 was for the civil servants to handle the routine business of the office, dealing with other civil servants and official matters. The others would tackle the more political items, dealing with ministers and people of political significance, liaising with them, conveying messages and handling their correspondence. The more senior the status of the secretary, the more important the business he dealt with, so the younger and less experienced had more of the chores to perform, while the most senior might be almost the *alter ego* of the prime minister, trusted as the voice and ears of his master, such as was Montague Corry for Disraeli.

1900s to 1916

In this period sharper distinctions came to be drawn amongst the secretaries at No. 10 and they became more specialized in their functions. The Principal Private Secretary emerged clearly as the head of the office, and he was not a civil servant but a personal and political appointee, such as Balfour's J. S.

Sandars, Campbell-Bannerman's Arthur Ponsonby and Asquith's Vaughan Nash and Maurice Bonham-Carter. The civil servants still handled the more routine business, and were the junior staff at No. 10, although some came to be trusted with more important policy issues involving the departments, for instance Asquith's Eric Drummond. A division of labour between the secretaries was clearer than in the past, yet there was still a blurring of roles. The staff acted as a team to help the prime minister, sharing often in the prime minister's social life, playing bridge and dining with Asquith, and in Bonham-Carter's case, even marrying his daughter.

1916 to 1922

The period of Lloyd George and of Bonar Law was critical and formative in the shaping of the prime minister's network of aides. The reverberations of that time are still throbbing today. Lloyd George cleared out all of Asquith's staff, and brought in his own. Into the private office he put his political and private secretaries with J. T. Davies as the Principal, taken from his previous department, and he also installed as a private secretary his mistress, Frances Stevenson. To provide him with policy advice he set up the 'garden suburb' of experts, at first headed by W. G. S. Adams and later by Philip Kerr, the first time a prime minister had sought a source of policy advice working solely to him. He also established the Cabinet Office under Maurice Hankey to prepare cabinet business, to take its minutes, to ensure its conclusions were acted upon by the departments and generally to coordinate government in line with cabinet decisions. Hankey and his staff were often indistinguishable in their advice and memoranda from those of the private office or of the new secretariat.

This major increase in the aides of the prime minister reflected Lloyd George's more interventionist view of the role of prime minister, but inadvertently he had set up the very institution that would inhibit the development of a Prime Minister's Department in this country: the Cabinet Office. If the private office had continued on the lines it had been evolving along under Asquith, then the work of servicing the cabinet would have fallen to the prime minister's private office, with the Principal Private Secretary carrying out the tasks later performed by Hankey. Instead, under Lloyd George it ran down two tracks. He enhanced the prime minister's side with the 'garden suburb' and the cabinet side with the Cabinet Office. At the time it seemed as if he was strengthening his own personal power and becoming an 'Imperial Caesar', since both the 'garden suburb' and the Cabinet Office were seen as sustaining prime ministerial power.

On his fall from office in 1922, it was expected that both these innovations would be demolished by Bonar Law. However, although he dismantled the 'suburb', he did not destroy the Cabinet Office or merge it with the Treasury as

Warren Fisher, its permanent secretary, wanted. The long-term significance of these events is that a counterbalance to the staff serving the prime minister alone had been established on a firm basis. The Cabinet Office had taken over functions that might otherwise have been performed by a Prime Minister's Department. Indeed, the creation of any such department was blocked by conferring on the Cabinet Office the very functions that would have been the core activities of such a department. The Cabinet Office, with its commitment to supporting the collective processes of British government, also helped to check the pretensions of prime ministers to become presidential. Prime ministers always faced a department constantly reminding them of the need to involve the cabinet.

1920s to 1930s

The significant change of this period was the achievement by the civil service of dominance in the private office and a downgrading of other personal and political aides of the prime minister to an inferior and dispersed status elsewhere at No. 10. The key figure of the period is the Principal Private Secretary, Sir Ronald Waterhouse. He was a soldier and Conservative sympathizer, and friend of Bonar Law who appointed him to be his Principal Private Secretary in 1922. He remained in that position for Stanley Baldwin and more significantly for Ramsay MacDonald, the first time that a private secretary of one prime minister stayed on to serve a prime minister of a different party, establishing a precedent of impartial civil service continuity. Waterhouse was also retained again by Stanley Baldwin in 1924 on the collapse of MacDonald's government. He was thus Principal Private Secretary to three prime ministers from 1922 to 1929, and in that time it became the practice for the other private secretaries to be civil servants, seconded from their departments for a stint at No. 10 lasting usually about three to four years. They were normally young men in their late twenties or early thirties who would rise soon to top positions in their departments on their return from No. 10. The work in the private office became more specialized: for instance, one private secretary tended to handle all the prime minister's Parliamentary questions, and, as we have seen, a press and information officer was appointed for the first time in 1931.

Prime ministers still found it necessary to have close to them personal and political advisers who were not part of the civil service nor of the private office. Bonar Law and Stanley Baldwin brought to No. 10 Sir Geoffrey Fry, a wealthy barrister, who helped them both in an unpaid capacity, handling correspondence, acting as a channel of communication and generally being available for whatever duties the prime minister asked him to undertake. Ramsay MacDonald took to No. 10 Herbert Usher as his political secretary. He had been a political journalist and Parliamentary candidate. Also at No. 10 was MacDonald's personal secretary, Rose Rosenberg. Such aides were separate from the private office, and were not regarded as so important. Neville Chamberlain introduced to No. 10 as his adviser Horace Wilson, who had been the government's industrial adviser. For Chamberlain he ranged much more widely, especially on foreign affairs. Prime ministers relied a great deal on the Cabinet Secretary, Hankey, and on Warren Fisher of the Treasury, who was also official head of the home civil service. They were the two leading civil service advisers to the prime minister. Outside the staff in the private office, they were also the civil servants who most often came into contact with the prime minister: the former encountered the prime minister in his capacity as chairman of the cabinet, and the latter as the First Lord of the Treasury and thus the ministerial head of the civil service.

1940 to 1945

The Second World War did not witness such a great upheaval in the arrangements at No. 10 as had the Great War, but there were important developments. Churchill ejected most of Chamberlain's secretaries and aides and brought in civil servants who had been helping him at the Admiralty, but he did retain John Colville, the most junior of the private secretaries, who later became one of his most trusted assistants. The insertion of Churchill's private office from the Admiralty into Downing Street is said by some to be the occasion for the first use of the term 'private office' at No. 10. Before the word came from the Admiralty, it is suggested, no one would have spoken of the 'private office'; they would have talked of serving the prime minister, or of working at No. 10. Official language takes some time to catch up with practice, for there had clearly been at No. 10 since the early twenties a group of civil servants constituting a distinct, private office.

Churchill's big innovation was to repeat the experiment of Lloyd George by creating his own team of advisers, under the Oxford academic Lindemann. His Statistical Section was very similar to the 'garden suburb', a group of experts working only for him. He continued to rely on the Cabinet Office, on Edward Bridges for the civil side and on 'Pug' Ismay for the military. He also made use of confidential aides, or cronies, like Desmond Morton, for liaison with foreign governments in exile and views on intelligence matters, and on late-night drinking companions, like Lord Beaverbrook and Brendan Bracken.

Thus Churchill maintained a loose network of aides, yet at the heart of it was the private office. It sought to ensure that the prime minister had available all the information he needed to take his decisions, that he was where he was supposed to be at all times, and that his daily life ran smoothly. It provided the disciplined framework within which the prime minister could function.

1945 to 1964

The set-up at No. 10 in this period presents a picture of stability, disrupted only occasionally by the intrusion of outside elements. Although Clement Attlee began his term by bringing in a few personal aides, such as Douglas Jay, he soon found that he could depend on the civil servants in his private office for whatever help he needed, as well as the Cabinet Office. The private office itself became more structured and its work allocated more specifically between the private secretaries. There were normally four private secretaries: at the head was the Principal Private Secretary, in charge of the office and the civil servant closest to the prime minister; then there was a private secretary handling foreign affairs, usually from the Foreign Office; a private secretary from a home department dealing mainly with economic issues; and one responsible for Parliamentary affairs, especially the prime minister's Parliamentary questions. As we have seen, advice to the prime minister on a range of appointments had, under Churchill, been hived-off to one private secretary, Anthony Bevir; he built this task into a full-time occupation, symbolized in 1947 by the title 'Secretary for Appointments' appearing for the first time in the *Imperial Calendar* as a distinct position at No. 10. Attlee, as we have also seen, established the post of 'Public Relations Adviser', and his section grew over the years. The prime minister relied heavily on his cabinet secretaries, first Bridges and then Norman Brook, not only for administrative help but also for policy advice, even on the most controversial issues of the day.

Churchill's return to power in 1951 produced a slight hiccup in No. 10. On seeing his civil service private office for the first time he is reported to have exclaimed they were drenched in socialism and that he wanted back his old team of Leslie Rowan and John Colville. His obduracy meant that there was a sharing of the position of Principal Private Secretary between Colville and the official in post, David Pitblado. Otherwise Attlee's structure was retained, except that Churchill relied considerably on his son-in-law Christopher Soames, who was his Parliamentary private secretary and acted very much as some of the political and personal secretaries to prime ministers in the late nineteenth century.

Anthony Eden adopted the Attlee system and made no real change, but Harold Macmillan instituted some small yet significant adaptations. He added to the private office an outsider, John Wyndham, the first to invade the civil service preserve since the twenties. He sat at a desk in the private office rooms, handled business like a private secretary and was generally available to give advice to the prime minister. He was a genial companion who relaxed the prime minister with his wit and humour. Mr Macmillan also drew on the services of aides from Conservative Central Office for help in speech writing, as did his successor Sir Alec Douglas-Home. Wyndham and these party assistants were not paid from public funds: the former had a private income and the latter were financed by their party. Mr Macmillan's other major change was to introduce into the cabinet room his Principal Private Secretary while cabinet meetings were taking place. He would sit by the door ready to convey urgent messages. Mr Macmillan felt it saved time by having the secretary present at cabinet: he would not have to tell him later what had happened.

1964 to 1976

In this period attempts were made by prime ministers to counterbalance the long-established predominance of civil servants at No. 10 through the introduction of a more explicit personal and political set of advisers. Indeed, it might be said that they sought to return to the older tradition of having their personal adherents with them. Their motives were suspicion of possible civil service lack of enthusiasm rather than of overt sabotage of the politicians' policy proposals, and the need to strengthen the resources available to the prime minister to push the government in the direction he wanted it to go. Harold Wilson said he hoped to turn No. 10 from a monastery into a power house. His most widely commented-on action was to bring to Downing Street in 1964, as his political secretary, his secretary while in opposition, Mrs Marcia Williams. He located her in an office on the other side of the cabinet room from the private office. Thus the political and administrative aides of the prime minister were positioned on opposite sides of the cabinet. He also was widely reported to have had frequent discussions on policy with an informal group of secretaries, advisers, aides and cronies, of fluctuating composition, popularly dubbed the 'kitchen cabinet', in which Mrs Williams was said to be prominent. She was depicted as having more power than some ministers and to have had blazing rows with civil servants who were supposed to have been frustrating Labour's policies. Mr Wilson sought to inject a stronger political element into No. 10 by appointing as his heads of the press and information divisions politically sympathetic journalists rather than civil servants from the Government Information Service. He sought alternative sources of policy advice in the 1960s by placing Thomas Balogh in the Cabinet Office, and in the 1970s by creating the Policy Unit under Bernard Donoughue in No. 10 itself: both were to provide advice to the prime minister so that he would not be at the mercy of advice from the civil service and ministers alone.

Mr Wilson also increased the size of the private office by one to give him an extra secretary on the domestic front. However, his most disruptive action was his interference in the selection procedures of the private office. The usual way in which secretaries had been chosen was for the civil service to take the initiative and send the prime minister about three candidates he might consider. After interview, he would select. Mr Wilson, however, was not as ready to accept the choices of the machine, especially over the position of Principal Private Secretary. The civil service tried when submitting their names to find people who might be expected to work easily with the prime minister. They sought to find a point of contact, as with Derek Mitchell's Fabian sympathies for Mr Wilson's and the Labour government's objectives, or with Robert Armstrong's love of music, which was thought to give him a close connection with Edward Heath. The civil service tried to anticipate the sort of Principal Private Secretary a prime minister would choose. However, Mr Wilson was not very happy with Mr Mitchell, who did not get on well with Mrs Williams, and when a successor was mooted he rejected the advice of his civil servants and insisted on having at No. 10 his former private secretary from the Board of Trade in the 1940s, whom the civil service regarded as unsuitable and not up to the requirements of the job. In the event the secretary died under the strain. For the appointment of his successor, Mr Wilson again went against civil service advice and insisted on his own choice. When Edward Heath became prime minister this secretary was removed prematurely from No. 10 to be replaced by one of whom the civil service approved. When Mr Wilson returned to power in 1974 he did not engage in similar attempts to select private secretaries whom the civil service thought inappropriate.

Mr Heath maintained the office of political secretary, locating his choice, the former foreign office official and his political secretary in opposition, Douglas Hurd, in the room previously occupied by Mrs Williams. He sought to distance himself from Mr Wilson by playing down the more obvious political elements at No. 10. In the press office he dispensed with politically sympathetic journalists and oppointed members of the civil service, especially those who had served in the Foreign Office news department, like Donald Maitland and Robin Haydon. He placed a team of businessmen under Richard Mejyes in the Civil Service Department to encourage the use by government of the best business practices, and in the Cabinet Office he created the Central Policy Review Staff under Lord Rothschild to conduct analyses of policies and policy issues that crossed departmental boundaries, and to keep under review government policies to ensure they conformed to the government's strategic objectives. This 'think-tank' was located deliberately in the Cabinet Office and not in the prime minister's office at No. 10 to fend off criticism that he was seeking to aggrandize his status with the establishment of a Prime Minister's Department.

In 1974 Mr Wilson put Mrs Williams back in her old room beside the cabinet room, appointed a politically sympathetic journalist, Joe Haines, as his press and information officer, and set up the Policy Unit under Dr Donoughue, but other than changing these political elements, he retained the structure and personnel of the civil service secretaries.

The next two sections will examine in detail the working arrangements of

James Callaghan and Margaret Thatcher. First is a snapshot of how the network was made up in 1979, on the eve of the general election.

Mr Callaghan's System, 1976 to 1979: the Wider Network

There are three central functions that prime ministerial departments, and presidential and chancellor's departments, often perform: first, control over the machinery of government; second, coordinating policy formulation and implementation; and third, controlling and allocating resources. In Britain in 1979 these functions were scattered among a number of departments. Control over the machinery of government and the civil service was given to the Civil Service Department, established in 1968; policy coordination was performed by the Cabinet Office, set up in 1916; and resource allocation was overseen by the Treasury. The ultimate political responsibility for each of the three departments was in fact the prime minister's, because the prime minister was the minister for the civil service and the political head of the Civil Service Department, although he left the day-to-day ministerial running of that department to the Lord Privy Seal. The prime minister was also the first minister in the cabinet, its chairman and thus the political head of the Cabinet Office. He was also the First Lord of the Treasury, his official title on the name-plate at No. 10 Downing Street. He was, in fact, the political boss of the three central departments and he had reporting to him the three most important civil servants in Britain: the Permanent Under-Secretary of the Civil Service Department, Sir Ian Bancroft, the official head of the home civil service, reported to the prime minister in the prime minister's capacity as the minister for the civil service; the official head of the Cabinet Office was the Secretary to the Cabinet, Sir John Hunt, who again reported directly to the prime minister; the Permanent Under-Secretary of the Treasury was Sir Douglas Wass, who would report directly to the prime minister. They were the most highly paid civil servants, receiving more than other permanent secretaries. There was a fourth in this category: the Permanent Under-Secretary of the Foreign and Commonwealth Office, Sir Michael Palliser, the head of the diplomatic service. These were Britain's top mandarins.

Of these four, the two who had the most regular and closest contact with the prime minister were the Cabinet Secretary and the official head of the home civil service. The relationship between the prime minister and these two, and indeed the four, fluctuated depending as much on their personal relationships as on the issues uppermost at the time. The prime minister also had reporting to him the head of the Central Policy Review Staff (the CPRS), the 'think-tank' located within the Cabinet Office. Sir Kenneth Berrill, the head of CPRS, had direct access to the prime minister. The prime minister, if he wanted and had informed the relevant minister, could also call in for help the permanent secretaries of other departments, when he was concerned with a problem that fell within the responsibility of a particular department. He had access not only to generalist administrators but also top specialists in Whitehall, scientific, military or other professionals located in different departments, and was in close contact with the security services.

Although the levers of control were not all gathered together into one Prime Minister's Department, the prime minister could touch these levers if he wanted to engage them, and the prime minister could also draw on contacts with his ministerial colleagues. They met formally in cabinet and cabinet committees and also informally. Each day the Chief Whip moved through the corridor from No. 12 to No. 11 into No. 10 Downing Street. The doors between 10, 11 and 12 were open, with constant interchange. The prime minister was not locked into monastic seclusion. He went regularly to the House of Commons. He had a room in the House of Commons, he walked in the corridors, where he could be lobbied and contacted by Members of Parliament. He travelled around the country and received many deputations. There were numerous people coming into contact with him whose services he could draw on. However, the individuals mentioned so far did not have a primary loyalty to him. They had their own main functions to perform, and their own careers and ambitions to pursue independently of the prime minister.

The people who served only the prime minister made up what was officially called 'the Prime Minister's Office'. This staff totalled about 80 and could be divided into four main groups. Each of these groups had its own chief responsibility, although the work of one group impinged very closely on the work of another.

The Private Office

The first group, the core of No. 10 Downing Street, was the private office, consisting of six civil servants. They inhabited two rooms adjacent to the cabinet: two rooms between which the inter-connecting door was always open. In the first room, the one next to the cabinet room, was the head of the private office, the Principal Private Secretary, Mr Kenneth Stowe. He had been in this position since 1975, rather longer than the usual term of about three years. He could be regarded as the prime minister's chief of staff. His rank was equivalent to deputy secretary and his role was to oversee No. 10 as a whole. He coordinated the submissions that went to the prime minister. He was in charge of the box which contained all papers for the prime minister, seeing it last before it went to the prime minister. He was always involved in the most important items that interested the prime minister. Whatever was uppermost in the prime minister's mind, Mr Stowe would be handling, and as the head of No. 10 he kept in close touch with Sir Ian Bancroft, the head of the home civil service, and with the Cabinet Secretary, Sir John Hunt, and although a deputy secretary, he could contact freely any permanent secretary. He was responsible for linking the prime minister with Buckingham Palace; he handled business with the Queen's private secretary, preparing the weekly audience between the monarch and her chief minister. He took a particular interest in the machinery of government, in the appointments that the prime minister made and the honours granted.

In the same room as the Principal Private Secretary was the private secretary who handled overseas affairs, defence matters and Northern Ireland. He invariably came on secondment to No. 10 from the Foreign Office and was of counsellor (Assistant Secretary) rank. In the second room, beyond the door which was always kept open, were crowded together the other private secretaries. There was an assistant secretary from one of the economic departments who handled economic affairs. There were two principals: one dealt with other domestic issues, usually not of an economic nature; the other focused on the prime minister's relations with Parliament. His main job was to prepare the prime minister for his question periods that came twice a week, Tuesdays and Thursdays. He had to process the prime minister's Parliamentary questions, especially to provide him with the possible answers he would need to supplementary questions. The sixth person in these two rooms was a higher executive officer, who dealt with the prime minister's correspondence with the public. He kept his diary and fixed up his engagements and travel arrangements.

These six civil servants made up the private office. Each had his own main concern, but was not limited just to sticking to his range of responsibilities. Each had to be ready to take over the work of the others. This flexibility was encouraged by the nature of the room. The six were crammed together: they overheard conversations; they chatted together about business and dipped into each other's work trays. When work was finished it was put in a tray, the 'dip', and each secretary could go along and 'dip' in and see what the others had been doing. In this claustrophobic setting it was very easy to pick up what was going on, and it was very important to get on well together. Secretaries frequently talked about the team spirit at No. 10, and how they had to act like the rugby pack, and be ready to pick up the ball and run with it. This need to interchange with each other was reinforced by a rota system for the evenings and holidays so that one of them was always available to take over the work of another.

Members of the private office were seconded on loan from their departments and usually served about three years at No. 10. This temporary secondment avoided building up a 'No. 10 view' or a Prime Minister's Department. It was also thought to be important because three years was about all that one could stand at the top. Private secretaries in the private office were usually in their early thirties, 'high-flyers', thought to be the most able in the civil service. They were given a taste of what it was like at the top and the danger was that it could be too 'heady', too attractive, which made it difficult for an official if he stayed too long to go back into his department to routine, dull work. Three years were felt to be about enough to avoid that kind of 'corruption'. The other sort of 'corruption' that could take place was that private secretaries might become too attached to the prime minister, as happened with some of the private secretaries of Lloyd George and Harold Macmillan, who found it impossible to go back into their departments and so left the civil service.

Below these temporary denizens of No. 10 and supporting them were the more permanent staff. There were four assistant private secretaries, all women, who provided continuity at No. 10. They were the repositories of very long experience about practice and procedure. Some went back in their experience to the 1940s, and when they first came they had been working with colleagues who were at No. 10 in the 1920s. The continuity of the No. 10 assistant private secretaries can be traced back to 1916. These redoubtable 'Queen Bees' headed sections on honours, on confidential filing, on records and correspondence. Underneath them in the hierarchy were 'the garden-room girls' who inhabited a room that looked out onto the garden of No. 10. They constituted a pool of shorthand-typists who served the prime minister and private secretaries. The prime minister did not have his own typist. There was a pool of constantly interchangeable women. Also making up this official element at No. 10 were the duty clerks, executive officers who were there 24 hours a day. They formed a back-up staff, performing a range of supporting tasks.

The private office never slept. A private secretary, one of the six, was always on call, and the office was always manned at least by an executive officer. The telephone switchboard responded throughout the 24 hours. The private office was the operations room of No. 10. Everything going into and out of No. 10 went through the private office. The private secretaries saw their role as to ease the burden on the prime minister, to help the prime minister think and act, and to ensure that he had all the necessary advice and information he required for his decisions. They saw their job as being to smooth the prime minister's way, clearing away the trivial and routine so that he could concentrate on the essential. So they performed, at one extreme, somewhat minor tasks – keeping his diary, arranging his day, seeing he got to where he ought to be – and, on the other hand, briefing him on important current issues and prospective developments. They helped to draft his speeches, prepared him for meetings and engagements and in particular they were a channel of communication with Whitehall. The private secretaries of Whitehall constituted the 'bush telegraph' of government. There was a network of private secretaries in the other departments who were closely linked with the prime minister's private secretaries at No. 10. On this network they could signal out how the prime minister was thinking, what he was intending to do, what he had done; and they could collect in from the departments what the other ministers were doing, how departments were reacting, and ferry this information to the prime minister. No. 10 was at the centre of this 'bush telegraph'. The private secretaries there thought of their job as being to ensure that the prime minister had before him full information so that he could take his decisions; and once his decision was taken, they then conveyed his views back to the departments.

They also acted as a filter, a sort of gatekeeper, because in their role of selecting what went to the prime minister, they could exclude what they thought inappropriate. They chose both the papers and the people that were to go before the prime minister. Most did not see themselves simply as a post-bag for others; before they sent items to the prime minister they would scribble a few words or lines on it, pointing out its significance, and perhaps commenting where they thought a submission was deficient or where something new had taken place. From their central vantage point, they might spot something, a consequence or implication, neglected by departments that might be somewhat blinkered. There were basically two streams of paper to the prime minister – those from ministers' departments directly and those channelled through the Cabinet Office. The private secretaries put more comments on the papers that came directly from ministers and departments than on papers that came from the Cabinet Office. The Cabinet Office itself was performing a filtering, commenting, coordinating role, and the private office felt less need, normally, to comment on their submissions.

The private office was much concerned with Parliament, which loomed very large in the eyes of civil servants. Much of their time was spent on preparing the prime minister for his Parliamentary activities. One private secretary worked virtually full-time planning for the prime minister's Parliamentary question period, and a great deal of attention was given to speeches and statements that the prime minister had to deliver in the Commons, above all alerting him to the pitfalls that might lie ahead.

The private office handled all his correspondence in and out, and private secretaries tried to be near the prime minister at all times, and at all meetings. He was the only minister to have his own staff in the cabinet room when a meeting was taking place: either the Principal Private Secretary or the private secretary who was handling the business being discussed at that point on the agenda.

The private office shadowed the prime minister, taking notes of all his important conversations, with ministers for example. They listened in on his phone calls, unless he expressly asked them not to. This eavesdropping was essential to record what was discussed, the prime minister's decisions and to ensure they could be followed up. Private secretaries have called this work 'watching the body', or acting as 'groom-in-waiting'. The essence of a good private secretary is 'never to be out of the way but never in the way'.

The private secretaries, then, carried out a variety of tasks. Their major objectives were to help the prime minister conduct his business efficiently, to do what the prime minister would do if he had the time and energy to do it himself, to provide extra hands, eyes, legs, mouths and arms for the prime minister. That was the private office, the core, the first of the four elements at No. 10.

The Political Office

While the private office linked the prime minister mainly to the world of officials at Whitehall, the prime minister needed also to be linked to the world of politics. Mr Callaghan appointed not a political secretary but a political adviser, Tom McNally, a former research official at Transport House on the international relations side, who first came to know the prime minister in the years of opposition from 1970. When Labour formed the government in 1974, Mr Callaghan took him to the Foreign Office as his political adviser, and from the Foreign Office the prime minister transferred Mr McNally to No. 10. Mr McNally was a temporary civil servant, paid from public funds, but he had a staff of four who were paid from a political fund financed by the Labour Party, the trade unions and the Co-operative Society. The people under Mr McNally constituted the political office.

Mr McNally's role was to deal with primarily party political matters, to liaise with party headquarters, the officials and the proliferation of committees at Transport House. He handled the correspondence with the party, from Labour supporters and MPs. He acted as a politically reliable channel to and from the prime minister. If one wanted to contact the prime minister and did not want the civil service to know, one would go through the political secretary. He commented on papers circulating around No. 10, added notes to the briefs, and on the papers that came in from different departments and ministers. He sat in on committees of ministers and civil servants if the prime minister so desired. He helped the prime minister in building up and drafting his speeches. He checked over speeches written by other members of the No. 10 outfit. His concern was with their party political dimension, but he was generally available to the prime minister for political advice.

The Policy Unit

The third element at No. 10 was the Policy Unit, created in 1974 by Harold Wilson, and taken over by James Callaghan. Mr Wilson's head of the Policy Unit was his senior policy adviser, Dr Bernard Donoughue, and Mr Callaghan continued with him. Dr Donoughue, a former journalist, political historian and lecturer at the London School of Economics, was a temporary civil servant, paid from public funds. He had a team of about seven, and could also call in other people as consultants on a part-time basis. His unit were specialists and therefore unlike the generalists in the private office. They were also Labour supporters, whereas the civil servants in the private office had no party affiliation. Dr Donoughue also sought people with some experience of government, perhaps as consultants or advisers earlier on.

The role of this unit was forward policy analysis, medium and long term, on domestic and overseas policy. They could act on their own initiative if they thought there was a policy area that required their contribution. They also acted in response to a prime minister's request. Their link to the prime minister was through Dr Donoughue, who from time to time put to the prime minister papers of about two or three pages on an issue, or else he talked to the prime minister. The Policy Unit gave the prime minister a view that was different from that of the official machine and from that coming to him from separate departments. They commented on and probed the advice coming in from these other sources.

Dr Donoughue attended ministerial meetings when the prime minister asked, and sat in on a number of official committees, including one of the most important committees in British government, that of deputy secretaries of the Cabinet Office, chaired by the Secretary of the Cabinet, which met every week to plan cabinet business for the weeks ahead. By 'cabinet business' is meant not just meetings of the cabinet but also of the many cabinet committees. The deputy secretaries arranged what cabinet committees were to be set up, who was to sit upon them and the timetabling of the business. They planned the cabinet's programme of work, the 'fixture list for the cabinet policy season'. Both Dr Donoughue and the Principal Private Secretary, Mr Stowe, went to this committee. Thus the prime minister had two people making an input into the agenda-setting function.

Dr Donoughue maintained contact himself and through his team with the specialist advisers in the departments. One of the features of the 1970s was the emergence of these special advisers, both the political advisers and the more expert advisers appointed by a number of ministers. They totalled about 25. They built up their own informal network of regular contacts, through which No. 10 could learn what was going on inside the departments and the problems that were arising. Although the Policy Unit dealt with the middle- and long-term policy, Dr Donoughue was also called upon to help in immediate crises, drafting white papers, government announcements and prime ministerial speeches. The Policy Unit provided the prime minister with a source of policy analysis uniquely loyal to him. Certainly the private office professed loyalty to him, but he probably felt that they had to have regard to their careers, and to the people who would be promoting them in the future. They might appear loyal primarily to the official machine and be reticent on certain issues, while the Policy Unit, with its political composition, could say the sorts of things that officials neither could nor would want to.

The Press and Information Office

The fourth element at No. 10 Downing Street was the press and information office, headed by the press secretary, Tom McCaffrey, with a staff of about ten. He first worked for Mr Callaghan when he was Home Secretary in the 1960s. When Mr Callaghan became Foreign Secretary in 1974 he asked Mr McCaffrey to be his press officer at the Foreign Office, and he subsequently took him with him to No. 10. The role of the press office was to link the prime minister to the press and broadcasting organizations. The press office and the press secretary handled the lobby correspondents, giving briefings each day about what was going on at No. 10 and generally in government. They planned the prime minister's broadcasts, and were the main source of advice to him about how to present his image and the whole range of government policy. They acted as general public relations advisers.

Other Aides

At No. 10 there were also the messengers, security staff, domestic staff and cleaning staff, and there were three other somewhat detached elements. There was the Secretary for Appointments, Mr C. V. Peterson, who occupied the best staff room at No. 10. He was a civil servant who handled the ecclesiastical and other Crown appointments, acting as 'heaven's talent scout'. He was involved very much with the many appointments to various bishoprics and deaneries. He also operated a number of charities. He acted as the personnel manager for the junior staff at No. 10, and looked after the structure and furnishing at both No. 10 and Chequers.

There was also the prime minister's Parliamentary private secretary (PPS), Roger Stott, who was a backbench MP and unpaid. He had a desk in Mr McNally's office but he worked mainly from the prime minister's room at the House of Commons. His job was to link the prime minister to the backbenchers in the Commons and keep him in touch with the comings and goings and the gossip in Westminster. The prime minister, if he wanted, could use him on special tasks. There was also the prime minister's constituency and personal secretary, Ms Ruth Sharp, who was paid by Mr Callaghan personally and who had been with him for years, from when he was a backbench MP. She handled his more private correspondence, his relationships with his constituency agent and his personal and family matters.

To summarize, the four main elements in No. 10 were the private office, the political office, the Policy Unit and press office. The heads of each had direct personal access to the prime minister and were in daily contact with him. Each had a main responsibility but there was no rigid demarcation of duties at No. 10. At the top in politics sharp distinctions do not count; all is ambiguity and shading. The private office, for instance, needed to be very much attuned to political factors; it had much political business to handle. The political office was often concerned with issues of future policy and with handling the press. The press office advised the prime minister on his speeches and on policy matters, and the prime minister depended very heavily on and listened a great deal to the influential Mr McCaffrey. The Policy Unit did not have its gaze fixed only on the future or the medium term. Dr Donoughue's unit was frequently engaged in quite short term problems – drafting a White Paper, handling difficult politicians and awkward trade unionists. At No. 10 politics and administration interpenetrated.

Mrs Thatcher's System, 1979 to 1984

The structure of the Prime Minister's Office under Mrs Thatcher remained, from 1979 to 1984, very much as it had been under Mr Callaghan, and its size was unchanged too, at around 80 people. Some slight modifications occurred, some titles changed and new people appeared. As in the past, the office adapted to the needs and style of the prime minister. She resisted advice from a number of outside observers, like Sir Alfred Sherman, to set up a Prime Minister's Department. She preferred not to restructure the administrative machine and set up a bureaucratic institution that would irritate her ministers and departmental civil servants. She felt she could obtain the advice and assistance she needed by maintaining a loose network of varied aides located in different places. This system would give her the support she wanted without alienating either her political or official colleagues.

She did, however, undertake two major administrative changes outside the Prime Minister's Office that altered the arrangements for providing advice to the very centre of government. In 1981 she abolished the Civil Service Department and retired prematurely its permanent under-secretary, Sir Ian Bancroft, who was the official head of the home civil service. The department's functions were distributed to the Treasury and the Cabinet Office, with the Management and Personnel Office established in the latter and responsible to the prime minister for running the civil service. From 1981 to 1983 there were two joint official heads of the home civil service: Sir Douglas Wass, Permanent Under Secretary at the Treasury, and Sir Robert Armstrong, the Cabinet Secretary, who had replaced Sir John Hunt in 1979. On the retirement of Sir

Douglas in 1983 Sir Robert became the sole official head of the home civil service, while remaining Cabinet Secretary.

Sir Robert was no stranger to the centre of government. He had been Principal Private Secretary at No. 10 to both Edward Heath and Harold Wilson. He was the first former Principal Private Secretary there to go on to be Secretary of the Cabinet, and the first Cabinet Secretary to have served as a permanent under-secretary elsewhere (the Home Office) before going to the Cabinet Office. His influence was further enhanced following the Franks report on the Falklands conflict, when the Cabinet Office was given an increased role in coordinating intelligence. (In 1982 Sir Michael Palliser retired as Permanent Under-Secretary of the Foreign and Commonwealth Office, to be replaced by Sir Anthony Acland; and in 1983 Sir Douglas Wass was replaced at the Treasury by Peter Middleton. So, by 1983, there had been a complete change of personnel among the most important civil servants from when Mr Callaghan was prime minister.)

Mrs Thatcher's second major administrative change was to abolish the Central Policy Review Staff in 1983. On the retirement in 1980 of its head, Sir Kenneth Berrill, Robin Ibbs, a top executive at ICI, took over. He was in turn replaced in 1982 by a merchant banker, John Sparrow. The prime minister, however, was finding that the CPRS was not useful for her purposes. She was relying for policy advice more on her aides at No. 10, and she felt that the CPRS was a leaky vessel, not fully committed to her. It was wound up after the election of 1983.

Within the Cabinet Office, the prime minister created a new post of 'Prime Minister's Adviser on Efficiency'. Its first holder was the joint managing director of Marks and Spencer, Sir (later Lord) Derek Rayner, who on a part-time basis conducted reviews of the performance of selected parts of the civil service. The second holder was Sir Robin Ibbs, who in 1983 returned to serve Mrs Thatcher.

At No. 10 itself the official side remained much as before in structure and functions. The Principal Secretary, Mr Stowe, was succeeded in 1979 by Clive Whitmore, who had served previously in the War Office, the Department of Defence and the Cabinet Office. In 1983 he was promoted Permanent Under-Secretary at the Department of Defence and was followed as Principal Private Secretary at No. 10 by Robin Butler from the Treasury. Mr Butler had been a private secretary at No. 10, both when Sir Robert Armstrong had been the Principal there and subsequently under Mr Stowe. Thus from 1983 the two top officials advising the prime minister were former colleagues who had served together at Downing Street under both Mr Heath and Mr Wilson, and they were both civil servants from the Treasury.

Four private secretaries covered overseas affairs, economic affairs, Parliamentary affairs and home affairs and the diary. In the 1970s the member of the private office who handled Parliamentary affairs moved on to home affairs, but under Mrs Thatcher the Secretary responsible for home affairs graduated to Parliamentary affairs. Mrs Thatcher was also eager to ensure that one of the private secretaries had a scientific background. A sixth member of the private office, Ms Caroline Stephens, was personal assistant to the prime minister. Whereas the others stayed for the usual three or so years at No. 10, Ms Stephens has been there since 1979. She does not handle policy; she looks after the personal requirements of Mrs Thatcher, such as ensuring the right clothes are packed. She keeps the diary of engagements under the supervision of the home affairs private secretary.

The Secretary for Appointments, Mr C. V. Peterson, was succeeded in 1982 by Mr J. R. Catford, who continues the role of preparing the background material for appointments on which the prime minister takes the critical decisions. The long-serving 'Queen Bee', Miss J. M. Porter, retired as assistant private secretary to the prime minister in 1983.

The chief press secretary since 1979 is Bernard Ingham, a former journalist who moved into the civil service as a chief information officer at the Department of Employment and Productivity, and was later at the Energy Department in charge of the conservation division. He is a vigorous exponent of the prime minister's views to the media.

Within the political side of No. 10 there have been more significant changes. Indeed, for the first time, the 1983 edition of the *Civil Service Yearbook* recognized a distinct part of the Prime Minister's Office as the 'political office'. One of Mrs Thatcher's innovations in 1979 was to appoint a political 'chief of staff'. He is David Wolfson, a former businessman from Great Universal Stores, and secretary to the Conservative Shadow Cabinet when Mrs Thatcher was leader of the Opposition. He acts as a general-purpose political adviser, an emissary and a discreet aide with whom the prime minister can have a relaxed conversation. As political secretaries, she had first Richard Ryder, a former journalist on the *Daily Telegraph*, who had worked in Mrs Thatcher's private office during her years in opposition. He is married to her personal assistant Ms Stephens and left No. 10 to pursue his own political career in 1981, becoming an MP in 1983. He was succeeded by Derek Howe, a Conservative Party press official, and then in 1983 by the current political secretary, Stephen Sherbourne, from the Conservative Research Department. The main tasks of the secretary are to link Downing Street to the Conservative Party, and to watch over the political aspects of the prime minister's activities.

On taking office in 1979 Mrs Thatcher retained the Policy Unit, but slimmed down its size. From 1979 to 1982 it was headed by the special adviser John Hoskyns, a former army officer, a businessman who had built up his own computer firm and an adviser to Conservative Central Office. Up to 1981 he was helped by another special adviser, Norman Strauss, a systems specialist from Unilever, and by one or two civil servants on secondment from their departments. They concentrated on economic, industrial, employment and trade union policies. From time to time they called for advice from individuals outside government, such as academics and businessmen. The placing of civil servants in the Policy Unit was something of an innovation and represents Mrs Thatcher's greater concern to have the right people near her than for the niceties of administrative protocol. It matched her placing of Ms Stephens in the private office, although she was for a time paid by the Conservative Party. Rigid barriers crumble at No. 10. It is a place of distinct entities but not rigid demarcations.

As head of the Policy Unit, John Hoskyns was succeeded by Ferdinand Mount, who had been at the Conservative Research Department and was a former journalist working on the *Daily Mail* and as political editor of the *Spectator*. His appointment was thought to signify that Mrs Thatcher wanted advice specifically about the presentation of policy for the coming general election and especially on policy towards the family, on which Mr Mount had written a book. Under Mr Mount the Policy Unit expanded in size and scope, acquiring, for instance, the services of Christopher Monckton from the Conservative 'think-tank', the Centre for Policy Studies, and Peter Shipley from the Conservative Research Department. A more obvious partisan element was implanted in the unit.

In 1980 Mrs Thatcher felt the need to have at No. 10 an adviser to focus on economic issues, to explain to her from an independent and economically impeccable standpoint what was significant, and either to reassure her that the departments were on the right lines or to mount a critique. She appointed Professor Alan Walters, a leading monetarist economist, from Johns Hopkins University in the United States. He was not located in the Policy Unit, because of his seniority, and to symbolize his independent status. He was called the economic adviser. So successful did this appointment seem to the prime minister that she established two similar positions in different fields where she felt she needed her own advisers. After the Falklands crisis in 1982 she brought to No. 10 as her foreign affairs adviser Sir Anthony Parsons, a former diplomat who had been Britain's representative at the United Nations during the Falklands conflict, and as defence affairs adviser she selected Roger Jackling, a civil servant from the Defence Department.

These appointments, and the expansion of the Policy Unit, reflected the more directive and interventionist style of the prime minister. She felt a personal responsibility for the policy of the government. To watch over the work of the separate departments and to monitor issues that crossed departmental boundaries she sought aides working directly for her. The growth of her assistance personnel at No. 10 counterbalanced her elimination of the CPRS, which had provided policy advice for the Cabinet as a whole, and it may also have been her way of responding to calls that she set up a Prime Minister's Department. In this way she could achieve the substance without the troublesome form.

In 1983 there were further significant changes on the policy advisory side of the Prime Minister's Office. In January, the economic adviser Professor Walters returned to the United States but was retained as a part-time adviser, coming to Britain each month for about a week. Sir Anthony Parsons was replaced in December 1983 as foreign affairs adviser by Sir Percy Cradock, another former diplomat, who had been the ambassador to China and was an expert on the looming problem of the future status of Hong Kong. The defence adviser returned to his department and his position was not filled. An expansion of aides at No. 10 took place in the Policy Unit. Mr Mount increased its members to nine, including himself. They were young, mainly in their twenties or thirties, and had had experience as civil servants or in commerce or industry, or in the Conservative Research Department or Centre for Policy Studies. Some in the unit had served in the CPRS, like David Pascall and Robert Young, and one, Oliver Letwin, was the special adviser to the Secretary of State for Education and Science. They specialized in distinct policy areas, and provided a check on what departments were proposing, even initiating ideas themselves. At the end of 1983 Mr Mount left the unit and was replaced as its head by Mr John Redwood. He is a Fellow of All Souls, a banker, author of books on industrial policy and a defeated Conservative candidate.

The prime minister's Policy Unit was said to be at full strength in November 1984. It comprised nine members:

John Redwood (head)	Jobs, privatization, tax, public sector.
Hartley Booth	Home policy, law and order, environmental pollution.
David Hobson (part-time)	Export credits, Scottish and Welsh affairs, accountancy.
Oliver Letwin	Education and science, employment, local government.
Christopher Monckton	Housing, Parliamentary affairs.
Nicholas Owen	Defence, competition, agriculture, civil service.
Peter Warry	Deregulation, pay, trade and industry.
David Willets	Health and social security, Treasury affairs.
John Wybrew	Energy, transport, financial management initiative.

The topics covered indicate the wide range of the prime minister's concerns and show what she wishes to monitor. One might expect her to make policy interventions in any and all of the fields mentioned. The Policy Unit represents the most comprehensive coverage of the work of government by any British prime minister in peacetime. The allocation of responsibilities is the most structured and formal since the secretariat of Lloyd George and the statistical section of Winston Churchill. However, there must be a question mark over whether such a small group spread so thinly can make a significant impact on policy-making and overshadow or even overturn the contributions from the departments.

When Mrs Thatcher first took office she was no enthusiast for special and political advisers and said that she intended to rely for political advice on her ministers, and by implication for policy advice on their departments. At No. 10 she cut down the number and seniority of her political aides and reduced the size of the Policy Unit. Over the period of her term of office, however, she revised her earlier judgement. She increased the political and policy components of her staff in the Prime Minister's Office. Indeed the current Policy Unit looks like a reconstituted and larger version of that run by Dr Bernard Donoughue for Harold Wilson and James Callaghan.

Between 1979 and 1983 the prime minister's Parliamentary private secretary, Ian Gow, achieved a degree of prominence unusual for holders of that position. He acted as the prime minister's eyes, ears and mouth amongst the Conservative backbenchers in the Commons. Mrs Thatcher realized it was important for her not to appear out of touch with her supporters, and although she maintained close personal contact with MPs, she depended a great deal on her PPS. Perhaps as a woman she needed a gregarious male to consort with his mostly male colleagues in ways and places thought inappropriate for her. More than earlier PPSs he was active in giving the prime minister political advice at No. 10 Downing Street. For his services he was awarded a place in the government after the 1983 general election. His role as PPS was taken over by Michael Alison.

The prime minister also drew on the advice of people who held no position at Downing Street, for instance from Lord Thomas and Sir Alfred Sherman at the Centre for Policy Studies, who could bring to her their ideas, respond to her queries or undertake missions on her behalf. Others might help with their particular expertise, advising for instance on her appearance or style of speaking, or assisting in the writing of speeches, such as Sir Ronald Millar, the playwright, or Gordon Reece, the PR specialist.

In October 1984 the prime minister introduced into her cabinet as Minister without Portfolio the former head of the Manpower Services Commission, David Young, who was created a peer. There had been speculation that Mrs Thatcher intended to set up a Prime Minister's Department with David Young as its head. In the event it was not established and Young was given responsibility for jobs and training initiatives, assisted by a small secretariat in the Cabinet Office, the so-called enterprise unit.

The way Mrs Thatcher has shaped the flexible elements that make up the Prime Minister's Office to suit her requirements reveals the adaptability of the British system. There has been no need for her to create a Prime Minister's Department to obtain the service she felt she needed. She is the most interventionist prime minister into the work of government departments since

Lloyd George and has sought to mould the staff around her to enable her to find out more of what the departments are doing, to scrutinize their activities and to provide other options to counter their proposals. While she has been strengthening her own personal staff resources, she has weakened those at the disposal of her cabinet colleagues for the performance of their collective deliberations by abolishing the CPRS. So she has tipped the system slightly away from collective and towards presidential government. But the shift is only slight. The political and policy aides who serve her are few, junior, inexperienced in government and fluctuating. They do not stay for long. They are not as stable a component as the private office nor any real rival to the formidable array of bureaucratic resources available to ministers in their departments.

Does Britain need a Prime Minister's Department?

The advocates of a Prime Minister's Department fall into three groups: first, those who positively want a more presidential prime minister and seek to build up a department as a personal administrative resource for the chief executive; second, those who feel that the modern prime minister will inevitably intervene in the work of ministers and of their departments, and that a Prime Minister's Department is needed to assist the prime minister to make sensible and effective decisions; third, those who support collective cabinet government and believe that the way to strengthen it is to create a department to help its chairman as the promoter of collective decision-making. Against them are those who fear that to establish a Prime Minister's Department would disrupt collective decision-making, and that the way to enhance the capability of the centre of central government is to strengthen the resources available to the cabinet as a whole.

The preceding historical survey has shown how there has evolved a loose network of aides to serve a prime minister. In a flexible way each prime minister has been able to shape and mould the system to his or her own distinctive requirements. Prime ministers have very variable styles, modes of working and conceptions of what they want to achieve as prime minister. They have been able to obtain the different forms of assistance they wanted because of this unstructured set of arrangements. If there had been a formal, bureaucratic Prime Minister's Department, it would not have been so amenable to the personal wishes of the prime ministers. Its structures would have offered resistance.

The present system hinders the emergence of any one person who has the prime minister's ear. Now there exists a group of people, probably about nine, who are in constant daily touch with the prime minister. Amongst them he or she can pick and choose on whom to rely, and can counterbalance one against the other. There is a danger in having a single head of staff at No. 10: everything might be channelled through that one person. The present system enables the prime minister to be in charge, not a single subordinate. A more structured department would generate a large amount of paper, which the prime minister might find difficult to master, whereas the present system, operating informally with a word here, a chat there, staff dropping in for drinks at the end of the day, enables the prime minister to keep on top of business.

Not only does this flexibility serve the purposes of the leader of the government, it is ideally suited to the environment in which the prime minister has to operate. He or she faces a fluid, volatile external world, of ever-changing and highly charged issues, of crises constantly bursting out and impinging on one another, and of unexpected events and problems for which there are no predetermined answers. It is an advantage for the prime minister to be served by an organic system rather than a mechanistic organization. It is better fitted to deal with an inchoate environment. Free from rigidities, it is more likely to innovate.

Further, the very looseness that characterizes the British arrangements encourages informal teamwork at No. 10. It exudes the atmosphere of a house (in fact it is two houses joined together). It does not have the feeling or look of a department. Doors are open, people pop in and out, chat and look through each other's trays. It is a very informal, not bureaucratic, atmosphere. When people are so close, those who are at the top of the various units play a very personal role for the prime minister.

There are also political objections to setting up a Prime Minister's Department. Whenever prime ministers have appeared to be embarked on a presidential course, building up at No. 10 their own groups of advisers on policy, as with the 'garden suburb' or the Cherwell Statistical Unit, there has been an outcry from the departments, both from civil servants who felt their close involvement in an issue was being challenged by inexperienced and remote outsiders, and from ministers who resented the intrusion into their responsibilities by people who were not publicly accountable. These objections by civil servants and ministers are not merely motivated by self-interest. They reflect more fundamental constitutional anxieties. Prime ministers have so far pulled back from establishing a Prime Minister's Department, however much they were initially inclined to do so, not only because they did not want to provoke hostility from their ministerial colleagues and civil servants, but also because they appreciated the force of the constitutional arguments.

Whether the UK should establish a formal, structured and bureaucratic Prime Minister's Department is a significant constitutional question. If one were to be set up, a major constitutional change would have occurred, which is why the issue is so hotly debated and so fiercely resisted. Those who advocate such a department seek more than a trifling administrative alteration. They view the British prime minister as a 'chief executive' who should be assisted by a chief executive's department. However, this analogy is false. The prime minister executes nothing, except making some appointments and allocating honours.

These people wish to reshape government to meet the needs of prime ministers who want to intervene in detail in the policy process. Thus, the implication of their proposal is to shift responsibility from ministers and the cabinet to the prime minister. In the British constitution, government is ministerial government. Powers and duties are laid on ministers, not on the prime minister. They come together in cabinet to resolve disputes between themselves and to determine a common line. The prime minister's task, among others, is to help colleagues reach agreement, to promote collegiality and a collective strategy. From time to time prime ministers may try to push their own particular line, and are encouraged to do so by those who favour it. But such personal initiatives come up against the constraints of cabinet government. The urging of the prime minister's own policy may hinder the achievement of a united cabinet. The logic of the British constitution is that prime ministers do not intervene in the policy responsibilities of specific ministers in order to advance personal prime ministerial objectives. Their intervention makes constitutional sense only if it is to enhance collective cabinet government. Setting up a Prime Minister's Department by increasing the administrative resources at the personal disposal of the prime minister would encourage that prime minister to intervene to advance his or her own proposals.

If a prime minister is sceptical of the policy direction proposed by a minister, he should not intervene and take over that policy area. The course of action appropriate to the British constitution is for the prime minister to confine and redirect the minister through the cabinet and a cabinet committee, or else to replace the minister with one prepared to conform with the collectively agreed policy.

A prime minister in practice usually has a dual motivation: the primary one is to help engineer a consensus between colleagues; the secondary motivation is to promote a personal policy. Too much emphasis on the latter can frustrate the achievement of the former, since as the protagonist of a particular line a prime minister will be a pressure for dissension, acting as a contestant against the interests of others. He will sow distrust and not facilitate the attainment of a united front.

It has long been argued, by for instance Leo Amery, Barbara Castle and Richard Crossman, that the cabinet usually fails to plan a collective strategy. It tends to respond to specific ministerial initiatives and to focus on the short term. Some prime ministers guide cabinets to have more regard for a collective strategy; others seem to drift from case to case. The weakness at the centre of British government lies not in the staff serving the prime minister personally, but in the staff serving the cabinet as a whole, and the prime minister as chairman of the cabinet. What is required is to build up the Cabinet Office, especially its analytical resources. This enhancement of the Cabinet Office is less likely to incite discord with departments than the creation of a Prime Minister's Department. Challenge to departmental proposals is likely to be more acceptable if emanating from an office without a personal, prime ministerial axe to grind. Such a development will fit in with Britain's constitutional evolution. It will not be seen as the personal instrument of the prime minister, but rather as an entity serving all ministers and seeking to advance a collective view. It will keep the prime minister's attention focused on collective and strategic aspects, constraining not only his aspirations to pursue an individual line but also the ambitions of ministers to push their departmental causes against the collective strategy.

The distinction between staff serving the prime minister alone and those serving the cabinet and sustaining collective government is critical in British government. It is symbolized by the fact that the door between No. 10 Downing Street and the Cabinet Office is locked. It has mattered a great deal to staff on which side of the door they were located. Those committed to the prime minister wished to be on the No. 10 side for ease of access to the prime minister. If placed on the Cabinet Office side, they felt cut off. Cabinet Office staff do *not* constitute the personal department of the prime minister.

At the present time what the prime minister needs is a loosely structured and flexible arrangement of assistants that can be easily adapted to his/her style of working and to changing needs and problems. There should be: (*a*) her personal, 'household', staff responsible for her daily schedule and acting as her gatekeeper; (*b*) her political staff, linking her to her party, providing political comment, and probing the political implications of policies; (*c*) her public relations staff, linking her to the media and advising on the presentation of policy; and (*d*) her civil service staff, linking her to the departments and the ongoing processes of government, providing data and ensuring she is fully informed from the administration.

For policy advice the prime minister should turn not to her own department but to a unit available to all cabinet ministers, a central Cabinet Office, or body within it, covering both short-term and longer-term perspectives. Its role would be to process departmental submissions for Cabinet consideration, ensuring that relevant options are taken into account, that issues are defined and clarified and that aspects missed by ministerial departments are expressed. Such a central office will serve not only the prime minister but her colleagues too and be a force to strengthen not weaken collective decision-making processes. Any augmentation of the centre of government should seek to enhance the analytical and evaluative capability of this Cabinet Office, which serves all ministers, and not to create a Prime Minister's Department.

Note

This contribution is based on a very wide range of sources, including official lists of civil servants, official publications about central government, biographical references, biographies, autobiographies and memoirs, Hansard and interviews with people who served prime ministers back to 1913. Parts of this chapter have appeared in A. King (ed.), *The British Prime Minister* (London, Macmillan, 1985), pp. 72–95.

Lord Hunt of Tanworth

In introducing his interesting and informative paper, Professor Jones has added a number of points that I cannot support. I agree that in the UK we have had an evolutionary process; indeed in modern times, apart from that one brief period under Mr Heath, we have never really concerned ourselves with central government organization in the way that, say, the Canadians have. Perhaps at times the Canadians have been too concerned with organization, but one needs to look at why an evolutionary process has happened here, and I am not sure that Professor Jones's paper provides the answer. Of course he is right that personality comes into it; but it is not only the personality of the prime minister. It is also the personality of the cabinet – whether it is a united or a fragmented cabinet; whether it has a strong manifesto for change, or a manifesto of continuity; whether it has a working majority or whether it has not. Indeed, all sorts of personalities come into play. However, I also think that over the years since the last war one can detect a number of fundamental external changes which have caused the increase in staff at No. 10 and in the Cabinet Office. It was not the overweening ambition of prime ministers that caused this. Look at Mr Callaghan: he did not want to involve himself in every issue; he would have liked almost an Attlee role – presiding as chairman of the cabinet and concentrating his efforts on the things of greatest importance and interest to him. He found this was impossible, however, and he had to get involved in all sorts of detail. Why? This brings me to the external changes I have detected and I will run through them very quickly.

First, after the Second World War, there was a great change from the time when departments were small and homogeneous and largely non-technical. The change came with the extension of the public sector, the introduction of the welfare state, Keyensian economics and the government feeling that it was responsible for everything. All this imposed a greater burden on the centre, but the machinery of central government was not adapted to cope with it, other than by setting up cabinet committees – trying to take some of the load off the cabinet. However, we managed, and we got away with it. But it increased the coordinating and strategic role of the prime minister.

The second stage came towards the end of the first Wilson government, and the succeeding Conservative government had reflected on it in opposition. There was considerable dissatisfaction among ministers with the advice they had been given; they had the feeling that they were being blown off course needlessly, that the whole bureaucratic system was designed to produce compromise and nice 'ironings out' of differences between officials and that the system led not only to compromise, but to great delay. Thus there were the experiments under Mr Heath – a 'think-tank' serving ministers collectively and very much concentrating on strategy; a system of programme analysis and review; and the introduction, by both parties, of political advisers, who have been retained. The latter are some help, but prime ministers, again of both parties, have always severely limited their role. The programme analysis and review system created a great deal of work but not much in the way of results, and was abolished. The 'think-tank' also, sadly in my view, has been abolished. These events illustrate the difficulties in running our system of a collective cabinet in modern times, with all power vested by Parliament in departmental ministers, as Professor Jones quite correctly says, in the absence of a chief executive. It is what has been described as the 'hole in the centre', and I think there are very few people who are really satisfied with the present position, although there is great disagreement about what the possible solutions are. Under the present system there is a cabinet which has collective responsibility, without sufficient information or power to exercise it. This is partly because of the lack of adequate collective briefing, and partly because of the impossible overload on ministers in their own departments and the very little time that they can give to their collective responsibilities. Hence, again, the tendency to involve the prime minister more.

There have been other pressures also which underline the difficulty of running a collective executive. These include modern communications and the pressures of the media, which make governments feel – rightly or wrongly – that they have to react to everything very quickly. It's a great pity that they feel that way, but they do. And if they are to react, that necessarily involves the prime minister, whether in a coordinating or a personal role. We also have, as do few if any other countries represented at this conference, the extraordinary arrangement whereby the prime minister has to go to the House of Commons twice a week and answer questions without warning on any subject at all. This necessarily involves briefing the prime minister on almost everything that is going on. There are now also departments that are much less homogeneous, and it is therefore much less easy to leave them free to get on with the things they ought to be getting on with. Take energy for example, which also involves industrial, environmental and foreign policy considerations. Another development has been the rise of summitry. You may deplore it or not, but it is a fact of life. Again, the prime minister is involved constantly in discussing issues which are partly domestic and partly foreign. And in the case of the UK, of course, this has been greatly accentuated by joining Europe and the interplay in the EEC between domestic and foreign policy issues. There is another domestic factor. It is probably true that 20 years ago a lot of civil servants felt a dual loyalty – a loyalty to their own department and a loyalty to the Treasury. Nowadays this kind of Treasury power is weaker and the role of the Treasury in holding the show on the road is correspondingly less.

All these changes mean that the *role* of the prime minister, as distinct from the *power* of the prime minister, has inevitably evolved. It is a role that involves a need to be kept informed, not waiting for trouble to come along; a need to initiate and to call others in for collective discussion; a need to act as the guardian of the cabinet strategy, although not necessarily as the architect of it. It is the prime minister only who can keep an eye on strategy as a whole and ensure that the constituent parts of that strategy are consistent and coherent. The prime minister must steer, but in a direction that the cabinet as a whole supports. I do not think it is possible any more – regrettable as it may be – to think of the prime minister in this country simply as holding the ring as a neutral chairman. This has nothing to do with whether there happens to be a pushy prime minster or a less pushy prime minister. I think it would apply equally if you had a very different character to our present prime minister, for example.

I now turn to the question of advice. I was interested in the discussion between our Canadian colleagues, and in the extent to which it was about optimum organization, and not about whether ministers were pleased or not pleased with the advice that they got. Of course, in theory, advice to the prime minister is given by departmental ministers, but that tends to bring the prime minister in very late, and I am afraid that events over the past 20 years or so have shown that prime ministers want some staff whom they feel are their own – whether they are in No. 10 or in the Cabinet Office – and to whom they can look to watch their interests and to bring to their notice options that have perhaps been buried away and ought to be examined. I was very struck during my seven years as Secretary of the Cabinet – and this was not peculiar to me because I am perfectly sure that Robert Armstrong would say the same – by the relative increase in the proportion of the time that I had to give to the prime minister as compared to the time that I could give to running the ordinary business of the Cabinet Office. Yet I always at the same time was conscious of how thin that advice was.

Other present or former members of the Cabinet Office may disagree with me, but I think it is still run on a shoe-string. The people in the Cabinet Office actually concerned with policy – whether it is processing policy, or advising on policy – number about 35, if one disregards the Central Statistical Office, the intelligence world, the clerks and the other ancillary staff. Of those 35, the majority are making comparatively little input to policy advice: they are basically concerned with taking minutes, arranging cabinet committee meetings and so on. So advice to the prime minister from the Cabinet Office is thin, and the question is whether it is adequate. Personally, I do not think it is. I doubt whether prime ministers on the whole have felt that it was adequate either.

So what can be done about it? The logical argument is to go for a Prime Minister's Department. Recent prime ministers have looked at this and then shied away from it because of what would be said (that they were seeking to increase their own power, becoming presidential etc.). The other objection, where I completely agree with Professor Jones, is that if we did go down this road it would have a very considerable effect on prime ministers' relations with their colleagues. At the moment they may suspect that on occasion what the prime minister says was either drafted in the Cabinet Office or results from a Cabinet Office brief, but nevertheless it is the prime minister who says it directly to his or her colleagues. If a Prime Minister's Department were to be set up, there would inevitably be officials going to meetings and speaking to other officials as it were on behalf of the prime minister, and I think that this would have a considerable effect on relations within the cabinet.

Towards the end of my time as Secretary of the Cabinet, at the annual Sunningdale Conference of permanent secretaries, I was asked to reflect on my seven years in the job and on the organization at the centre. I talked about the need for what I felt to be not more advice but advice given earlier and in greater depth. I disagree with Professor Jones's view that prime ministers do not want advice: they do want it. They do not look to their Cabinet Secretary for political advice and they will rightly in most cases pay much greater heed to the departmental minister's advice. But practice shows that they also want advice from someone they regard as their own.

At the Sunningdale conference, after I had put the pros and cons of a Prime Minister's Department, I very well remember a remark which a colleague of mine, who has now retired, made at the end. He said: 'Of course, it is perfectly obvious we need a Prime Minister's Department, so long as it is still called the Cabinet Office'. I think that may be the answer. The worry is how long you can go on applying sticking plasters and beefing up the Cabinet Office, which I think is Professor Jones's solution. Under the present government there has been some further beefing up and we have also seen the introduction of more people into No. 10, not just into the Policy Unit but into what is rather loosely called the Prime Minister's Office. We have also seen the disappearance of the 'think-tank' and the absence now of collective briefing for cabinet ministers. The think-tank, though part of the Cabinet Office, was able in a way to be separate from it.

How long the Cabinet Office can go on riding this sort of double bicycle – providing the sort of service which the prime minister wants and at the same time preserving its neutrality policy and playing its 'honest broker' role as a collective service to departments – I do not know. I hope that it can continue, because I agree with Professor Jones that this may be the right answer in present British circumstances. But I do not think that you can ignore the external events which, whether you like it or not, have pushed more load, more coordination and more strategic oversight on to the prime minister, and the fact that prime ministers do require people of their own to make sure they are being given all the facts.

4

The United States

Stephen Wayne

US presidents do not govern alone. They need help in making, promoting and implementing their decisions. They need help in articulating their beliefs, communicating their policy and responding to public moods, opinions and expectations.

The heads of the executive departments and agencies were originally intended to provide such help, but they have not proved sufficiently responsive to the president for him to depend on them alone. Increasingly, the interests, needs, and responsibilities of senior executive officials have diverged from those of the chief executive. Department secretaries and agency directors serve a number of masters and are dependent on the expertise of a multitude of individuals both inside and outside their agency. Their responsiveness must eventually detract from their loyalty to the president.

With an increasing number of issues overlapping departmental jurisdictions, and an increasing number of matters requiring presidential attention, presidents have found it necessary to turn to their own institutional structure and personal advisory system for assistance and support.

This paper will discuss that structure and system. It will focus on their influence on the policy-making and policy-mobilizing capabilities of the presidency. Particular emphasis will be placed on the White House and the Office of Management and Budget (OMB). First, however, the evolution of the cabinet, the president's initial advisory body, will be examined.

The Cabinet

The cabinet is not mentioned in the US Constitution. It was created by George Washington to provide a decision-making capacity in his absence and an advisory body in his presence. Consisting of the heads of the executive departments, it functioned as the president's principal council for approximately 140 years. When the party system developed during the Washington administration, the cabinet took on a partisan cast, which it has, for the most part, maintained.

Throughout most of the nineteenth century, presidents depended on the advice of their cabinets when developing positions and making major policy decisions. Presidents also turned to cabinet members for help in gaining Congressional support. During much of this period, power resided in the cabinet collectively rather than in the person of the president.

The latter's position began to change at the beginning of the twentieth century. As the president's ability to shape public opinion and build partisan support improved, his success in influencing Congress and his own department heads increased. From 1921, the power to affect department and agency decision-making through the budgetary process also contributed to a stronger chief executive.[1]

As a consequence of these changes, the cabinet declined in importance. Its meetings, once the principal vehicle for administrative decision-making, deteriorated to a forum for informing colleagues, floating new ideas and occasionally airing departmental views. Presidents, beginning with Franklin Roosevelt, preferred to deal substantively with cabinet members on an individual basis.

Eisenhower was the last president to use his cabinet as a group in a policy-advisory capacity. He presided over meetings that featured elaborate presentations of proposals by individual department heads and their staffs. These presentations, replete with visual aids and supporting materials, were the prelude to final decisions on the administration's legislative programme before it was sent to Congress.

Following Eisenhower, presidents paid lip service to their cabinets but did not employ them as their principal advisory group. The reasons for this stem from the size of the cabinet and the increasingly technical nature of policy-making. The need for highly specialized information made it difficult for the various secretaries to be sufficiently versed in the intricacies of issues outside of their areas of expertise to carry on an intelligent discussion in a general setting. Moreover, increasing pressure from outside groups forced department heads to assume more of an advocacy role for their respective agencies (referred to in Washington as 'going native'), particularly in on-the-record meetings or even in closed sessions in which minutes were kept (and thus could be leaked to the press). This 'going native' syndrome made the cabinet less useful for the president.

As a result of all these factors presidents have turned to their cabinets less frequently as their administrations have progressed. Carter, for example, met his cabinet every week during his first year, every other week during his second year, once a month during his third year and infrequently during his final year. The Reagan cabinet averaged three meetings a month during its first year and a half in office.[2]

Instead of using the full cabinet, the Reagan administration has created a system of cabinet councils. Organized on the basis of broad policy areas, seven councils deliberate policy, make recommendations and coordinate the implementation of key presidential decisions. Composed of six to eleven agency heads, they have not as a general rule set the administration's agenda as much as convert it into policy options.

President Reagan officially chairs each of the councils. During his first year, however, he attended only a small portion of the meetings, usually those dealing with the final stages of deliberation.[3] In the president's absence, the councils were run by one of the agency heads who was designated chairman *pro tempore*. Staff support has been provided by the White House. An office of cabinet administration coordinates activities of working groups that explore agenda issues and implement council decisions.

During President Reagan's first term, the councils functioned unevenly. Some, like the one on economic affairs, met regularly and helped fashion administration policy. Others, such as the ones on human resources, agriculture and natural resources and the environment, rarely met. The key to any council's functioning seemed to be the willingness of the chairman to work in a group setting and the priority which the administration placed on the issues which the particular council considered – the higher the priority, the greater the council activity.

The Presidential Office

The decline of the cabinet at a time when the activities of the presidency were increasing required that another advisory and administrative structure be established. This occurred in 1939 when the Executive Office of the President (EOP) was created. The charge of the EOP was to help the president perform certain central, non-delegable tasks. It was conceived as an in-house operation, one that would maintain a presidential perspective in its operation.[4]

Over the years the EOP has grown in size and responsibilities, but it has not done so in a carefully planned, systematic way. Rather, its development has been a product of historical accident, 'the needs of different administrations and the goals and operating styles of individual presidents. Today it consists of ten units. Figure 1 details its composition and size.

The transformations that have occurred in the EOP have produced a larger, more specialized and more politicized office; an office that has become more responsive to the policy goals and political needs of the president. It has extended the reach of the presidency and the influence of the president, but it has done so at the expense of the other executive departments and agencies.

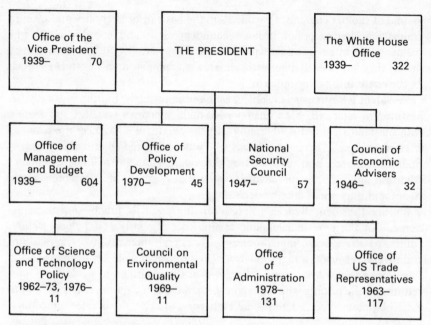

Figure 1   The Executive Office of the President (EOP). The Office of Management and Budget was called the Bureau of the Budget from 1939 to 1970. The Office of Policy Development was called the Domestic Council from 1970 to 1976 and the Domestic Policy Staff from 1977 to 1980. The figure given for size is determined by the number of permanent positions in the 1983 fiscal budget.

The White House

Of all the units within the EOP, the White House is the one that is closest to the president and exercises the greatest influence on his political and policy decisions. It is the second largest office (the OMB is the largest), with a budgeted staff of approximately 320 plus others detailed to it for short periods from other executive agencies.

The senior White House staff consists of between ten and twelve individuals (the number varies with each administration) who hold the title of assistant to the president, and who supervise semi-autonomous administrative units. Each is assisted by at least one deputy. The remainder of the staff consists of middle and low ranking officials and support personnel.

The White House is thoroughly political, with very few civil servants. Practically the entire staff is appointed by a new president except during a non-electoral succession when the need for continuity requires stability of office holders. Over time, however, most of the appointees of the previous president leave. Ronald Reagan went so far as to remove long-time secretaries and clerical aides when he took over in 1980.

The presidential campaign provides the pool from which senior White House aides are usually chosen. Partisan and personal loyalty seem to be the primary criteria for selection. For the Reagan administration this meant being a conservative, a Republican and an active Reagan supporter. These criteria were extended to department and agency political appointments as well.[5]

The partisan character of the White House extends into the EOP. Top positions in the OMB as well as other EOP units are also subject to presidential appointment. Here too partisan factors figure prominently in the selection. Since the heads of the principal staffs in the EOP also have White House appointments as presidental assistants, the EOP remains well attuned to White House opinion.[6]

In addition to its political character, the White House has become a highly specialized office, performing a variety of policy-making and policy-mobilizing activities. It was not always that way. During the first three decades of its existence, the White House functioned as a highly personalized office, reflecting the operating style of the president. Although the Roosevelt, Truman and Eisenhower White Houses differed somewhat in size and organization, they had much in common. By contemporary standards they were small, composed primarily of generalists, who performed action-forcing assignments, that is, those dictated by the need for a specific presidential decision or action. These staffs operated more as a personal extension of the president than as an institutional extension of his office.

Only Eisenhower had a chief of staff; Roosevelt and Truman supervised their assistants themselves. With the exception of Eisenhower's chief, Sherman Adams, presidential aides of all three White Houses did not possess the status and authority of department secretaries. Their influence in those days stemmed primarily from their mediating role, their ability to obtain information and their proximity to the president. When the White House called, the president's personal interests were usually involved.

Changes began to occur in the 1960s. These changes had a profound effect not only on the way the EOP was structured and how it worked, but on the operation of the entire executive branch itself. Presidential aides became better known, exercised more power and tended to monopolize the president's time. During the Kennedy–Johnson period policy-making staffs were created and institutionalized. Senior White House aides became the president's principal policy advisers. They supervised their own staffs which were based in the EOP. These staffs competed with the departments and agencies for influence.

The institutionalization of policy-making in the White House had three major effects. First, it gave the presidency a separate capacity to formulate policy distinct from and independent of the departments and agencies. Second, it allowed the president to take more credit for policy developed in his administration. Third, it accelerated the shift of power from the departments and agencies to the White House. Cabinet secretaries were no longer the president's only advisers within their respective spheres; in some cases they were not even principal advisers. Their status declined accordingly while that of the president's assistants increased.

In the 1970s the decentralization of power in Congress, the growth of single-issue groups and the weakening of partisan coalitions increased and diversified pressures on the presidency. To overcome these pressures, presidents were forced to make the formulation of policy more sensitive to outside interests. Before this period, the White House had been relatively invulnerable to most organized external forces; presidential aides worked within a relatively closed environment and while the leaders of the president's party, influential supporters and friends could and did gain access, the general public, including most of the interest groups' leaders, had more difficulty. Congress and the bureaucracy were the principal turfs on which outside groups fought their political battles.

With the proliferation and professionalization of interest groups, a host of individuals were able to gain direct access to the White House. The White House, in turn, began to organize groups into policy coalitions.

The increased sensitivity to outside forces has both detracted from and contributed to the president's power. On one hand it has worked to limit his discretion in that more interests have to be considered in formulating and implementing policy. More than one-third of the people who work in the Reagan White House service the president's five principal constituencies – the general public, Congress, state and local governments, interest groups and political parties. On the other hand, the capacity to mobilize groups into policy majorities has helped the White House overcome the increasing pluralism of the American polity. Issue majorities rarely emerge on their own; they must be created. Coalition building is thus an essential function of an increasingly specialized White House staff.

The growth of a large, functionally differentiated presidential office has strengthened the institution but it has also made it more difficult for the president to oversee that office directly. The experience of Presidents Ford and Carter attests to the need for a central manager, a chief of staff. Initially, both had hoped to establish a structure in which their top aides operated autonomously within their own offices and collegially as a staff. These aides were to have direct and easy access to the president. White House officials likened their position to the spokes of a wheel with the president at the centre. The system did not work well, however. Battles over areas of interest and authority, so-called 'turf battles', erupted both within the White House and between it and other executive agencies. These internal disputes plagued both administrations for most of their time in office. Advisory functions were also adversely affected. The presentation of a wide range of options to the president was not assured. Each administration had difficulty establishing and articulating its priorities.

While President Reagan maintained a large, structurally differentiated White House, he imposed a more centralized system. In his first term a chief of staff oversaw White House operations and a counsellor coordinated administration policy.[7] The policy and operational sides were linked by a triumvirate consisting of chief of staff James Baker, deputy chief of staff Michael Deaver and counsellor Edwin Meese. Together, they orchestrated staff activity, monitoring the operation of the different White House units, briefing the president and acting on his behalf. A legislative strategy group, operating out of the chief of staff's office, coordinated the administration's congressional initiatives. Figure 2 indicates the principal lines of authority during this first term.

The departure of Baker, Deaver and Meese at the beginning of the second term, however, forced changes in the structure, particularly at the top. The informality of the triumvirate was replaced by a chief of staff, Donald Regan, who preferred precise lines of authority and more formal operating procedures.

President Reagan's style in working with his principal White House aides remained essentially the same. His practice was to delegate considerable power and responsibility to senior staff. This exposed him to the charge that he was being manipulated by his staff and that his decisions were theirs. On the other hand, it distanced him from the problems that resulted from these decisions and from the people who made them.

Jimmy Carter took the opposite tack – with disastrous results. Finding it difficult to delegate, he spent considerable time becoming a policy expert on almost every decision he was forced to make. At the beginning of his administration Carter read upwards of 400 pages of papers and memos a day! James Fallows, a former Carter speech-writer, described his boss as 'the perfectionist accustomed to thinking that to do a job right you must do it yourself'.[8] Fallows provided the following illustration:

> He [Carter] would leave for a weekend at Camp David laden with thick briefing books, would pore over budget tables to check the arithmetic, and, during his first six months in office, would personally review all requests to use the White House tennis court. . . . After six months had passed, Carter learned that this was ridiculous, as he learned about other details he would have to pass by if he was to use his time well. But his preference was still to try to do it all.[9]

Naturally this prodigious effort took its toll on Carter and his policy.

Four trends in White House staffing are evident in the modern presidency. First, over time the White House becomes more important to the president. His need for a more centrally managed and efficiently run staff becomes obvious in

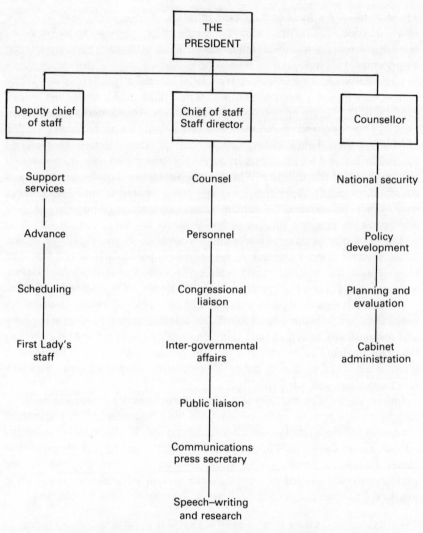

Figure 2 The Reagan White House, 1980–4.

large part because a president finds that he has to depend increasingly on his assistants, not on his department and agency heads, for information, advice and operational needs.

Second, White House staffs tend to expand over the course of an administration, and presidents come to rely increasingly on their staffs as leaks and loyalty problems surface and as press and public criticism mounts. Ironically, the larger and more powerful the staff becomes, the more resistant it is to the president's personal control. Like any large organization, it develops a structure and a routine of its own.

Third, the staff operation tends to exhibit self-perpetuating tendencies. These tendencies may even be reinforced as personnel leave and subordinates are promoted to replace them. 'Territories' are established and protected; standard operating procedures evolve. The White House achieves greater autonomy over priority decision-making and begins to engulf the president as he depends increasingly on it.

Finally, the White House itself may become isolated with time. Not only do the long hours aides work reduce their tolerance and aggravate their personal ambition, but they also seem to encourage withdrawal tendencies on the part of the staff and even the president himself. These tendencies can heighten the temptation to see the work in terms of 'we and they'. They can work to distance the president and his entourage from public criticism. They may also exaggerate other psychological proclivities such as Carter's pessimism and Reagan's optimism. Finally, they encourage turnover. Aides quickly burn themselves out. Few stay in their positions for a whole administration; most do not even remain for an entire presidential term.

While a centralized approach to presidential staffing can contribute to the isolation of the president, it is not the determining factor. The president's attitude and demeanour, his system of rewards and sanctions, have the most effect on the way staff feel and work. While not necessarily eliminating the incentives or disincentives of the job, a president can either reduce or enhance their effect. In general, the more personable, accessible and tolerant the president, the happier the staff. Efficiency, however, is not always promoted by the chief executive's being 'a nice guy'.

Each White House has its own style. During the Nixon years, especially during the time H. R. Haldeman was chief of staff, that style might be described as 'macho'. Aides had to prove how tough they were, how long they worked, how many sacrifices they made. There was little compassion, from the president downwards and no patience for poor quality work or late performance. Presidents Ford and Carter were more tolerant, more open and less imposing. They permitted a 'looser operation'. There were fewer penalties for non-performance and senior aides who did not produce quality staff work were circumvented rather than asked to leave.

Temperamentally, President Reagan has been more like Ford and Carter. Well liked and easy-going, he is not a disciplinarian. He has tended to rely on the judgements of his senior aides with respect to personnel decisions. He is, however, less tolerant of internal dissent than Ford and Carter and has been particularly sensitive to national security leaks within his administration. Those who are not team players are asked to leave by senior White House aides.

The Office of Management and Budget

The largest single unit in the EOP is the Office of Management and Budget (OMB), known before 1970 as the Bureau of the Budget (BOB). With a staff numbering about 600, it performs a variety of budgetary, legislative and management functions for the president. As with the White House, the OMB has become increasingly politicized.

Until the 1960s, the budget agency had only two political appointees, the director and the deputy director. The latter, by tradition, was chosen from the ranks of the professionals who had worked their way up in the agency. Senior civil servants helped make and implement major policy decisions. In exercising their judgements, these professional bureaucrats used presidential campaign statements, major addresses and reports, and special messages to Congress as a guide. If there was a major issue on which the Budget Bureau was uncertain how the president's programme applied or what the programme actually was, the White House would be consulted.

As a consequence of its non-partisan character, the Budget Bureau was particularly well suited to provide the president with 'advice on the merits' as opposed to 'advice on the politics' of an issue. Moreover, its invulnerability to outside pressures, relative invisibility to the press and accessibility to the president and his senior aides heightened its mystique and enhanced its authority. The Budget Bureau's decision was usually final. Although an appeal could be made to the White House by the departments and agencies, this practice was not encouraged and was rarely successful.

Changes in the organization, influence and roles of the BOB began to occur in the 1960s. These changes were a consequence of the increasing size of the White House staff, the increasing number of initiatives that emanated from it and the increasing suspicion of the political loyalties of civil servants by new presidents and their staffs.

Singly and together, these factors changed the character of the agency and the way it operated. Political positions were created on top of the OMB hierarchy. Presidents staffed them with people who shared their beliefs and perspectives. Civil servants who had previously exercised policy judgements on budgetary and legislative matters were relegated to positions of lesser importance.

These changes had two principal effects. First, it lowered morale in the agency and increased turnover. With political appointees serving an average of two years or less and civil servants exercising less influence, the OMB and indirectly the president were placed at a competitive disadvantage when dealing with senior officials from other executive departments and agencies. Secondly, it introduced political factors into the OMB's policy judgements. No longer could the president depend on the budget agency to present advice *solely* on considerations of merit. Greater discontinuities in policy, not only between administrations but within them, have resulted.

The politicization of the OMB has also subjected the agency to outside influences. It has made it more sensitive to the political concerns of the president. To some extent this has increased the willingness of presidents to use the agency to promote their policy objectives not only in budgetary and legislative areas but in administrative spheres as well. Presidents Nixon and Ford used it to improve management techniques and to evaluate existing programmes. Carter established a division within the agency to oversee reorganization efforts. Reagan has used the office to help decrease the size of the federal work force, extend presidential oversight over regulations issued by departments and agencies and achieve sizeable cuts in domestic programmes.

The OMB's ability to promote the president's objectives varies over the course of an administration. Initially its institutional resources are most valuable in overcoming departmental interests and Congressional opposition to achieve presidential goals. In the end, its nay-saying abilities are apt to be most effective in maintaining the president's course within the executive branch.

How the Reagan administration achieved its 1981 budget cuts illustrates the advantage the OMB can give a president in his first year in office. In January 1981, before many of the departments and agencies were fully staffed or their secretaries briefed about their budget needs, the OMB proposed major reductions in domestic programmes. Almost immediately, budget working groups were established. Composed of key White House personnel, budget officials and appropriate department secretaries and their aides, the groups reviewed the proposed cuts and made recommendations to the president. In most cases the recommendations supported the cuts. Why? The president had stated his goals, the OMB had a near monopoly over budget information and the composition of the groups was stacked against the departments. The secretaries were not in a position to advocate their departments' interests. As a result in just three weeks sizeable reductions were proposed in twelve major entitlement programmes and in much discretionary spending. Although the Reagan administration has attempted to maintain a 'top-down' approach to budgeting, it has not been as successful in subsequent years. None the less, throughout the administration the budgetary process has driven domestic policy-making rather than the other way around.

In summary, the expansion of the presidential office has been a mixed blessing. Created to meet increased expectations, it has generated new ones. Designed to coordinate and facilitate executive branch decision-making, it has produced serious tensions between the White House and the departments. Tailored to systematize advice to the president, it has proliferated that advice, and sometimes worked to isolate the president from his advisers. Yet its expansion has obviously been necessary. It has been both a cause and an effect of the growth of government, of the executive branch and of the president's responsibilities. In the foreseeable future the shape of the presidency may undergo modest adjustment, but the institution is not likely to shrink.

Policy-making

Policy-making has been affected by the structural and political changes in the presidential office. It has also been influenced by the decentralization of power within the political environment. The structural developments have enhanced the presidency's influence but not necessarily the president's personal control. He is dependent on his staff for deciding when he should be involved, what options he should consider, how those options are presented to him and how they should be articulated and promoted inside and outside the government. The politicization of all types of policy has made long-range planning more difficult. The election cycle must be considered when calculating the effect of policy change. Policy-makers will key recoveries to their own benefit whenever possible.

Short-term considerations such as elections tend not only to motivate decisions, but also to enhance the pragmatic character of the decisions themselves. Presidents are thus more inclined to strive for what is politically feasible rather than theoretically optimal or ideologically desirable. The actions of the Reagan administration are a case in point. Coming into office with clear-cut views of how it wished to stimulate the economy, the administration was forced to compromise its initial budget and tax proposals in order to get them enacted into law. The compromises became more extensive as the next presidential election approached and presidential influence in Congress declined. Pragmatic considerations, in short, muted the administration's ideological perspective but, at the same time, enhanced the chances for its legislative success.

The impact of politics on most types of policy decisions has had another effect: it has made those decisions less stable over time. The increasing interdependence of the United States on international forces and events has worked to the same end. It has forced presidents frequently to adjust their programmes. Discontinuities in policy within an administration are now more frequent, particularly when a president lacks an over-arching ideological framework. This was a problem Carter faced. In the words of James Fallows:

> I came to think that Carter believes fifty things, but no one thing. He holds explicit, thorough positions on every issue under the sun, but he has no large view of the relations between them, no line indicating which goals (reducing unemployment? human rights?) will take precedence over which (inflation control? a SALT treaty?) when the goals conflict.[10]

In contrast, President Reagan has been more successful in adhering to his major policy goals.

Changes within the political system have also increased the president's tasks. Competing demands, complex issues and confrontational politics have made it more difficult for a chief executive to design policy and obtain support for it. There are more groups with a stake in public policy – more opinions to be heard, more interests to balance, more agendas to combine. Moreover, one policy decision affects another. Spheres of jurisdiction overlap. Distinctions between domestic and international concerns are no longer as clear-cut. All of this has increased the costs and consequences of presidential policy-making.

Presidents must therefore work harder and devote more resources to formulate and implement their policy goals. Their strategies of policy-making have also been affected. A president must now establish priorities quickly, even before taking office, and then package, promote and cycle them throughout his administration. Since his political influence decreases even though his expertise should increase, rapid action and quick mobilization provide the ingredients for early political success. That success, in turn, builds a reputation which contributes to the achievement of additional political goals. This was the formula Ronald Reagan followed with excellent results.

Upon taking office in 1980, he translated his campaign stands – government is too large and costly, taxes are too high, defence is too weak and regulations are too numerous – into two basic legislative initiatives, budget and tax reform, and two basic executive ones, a recruitment freeze and a reduction and oversight of regulations. These issues constituted the administration's principal agenda for its first two years in office.

Limiting the issues helps the president set the pace and shape the tone of public debate. It helps focus public attention on certain presidential activities. This contributes to the perception that the president is in command. But there is, of course, a negative side to limiting the agenda: some people's expectations will not be satisfied. For the Reagan administration it was the social objectives of the conservatives which were postponed during his first term in office.

Another related problem has already been noted – maintaining a long-range perspective. In making policy, everyday emergencies tend to push out future planning. Contemporary White Houses have attempted to design a longer-range domestic planning capability but without much success. In 1975 President Ford asked Vice President Nelson Rockefeller to provide leadership and direction for the establishment of social goals. Rockefeller's decision not to run for office one year later, however, abruptly ended this effort. The most ambitious attempt thus far was the creation of a small office for planning and evaluation in the Reagan administration. Consisting initially of six officials, it was charged with developing strategic plans for the president's agenda and schedule. At the outset, the office designed a series of six-month blueprints for the administration. As part of this effort scenarios of possible responses to international and national crises and events were designed. Within two years, however, the focus shifted from policy to politics.

One of the lasting legacies of the Reagan administration's development of its policy-making and implementing machinery will probably be its introduction of sophisticated information and communication technology. The Carter White House had begun to employ computers for tracking correspondence and grants, but the Reagan administration broadened their application to include drafting, editing and transmitting speeches and messages, processing presidential correspondence and scheduling meetings, tracking legislation and monitoring executive operations. The White House has also expanded its access to commercial and governmental data bases. An electronic mailing capability has been established within the Executive Office and among its various units and a growing number of departments and agencies. There is even a portable electronic mailing unit which travels with the president. In short, the White House is beginning to take advantage of advances in computer technology to make, communicate and sell its public policy.

Conclusion

Presidential policy expectations have remained large and have even grown during the past decade, but the capacity of the president to meet expectations has not keep pace. The pluralism of the American polity has unleashed a multitude of centrifugal forces that seek to affect most types of decision-making. A president cannot ignore these forces and merrily go his own way; he must co-opt them. That is why the policy-making and coalition-building staffs were created. That is also why the OMB and other presidential agencies have become more politically sensitive.

A president cannot dictate policy outcomes but he can affect them. To do so, however, he must exercise personal leadership. Richard Neustadt discussed this problem in 1960 in his book, *Presidential Power*. His dictum that a president must be personally persuasive is still applicable, but rarely sufficient in and of itself. Today, a president is more dependent on his advisers and his institutional staff. He has no choice but to establish a functionally differentiated, responsive presidental bureaucracy. He does, however, have a choice over the personnel who serve in that bureaucracy and the criteria by which they will be chosen. By emphasizing partisanship he ensures responsiveness in the short term, but not necessarily the formulation and implementation of sound policy judgements in the long term.

Notes

1 The Budget and Accounting Act of 1921 required the president to present Congress with an annual executive budget. No longer could the departments and agencies submit their financial requests directly to Congress. The act also established a bureau within the department of the Treasury to help the president administer this new responsibility. That bureau's domination of the budget review process greatly enhanced the president's influence over the departments and agencies.

2 Chester A. Newland, 'The Reagan Presidency: limited government and political administration', *Public Administration Review*, 43 (1983), pp. 1–21.

3 When he presided, President Reagan's style was similar to Eisenhower's. He tended to be more interested in arriving at a consensus than in exploring the complexities of policy issues. For an excellent discussion of the cabinet councils and the president's role within them, see Chester A. Newland, 'Executive Office policy apparatus: enforcing the Reagan agenda', in Lester M. Salamon and Michael S. Lund (eds), *The Reagan Presidency and the Governing of America* (Urban Institute Press, Washington, DC, 1985), pp. 153–61.

4 Its title, however, was a misnomer. It was not a single office nor have its functions been primarily executive in character.

5 According to Pendleton James, head of President Reagan's personnel operation during the administration's first two years in office, the principal factors considered in making appointments were 'compatibility with the president's philosophy, integrity, toughness, competence, and being a team player'. Hendrick Smith, 'Conservatives cite gains in top posts', *New York Times*, 8 March 1981, p. 24.

6 The politicization of the EOP has also made transitions more arduous and more expensive. Reagan had by far the largest transition staff. Almost one hundred groups operated in five broad policy areas: economics, national security, human services, resources and development, and legal and administrative matters. Serving on the teams were partisan supporters, including some who had experience in previous Republican administrations. Agency officials, both political and professional, prepared reports for the transition teams which, in turn, offered recommendations to new presidential appointees.

7 The senior aides run their own offices relatively independently of one another. At the beginning of the administration they met regularly as a group to discuss and coordinate the day's activities. Their meetings were often preceded by a deputies' meeting. Following the senior staff session, each of the presidential assistants would meet individually with his or her own staff. Typically, presidential aides would arrive between 7.30 and 8.00 a.m. and leave ten to twelve hours later. The president's day might be shorter. President Reagan has tended to begin around 9.00 a.m. and finish by 5.00 p.m. Frequently on Friday, he would leave in the mid-afternoon for the presidential mountain retreat at Camp David. Jimmy Carter worked longer hours. An early riser, Carter usually arrived at the Oval Office by 6.00 a.m. He preferred to read alone for the first hour and a half to two hours until he received his national security briefing. Carter concluded the West Wing portion of his day between 5.00 and 5.30 p.m., but usually brought material back to his living quarters for study after dinner, a practice many presidents have followed.

8 James Fallows, 'The passionless presidency,' *Atlantic*, May 1979, p. 38.
9 Ibid.
10 Ibid., p. 42.

Roger Porter

There are two points in Stephen Wayne's paper on which I would like to comment before turning to another issue. First, he draws attention to the lack of responsiveness to the president by department and agency heads. I fully share the view that agency heads are pulled in the direction of their constitutencies. In many respects they are, or quickly become, advocates of the constituencies they represent. I am not convinced that this phenomenon is new or increasing significantly. It is and has been a persistent feature of the American political system. I became even more convinced of this after spending a considerable amount of time in the Eisenhower, Kennedy and Johnson presidential libraries. Those administrations fought the same kind of fights we are currently fighting. I am also not persuaded that presidents must look outside their department heads, to other advisers, although it is certainly true that many presidents have done so in the past. I am convinced they can develop processes that will *include* department and agency heads rather than trying to exclude or supersede them.

The second point is that in certain parts of Stephen Wayne's paper there seems to be a sense of inevitability about the movement during the life of an administration towards more and more centralization, of an enlarging and increasingly powerful White House staff, and of an isolation at the centre of the president and his staff. Certainly, one can find instances in the past where this has occurred, but again, I would emphasize that I do not find this inevitable. The two administrations that I have served in, the Ford and Reagan administrations, are examples of where this has not occurred.

In thinking about the way in which policy advice is tendered at the centre, there are some half a dozen salient characteristics of the US political system that are worth noting briefly because they tend to distinguish the US system from the others we have noted earlier. The first is the simple fact of the separation of the executive and legislative branches. The United States has a genuinely bicameral legislature which is not, in any manner, shape or form, under the control of the executive branch. This tends to influence the deployment of staff resources within the executive branch, and the relationships between departments and agencies and the central institutions within the executive branch.

Second, in the United States the presidency is a highly personalized institution, not simply in the sense that individual personalities and styles make a difference, but in the sense that presidents make an enormous number of appointments of non-career officials. Moreover, there is, in the White House, relatively little institutional memory – certainly much less than in most other political systems.

My third point was touched upon by Stephen Wayne, that is the relative unimportance of political parties in the US system. Our electoral process revolves around candidates: candidates are elected by raising funds and putting together campaign organizations on their own and without reference to the party; party programmes are frequently ignored and rarely, if ever, binding; and legislative discipline – certainly party discipline – in our Congress is noticeably lacking.

A fourth distinguishing feature of the US system is the presence of a large number of what I call entrepreneurial advocates. These may be found in Congress, in the executive branch, or elsewhere. There is an enormous amount of scope in the US system given to these entrepreneurial advocates to try to push their ideas through the political process.

Fifth, the notion of collective responsibility, that the cabinet is the institution with collective responsibility for the government's programmes, and a notion which has been discussed repeatedly at this conference, is an idea that is not a feature of the US system. In many respects the US system is one of a presidentially orientated executive branch. The concept of a group of people being collectively responsible for policy is simply not there.

Sixth, and finally, in the US system it is the president who is looked to to set the national agenda, to serve as the architect of the nation's foreign policy and to prepare and present a comprehensive legislative programme. If you consider the needs of the president – and, I would maintain, of the other chief executives that we have been talking about – there are a couple of things that strike one immediately. The first is that they are expected to make a large number of decisions about issues on which they themselves are not expert, and therefore they are going to have to rely on other people for information, for analysis, for structuring alternatives and for an assessment of the advantages and disadvantages associated with those alternatives. Many of the issues coming at them, and on which they are expected to decide, are interrelated, in the sense that what they decide on issue A today will affect the choices, and the relative attractiveness of those choices, on issues B, C and D that they are going to be considering two weeks, three months or a year from now. Thus, one major organizational challenge they face stems from this interrelation of issues. The second organizational challenge in the US system arises from the fact that the line operating departments and agencies, which form the bulk of the executive branch, are headed by a small tier of officials at the top whom the president appoints. He therefore must ask himself three central questions. What staff do I need? What am I going to have my staff do? And how are my staff and I going to relate to the line operating departments and agencies? In responding to those questions various presidents have taken at least two basic approaches. One I like to call 'centralized management'. Its essence is a profound distrust of those in line operating department and agencies. Centralized management attempts to create at the centre relatively large, independent, objective, neutral staffs, who owe allegiance to no other constituency, who serve no other master. It is they to whom the president looks to mobilize the information, develop the analysis and structure the alternatives upon which he can then take his decisions, and inform the line agencies and departments. 'This is our policy; you are expected to follow it'. This is probably best illustrated by the Nixon–Kissinger National Security Council staff, which was a conscious and deliberate attempt to provide Nixon and Kissinger with a capacity that would allow them to reduce their dependence upon the State departments: There was an attempt to replicate this on the domestic side of the White House in mid-1970 with the creation of the Domestic Council staff under John Ehrlichman. This again was a conscious attempt to create a relatively large capability – about 55 to 60 professionals, with an equivalent number of support staff – at the centre to circumvent dependence on line departments and agencies for a great deal of information and analysis.

A second approach, taken by some presidents, I call 'multiple advocacy'. The essence of multiple advocacy is a recognition that department and agency officials are going to be advocates for their particular programmes in the sense that they have a vested interest in the outcome. They have a preference as to which way the policy goes, and will try to push it in that direction. The idea behind multiple advocacy is that you shape policy through a competition of ideas where the advocates tend to check and balance one another and the staffs are 'honest brokers'.

When one looks at the central institutions available in the Executive Office of the President to assist the chief executive in carrying out these roles, one finds some very interesting things. As Stephen Wayne has mentioned, there has been a great deal of confusion in many people's minds about the size of the White House staff. Many have been led to the erroneous conclusion that the White House staff has grown, and grown dramatically. This is in part because of the way in which counting goes on in the United States. I will share one anecdote with you in this regard. When Richard Nixon came into office in 1969 there were officially on the rolls in the White House somewhere around 250 people, but through the phenomenon of detailing there were actually over 600. Roy Ash, when he became Director of the Office Management and Budget, told Nixon he wanted an honest count. This was done, and furthermore, they decided to cut back the size of the White House staff to 585. Those who look back now at the official figures erroneously conclude that the size of the White House staff more than doubled in the transition from Lyndon Johnson to

Richard Nixon. In fact, it was cut by about 10 or 15 people. Gerald Ford said he would cut the size of the White House staff by 10 per cent, which he did; it went down to 485. When Jimmy Carter came in he decided to cut the size of the White House staff by another 30 per cent, but it is very difficult to cut 30 per cent from any organization. They therefore took the largest component of the White House staff, which was the correspondence unit, and shifted them to what Stephen Wayne has described in his paper as the Office of Administration. This brought the number down to 350. As Professor Wayne has pointed out, it is about 322 today. In fact, then, the size of the White House staff has changed very little.

The White House staff is in fact a collection of very small offices dealing with inter-governmental affairs, public liaison, Congressional affairs, the press, communications, the counsels office, the speech-writers office, the staff secretary's office, the scheduling office, the personnel office and the advance office. The number of policy advisers in the White House is, has been, and will probably remain, relatively small.

The largest, and in many respects the most important institution in the EOP, is the Office of Management and Budget. It has a total of some 580–600 employees, about 320 of whom are in the budget division. There are budget examiners for each department, each agency and most bureaux. Virtually all of the staff of the Office of Management and Budget, unlike the White House, are career civil servants, with a small tier of political officials at the top. They perform a number of important and crucial roles. First, they prepare the Unified Federal Budget; they maintain the budget estimates, report these quarterly, handle supplemental budget bills, rescissions and deferrals and coordinate the administration's strategy in the appropriations process. They do much of what is done in most other countries in the Ministry of Finance or the Treasury Department.

Second, they perform the crucial role of central legislative clearance. That is, they must clear every important piece of testimony that is offered by a cabinet or sub-cabinet level official. Third, they process all executive orders. Fourth, they review most important regulatory actions. Fifth, they exercise a great deal of management oversight. Sixth, a new function they have acquired during the Reagan administration, they maintain a high level of Congressional liaison and coordinate the administration's negotiations with the Congress in the appropriations process.

A third major institution within the EOP is the National Security Council staff. This body controls the flow of information to the president on national security issues and maintains the situation room in the basement of the White House, which operates 24 hours a day and enables the president to maintain constant contact if necessary with US posts abroad. They coordinate the inter-agency machinery on national security issues, handle all the preparations for foreign visitors to the United States and presidential visits abroad. The NSC maintains a very elaborate crisis management facility, and in general serves as the principal adviser to the president on national security issues. The National Security Council's role has varied a great deal. As I pointed out, during the Nixon–Kissinger period there was an attempt to use the NSC essentially to supplant the State Department. The National Security staff, which numbered eight professionals under McGeorge Bundy during the Kennedy period and had risen at the height of the Vietnam war to 18 professionals under Walt Rostow, suddenly mushroomed to between 55 and 60 professionals with an equivalent number of support staff. In line with the view that large entities rarely go back to becoming small entities, the National Security staff today numbers about 45 professionals with roughly 100 support staff.

A fourth major element in the EOP is the Council of Economic Advisers. This was created in 1946, against the objections of the president, in the Full Employment Act of 1946. Truman neither asked for nor wanted a Council of Economic Advisers and in his two volumes of memoirs he mentions it on only one occasion. It has followed the rather remarkable pattern of not increasing in size in more than 35 years. Its total size, including all support staff, in 1947 was 41 people. Today it has three members, 18 professional staff and approximately 13 support staff. It is relatively small, has no operational responsibilities and is designed to produce the economic forecasts for the administration in coordination with the Office of Management and Budget and the Department of the Treasury. It produces the Economic Report of the President which is sent to the Congress once each year, and it supplies the president with economic advice unfiltered by departmental or agency bias.

Finally, the fifth key element in the EOP is the Office of Policy Development, which Professor Wayne referred to. This is the successor to what used to be known as the Domestic Council staff or the Domestic Policy staff. The name was changed, as is frequently the case, when a new administration came into office, in order to emphasize new responsibilities. In this instance the term 'Domestic' was dropped from the title because it was given responsibility for all economic policy, both foreign and domestic. Its size has tended to fluctuate. A conscious decision was made at the outset of the Reagan administration to reduce it in size (a recommendation which I personally enthusiastically concurred in). It currently has approximately 18–20 professionals with about 15 support staff. It performs two key roles. First, it serves as the policy arm of the White House staff, helping prepare major presidential speeches such as the State of the Union speech; reviewing all presidential speeches, messages, proclamations, executive orders and enrolled bills; preparing questions and answers for press conferences; preparing a series of issue papers which are discussed at a weekly issue luncheon with the president, and generally providing policy advice to the president in the way that one would expect of a personal staff.

Secondly, it has the important function so often referred to at this conference of coordinating the activities of the cabinet councils. The seven cabinet councils created by the Reagan administration are collections of cabinet officials which advise the president over broad areas of public policy – economic affairs, natural resources and the environment, human resources, commerce and trade, legal policy, management and administration, and food and agriculture. This experiment in cabinet council government has been an interesting one. Many people doubted that it would last beyond the first year of the administration, in line with the fact that presidents have frequently followed the pattern of beginning their administration with great enthusiasm for looking to cabinet level advice, only to discover that they did not want it after all. These cabinet councils, however, have held well over 500 meetings and their level of activity today is as high as it has ever been. Attendance at the meetings by cabinet level officials remain as high as it has been over the four-year period and, on the whole, both the president and his senior cabinet officials seem pleased with the process.

One final word. It seems to me that what the US system has demonstrated is a good deal of flexibility and adaptability in responding to the wishes of the chief executive. It it hard to impose a system on a US chief executive that he finds incompatible with his style. A second lesson that has been learned, often painfully, is that the centre can never hope to duplicate the resources that are found in the departments and agencies. Presidents who have tried to create large, independent roles for a neutral staff at the centre, because they want to exclude or reduce their dependence upon the line operating departments and agencies, have inevitably been frustrated and disappointed in that effort. Presidents have looked to various central institutions – the White House staff, the Office of Management and Budget, the National Security Council, the Council of Economic Advisers, the Office of Policy Development – as counterweights or counterpoises to the advice they are getting through the line operating departments and agencies. But those presidents that have had the greatest success in governing and in shaping the course and direction of public policy, in my view, have been those that have tried to incorporate the line operating departments and agencies, and bring them into the policy process. This has enabled these presidents to develop a more unified team and to present a united front to the Congress, which is always anxious and ever ready to try to divide an administration and to play it off against itself.

5

France

Pierre Gaborit and Jean-Pierre Mounier

Although the Fifth Republic is now a quarter of a century old, it is still customary to say that it has not yet stood the test of 'coming under fire'. And yet everything goes on as if public life were in fact governed by an immutable regulatory system. In a political system of unequal institutional diarchy, we can see an increasing interaction between the head of state and the personal staff working for the members of the executive branch. However, the institutional mechanism in itself is not enough to explain the unusual character of the French system. One must also consider the personalities of individual leaders, as well as the details of the structures themselves. There is also another unchanging reality, that which some observers call 'the Republic of officials'. This takes account of two successive phenomena: the rise in power of the party-political general staffs at the expense of the general staff of the administration, and the rise in power of a caste of all-powerful senior officials who have taken the leading positions within these party general staffs, at the expense of the general staffs themselves. The whole process is cemented by the concept of 'legitimation through ability' and by the ideology of 'the general interest'.

The changeover in government in 1981, the first since 1958, gave rise to the idea that the existing regulatory mechanism would be questioned. It was expected that there would be a challenge to the primacy in political decisions of the caste of senior officials; that there would be a large-scale come-back by personnel with a stronger party-political commitment, a resurgence of the idea of a political programme and even a reform in institutions.

In reality, three years later, everything seems to be in place as before, with the power of the Elysée[1] all-pervasive in political decisions, a continued growth of administration of general staff type at every level and a re-establishment of the old system of values and representative functions at the highest level of the state.

The Growing Domination of the Elysée in the Decision-making Process

The Unequal Diarchy

The institutional system of the French Fifth Republic has for a long time been presented as a hybrid model incorporating possibilities of evolution in two distinct directions: neo-parliamentarism and presidentialization. On the whole, political observers have tended to see as the decisive factor the ability of the president to ensure the cohesion of the parliamentary majority. In fact, on the contrary, a quarter of a century of experience of how the institutions function has made it quite clear that, above and beyond the ups and downs of the changing political situation, the presidency of the Republic has become the dominant centre which sends out impulses to determine the policy of the state, and that the presidency has succeeded in getting the whole ensemble of the decision-making apparatus to work for it. Paradoxically, the weight of the prime minister, and of his general staff, in the state apparatus has been reinforced by this development, at the expense of the influence of individual ministers, who are limited to a purely managerial role. This is what is generally described as a diarchical system, characterized by a hypertrophy of the ministerial general staffs, and the setting-up of a relatively stable system for regulating the relations between the decision-making centres. The system is, however, unequal, because of a permanent tendency towards the reinforcement of the presidential pole in the whole apparatus of the state.

The Presidency of the Republic

The institutional entourage of the president consists of the General Secretariat of the Presidency, the civilian cabinet and of the president's personal military staff. The particular weight of these different elements has varied quite considerably from one president to another. All the same, the pre-eminence of the Secretary-General of the Presidency, of whom de Gaulle said: 'he is *au courant* of everything and at the centre of everything',[2] has become steadily stronger, at the expense of the *cabinet*,[3] where indeed the position of *directeur de cabinet* even disappeared during the presidency of Georges Pompidou. The influence of the chief of the personal military staff is more difficult to estimate, as it depends on the role he plays in the Supreme Council and the Supreme Committee for National Defence, and on the degree of direct access to the president available to him.[4]

The present set-up at the Elysée, however, does not allow us to appreciate all the nuances of the working mechanism of the presidential entourage. Indeed, ever since the presidency of General de Gaulle, successive heads of state have equipped themselves with advisers from outside the traditional hierarchy. This practice has even been institutionalized, with the establishment of the General Secretariat for Algerian Affairs and then of the General Secretariat for African and Madagascan Affairs, which were directly attached to the presidency (but which have now been abolished). On the other hand, the use by presidents of advisers from outside the hierarchy (whether in the General Secretariat or the *cabinet*), has continued, and has led to a *de facto* breaking-down of the formal hierarchy of the entourage.

The two most significant examples have occurred under the presidencies of Georges Pompidou and of François Mitterrand – two very different individuals. When Pompidou recruited advisers from outside the civil service – Pierre Juillet and Marie-France Garaud (both of whom had already been his aides when he was de Gaulle's prime minister) – and made a practice of consulting them daily on the whole range of governmental policy, he created a focus of competition to the Secretary-General of the Presidency.[5] Mitterrand, when he appointed six advisers from outside the hierarchy, set up a 'first circle' within his personal entourage, characterized by direct and very frequent access to the president. Even within this first circle, however, a hierarchy was established, within which the official designations corresponded perfectly to the reality: Jacques Attali, the president's special adviser, is consulted on government policy as a whole, and is present at meetings of the Council of Ministers; the three *chargés de missions auprès du Président* (Pierre Dreyfus, François de Grossouvre and Régis Debray) are responsible for giving the president advice on the mood of the different sections of public opinion, and for maintaining a dialogue with them; and the two *conseillers auprès du Président* (Michel Charasse and Guy Penne) are concerned with more specific areas of policy – relations with local councillors for the former and African affairs for the latter.

This current development symbolizes fairly accurately the evolution of the presidential entourage. Whereas it initially consisted of about ten people, it now numbers some 40 official advisers.

From a strict technique best described as 'raking-over',[6] the working methods used have developed into a situation where the president's advisers find themselves in competition with one another, sometimes without knowing it. The personal links of each adviser with the president are crucial to the degree of influence each can exercise on his decisions.[7]

This process explains both the need for strong coordination of the presidential team and the progressive weakening of the distinction between the General Secretariat of the Presidency and the presidential *cabinet*. Even if the influence of the director of the *cabinet* has varied according to his personal relations with the president,[8] the role of the Secretary-General has always remained an essential one.

The Secretary-General of the Presidency, who has an audience every day with the head of state, carries out a triple function. First, the coordination of the administrative arrangements of the presidency; second, links with the prime minister's *cabinet* and the General Secretariat of the Government; third, the task of organizing, with the General Secretariat, the ministerial meetings which prepare the way for policy decisions at the highest level. In these different roles, the Secretary-General of the Presidency has frequent contact with the prime minister and his staff, with the ministers and members of their *cabinets*, with certain senior officials and, of course, with the other members of the presidential staff, for whom he is in most cases an essential point of contact.

The Secretary-General is thus well placed to play an important role in resolving conflicts that arise inside the government or inside the presidential entourage. However, this influence should not be exaggerated, in view of the many different means of direct access to the president, and the tendency – which has been constantly reinforced in the present period – towards a direct and personal exercise by the chief of state of the functions of decision-making and arbitration. The Secretary-General of the Presidency can intervene in a decisive way on minor decisions, but he does this on the same basis as other advisers who are frequently consulted by the president; his function as a mediator is a real one, but it is essentially carried out within the presidential entourage.

This entourage, indeed, does not function like a collegiate organ. Meetings, which are generally held under the chairmanship of the Secretary-General or his deputy, are most often of a specialized kind, and only bring together a limited number of participants. Importance is attached to communication through written notes. Such working methods may be, in part, the result of the technical nature of the decisions to be taken; but it seems that they must be explained above all by two characteristics of the French political system. The first of these is the homogeneity of the president's entourage. The presidential team, which is totally renewed every time there is a change of president,[9] is chosen from among the group of close supporters of the head of state.[10] Total loyalty, both personal and political, is essential, even though it does not necessarily have to be confirmed by a party-political commitment.

Essentially, the choice is made from among civil servants. However, the personal life history of each president may bring in factors that will seriously modify this method of selecting advisers. Both Georges Pompidou and François Mitterrand, being distrustful of senior civil servants, considerably reduced the proportion of them in their respective general staffs. Mitterrand, having based himself on a political party which he had entirely renovated, drew to a considerable extent on the ranks of the party in building his presidential team, without, however, giving the team the flavour of a party-political caste. The internal cohesion of the presidential team of both Pompidou and Mitterrand was hardly affected by this broader recruitment, and this in itself confirms the influence over individual appointments of a deeper, institutional logic.

The second factor which explains the working of the presidency is the conception of the role to be played by the head of state. Being, as he is, at the centre of political power, he cannot risk being committed by the words of one of his advisers. At the same time, being assured of a mandate of long duration, he must take care not to 'wear out' his personal entourage in the eyes of the public. He is obliged to demonstrate his personal ability to devise his own policies, but he must not appear to be dependent on his collaborators.

The general staff of the president thus appears as a centralized apparatus, which leaves open certain routes of direct access to the chief of state, although these are strictly controlled by his immediate entourage. The prime minister, the members of the government who are given priority by the president himself and the main political and social forces of the country have direct access to the president, who will decide himself whether or not to bring in one or another of his advisers during this type of consultation. Any possible breakdown in relation to public opinion thus cannot be attributed in principle to the president's entourage. The president shares with the prime minister – though he himself is the final arbitrator – the task of maintaining the cohesion of the government's parliamentary majority.

L'Hôtel Matignon

At first sight, the apparatus for advice and support which is available to the prime minister may appear to be comparable to that for the president. There is the same type of structure, notably a prime minister's *cabinet* and the General Secretariat of the Government. The same increase of staff can be observed here as with the presidency, and the political personnel is similar. There is a difference, however, but it is more one of nature than of degree.

The advice apparatus available to the prime minister, however effective it may be in maintaining control over the activity of the government, still has the effect of reinforcing the pre-eminence of the head of state and his own general staff. The composition of the prime minister's apparatus, moreover, lies partly outside his own control.

The *cabinet* of the prime minister, originally conceived as an organization of modest dimensions, has continually increased its strength. From a staff of about 20 members at the beginning of the Fifth Republic, it rose to about 50 during the first two Mauroy governments. The third Mauroy government, and then in a more decisive manner the Fabius government, have proceeded with a more limited level of staffing. The reasons for the gradual increase in the staff are mainly related to the prime minister's wish to maintain control over the apparatus of government, one of his major tasks. Because of this, each department of government has been furnished with a technical adviser or an official attached to the prime minister, with the responsibility of following developments in the policy area of the ministry in question. This tendency reached a peak in the second government of Pierre Mauroy, which, even though it was not the first coalition government of the Fifth Republic, set itself the objective of ensuring strict control over an administration that had not seen a change of political leadership for a quarter of a century.

It is, however, far from certain that this aim was in fact achieved. Successive prime ministers, in wanting above all to have each sector of governmental activity systematically supervised by a member of their *cabinet*, have weighed down the decision-making process. In seeking, in the second instance, to allocate themselves the powers necessary for this, they have allowed the individual departments to place their own representatives within the prime ministerial *cabinet*, which has had the effect of putting the mechanisms of control into reverse. This is particularly clear in the case of the Ministry of Finance. In any case, the functioning of the *cabinet* itself has been weighed down, whatever the organizational form employed.

The *cabinets* of the prime ministers have always oscillated between two types, either acting as a 'rake', where his closest collaborators filter access to the prime minister, or as a limited collegiate system, characterized by a high frequency of meetings and by a multiplicity of avenues of direct contact between the prime minister and his principal advisers. The *cabinets* of Pompidou, Chirac, Couve de Murville, Messmer and Fabius correspond to the first type, and those of Chaban-Delmas and Mauroy to the second. In both cases, however, an essential role is played by the 'man in charge', who has been able, either alone or with the director of the *cabinet*, to enjoy direct and frequent access to the prime minister, and who constitutes a filter for other advisers who only communicate with the prime minister by written notes.

The director of the *cabinet* himself is much more than the leader of the team, a function which in any case he has to carry out with the cooperation of, or sometimes in competition with, the leading members of the *cabinet*, who are responsible for the major sectors of governmental activity.[11] The personality of the prime minister is a decisive factor in this respect: those like Georges Pompidou or Jacques Chirac who took their own decisions based on written notes submitted by the *cabinet*, relied extensively on the 'first circle' of advisers, who at certain times were even brought together on a daily basis. They thus took over, in a large measure, the function of coordinating the *cabinet*. The director of the *cabinet* is in this case essentially in charge of the general cohesion of the government's actions, and to carry out this function he frequently receives ministers or periodically brings together the directors of their *cabinets* as well as carrying out negotiations with the political parties and pressure groups, and exchanges of view with the presidency. The directors of the *cabinets* of the prime ministers who, as with Jacques Chaban-Delmas or Pierre Mauroy, made the contrary decision for 'polycentrism' and a form of team work, while keeping this role of political guidance, have had the additional task of the technical coordination of the *cabinet*.

A choice in this latter direction was made at the expense of cohesion and of efficiency. The hierarchy of the *cabinet* has generally been broken down into a juxtaposition of parallel hierarchies, and even a great increase in the number of meetings of the *cabinet* has not been able to cope with this development. The prime minister's advisers, on the other hand, have been able to gain in autonomy what the *cabinet* has lost in procedural rigour: they have engaged in direct dialogues with ministers, they have summoned senior officials for discussions, and they have involved themselves in every stage of the decision-making process. In this way, it has been possible for the process to be described in the following ironical way: Matignon gives the first impulse, then ministers hand over the execution of these general directions to their staffs, the general staffs re-make the original decisions, the ministerial *cabinets* rearrange them, and finally the *cabinet* of the prime minister takes hold of everything again.[12] The problem is that one can no longer determine with any certainty who has really taken the responsibility for a decision.

Originally conceived as a means of giving the head of government the technical assistance and support necessary for the definition of his policy, the prime ministerial *cabinet* has thus contributed in a large measure to the creation of a veritable 'administration by general staff',[13] with a party-political domination which has been superimposed on a managerial administration and on an administration by delegation; the establishment of this type of administration has been made easier by the fact that the personnel who run the political general staffs and those who occupy the highest positions of the administrative apparatus of the state are one and the same. As well as the dysfunctional effects of this on the management of the affairs of the state, it has also contributed in large measure to cutting the prime minister off from public opinion. The confusion between political and administrative elements which has thus been maintained has paradoxically damaged the control of the state apparatus by the prime minister, even though he has at his disposal one of the most effective instruments, the General Secretariat of the Government.

The General Secretariat of the Government, the central administrative apparatus at the service of the prime minister, is able, because of its great stability, to form the central pole around which the rest of the Hôtel Matignon revolves. Thus, even though there have been ten Secretaries-General of the Presidency in 30 years, there have been no more than six Secretaries-General of the Government in a period of more than 40 years. The function is reserved by tacit agreement for a member of the Council of State, and the staff which he directs consists of about 50 people.

The General Secretariat carries out a series of functions which are essential for preparing and carrying through policy decisions at the highest level. First, the General Secretariat keeps up to date the government's agenda for the preparation of meetings of the Council of Ministers, the contents of which are regulated by the six-monthly work programmes (a practice brought in under the presidency of Valéry Giscard d'Estaing), and by the directives sent by the president to his prime minister (not on a regular basis). It plays the role of legal adviser to the *cabinet*; it provides the secretariat for inter-departmental meetings held under the chairmanship of a member of the prime minister's *cabinet*, and it keeps the minutes of these meetings; it is responsible for recording the decisions taken by the government, and for presenting them to the Council of State, which is consulted on all important draft legislation; and finally, it acts as the memory of the government.

This omnipresence of the General Secretariat of the Government should not, however, be taken to mean that the officials it comprises have a tendency to supplant the advisers of the prime minister. For instance, they play no role in resolving conflicts that arise between different departments, or within the prime minister's *cabinet*. Their influence is exercised by means of the technical advice they provide to the prime minister on the quality of the plans worked out by the departments, and is thus influential only at the margin.

The position of the Secretary-General is quite different. This official is an essential cog in the apparatus of the state, thanks to the role he plays in ensuring the cohesion of the government's actions as a whole, the fact that he is present at sessions of the Council of Ministers (whose agenda and minutes are his responsibility) and his presence at meetings of the councils and committees which are held under the chairmanship of the head of state or the prime minister. The importance of his post explains why he is responsible 'in carrying out his essential functions' to the president.[14] However, he is neither at the centre of arbitration of political questions, nor in competition with the direct entourage of the prime minister, or, *a fortiori*, that of the head of state. The choice of a very senior official, always a product of the Council of State – an institution which guarantees independence of its members with regard to the political authorities – and the technical profile which successive secretaries-general have always adopted, constitute the most clear confirmation of his position. At the same time, however, they confer on him a functional and moral authority in relation to the whole administrative/political complex which has built itself up at the very top of the state apparatus, and which is tending to take on an essential role in the French political system.

The Regulating Mechanisms

The Council of Ministers, whose weekly meetings are presided over by the head of state, cannot be seen either as a point of arbitration for resolving the internal conflicts of the government, nor as a collegiate body which enables the president or the prime minister to air decisions they are thinking of taking. On the one hand, the reinforcement of the presidential pole in the institutional system leads in most cases to an announcement of the most important decisions by the president;[15] on the other hand, the Council of Ministers functions more often as a place for confirming decisions on measures that have been prepared long in advance than as a forum for reflection or discussion.

A change of government in 1981, however, raised the hope that a more substantial role in the process of deliberation would be allocated to the Council of Ministers; but in practice any tendency in this direction seems to have been undermined as early as 1983 with the formation of the third Mauroy government, in which, incidentally, the number of ministers in the Council was considerably reduced. On the other hand, however, the government developed the habit of 'working seminars' which presented the possibility – albeit at very long intervals – of less formal discussion of the general direction of state policy.

We thus have to look elsewhere for the regulatory mechanisms of the state apparatus. There is no lack of instruments that might carry out this function. A juridical analysis allows us to make a distinction between inter-ministerial or limited 'councils', which meet under the chairmanship of the head of state, inter-ministerial committees presided over by the prime minister, and inter-departmental meetings where the chairmanship is taken by a member of the prime minister's *cabinet*, or in exceptional cases by the Secretary-General of the Government.

Taking a longer-term view, we have to note a general increase in the frequency of meetings of these different types of regulatory bodies. There are several complementary reasons for this evolution. The overall lines of foreign policy, by their nature, are the responsibility of the head of state; this explains why the only inter-ministerial councils mentioned in the constitution are the Council and the Supreme Committee of National Defence, all other councils and committees being the result of custom and practice. In reality, moreover, the personal grip of the president on foreign affairs goes considerably beyond the existence of these councils, as he alone makes the final choices and decisions, without necessarily consulting the prime minister or the relevant departmental minister (but generally after taking advice from a special adviser close to himself).

Secondly, going beyond foreign policy, the Algerian crisis marked a critical turning-point. President de Gaulle, who had up to that point shown great respect for the role of the prime minister, took the decision at that time to give his own instructions directly to Louis Joxe, the minister responsible for this issue. This tendency towards the increase of presidential power gave rise to a theory put forward by a former prime minister of the Fifth Republic, who thought it was possible to distinguish three types of political domain: the domain reserved for the head of state, the domain which he supervised, and the domain which was entirely delegated to the prime minister. This theory – which in any case was very controversial – is certainly obsolete today. It would be more accurate to say that the president has at his disposal a power of strategic intervention which allows him to take up any governmental matter which seems to him to require a decision at the presidential level. Thus, for instance, François Mitterrand has brought in the practice of weekly inter-ministerial councils devoted to economic and social policy.

Lastly, we can see that the prime minister has thus been partially dispossessed of his power of arbitration and decision, a process that is reflected in the composition of his *cabinet* (where international relations occupy only a minor place), and in the frequency of meetings held under the chairmanship of the prime minister or of a member of his *cabinet*.

Tables 1 and 2, which are based on information given to the authors by the Hôtel Matignon, provide eloquent testimony on this point. They show the considerable growth in the frequency of meetings of every kind, with a tendency to increase sharply after each change of prime minister, followed by a considerable decline in frequency, above all for committees convened by the prime minister himself (although this fall never takes the frequency of meetings back to that prevailing before the change of government). This fact would seem to be the result of the institutional logic we have already described.

Indeed, at the beginning of a prime minister's term of office, the division of roles between the head of state and the prime minister is a balanced one. The prime minister, who does not have the benefit of guaranteed tenure of office, has to prove that he has a considerable capacity to govern. The consideration of a large number of policy issues by the prime minister and his office is also justified by the need to avoid committing the president irrevocably to the lines

Table 1 Inter-ministerial committees convened by the prime minister 1981–4

	1981	1982	1983	1984
January		14	10	6
February		8	7	14
March		14	5	5
April		11	5	9
May	1	10	5	1
June	2	11	5	8
July	13	20	9	3
August	5	2	7	
September	14	7	3	2
October	12	8	4	
November	9	8	4	
December	9	7	3	
Total	65	120	67	48
Monthly average	8.12	10.00	5.58	5.33

Table 2 Meetings and committees convened by the prime minister and his *cabinet* 1979–83

	Jan.	Feb.	Mar.	Apr.	May	Jun.	Jul.	Aug.	Sep.	Oct.	Nov.	Dec.	Total	Monthly average
Inter-departmental meetings														
1979	81	81	101	63	81	87	102	52	66	104	95	76	989	82.40
1980	95	106	86	105	81	88	85	25	79	112	90	115	1067	88.90
1981	97	106	105	73	26	66	86	61	110	149	154	130	1163	96.90
1982	133	154	172	164	137	188	137	70	135	172	186	188	1836	152.90
1983	178	157	144	86	102	116	109	67	138	130	137	125	1489	124.00
Inter-departmental committees														
1979	6	6	5	10	7	5	8	2	4	3	6	7	69	5.75
1980	5	6	5	2	8	3	5	2	3	1	4	5	49	4.08
1981	2	5	2	0	1	2	13	5	14	12	9	9	74	6.16
1982	14	8	14	11	10	11	20	2	7	8	8	7	120	10.00
1983	10	7	5	5	5	5	9	7	3	4	4	3	67	5.58
Total														
1979	87	87	106	73	88	92	110	54	70	107	101	83	1058	88.88
1980	100	112	91	107	89	91	90	27	82	113	94	120	1116	93.00
1981	99	111	107	73	27	68	99	66	124	161	163	139	1237	101.16
1982	147	162	186	175	147	199	157	72	142	180	194	195	1956	162.92
1983	188	164	149	91	107	121	118	74	141	134	141	128	1556	129.68

The rate of increase of inter-departmental meetings and committees convened by the prime minister and his *cabinet* 1981–3 is as follows:

Meetings: 1981, 1163; 1982, 1836; increase = 57.78%.
Committees: 1981, 74; 1982, 120; increase = 62.16%.
Total: 1981, 1237; 1982, 1956; increase = 58.04%; 1983, 20.45%.

In 1982, 12 committees were presided over by P. Mauroy out of 120; in 1983 he presided over 49 committees out of 67.

of policy adopted. This tendency also corresponds to the need for the prime minister to get a grip on an administrative apparatus that runs the risk of being affected by the political changes of the time, and not all of whose members are committed to the same political ideals. (This is confirmed by all inquiries undertaken before 1981 among members of ministerial *cabinets* and among senior officials holding posts filled at the discretion of the government.) On this last point, as explained above, the prime minister is better placed than the president, in view of the size of his general staff and the logistic resources of the General Secretariat of the Government.

The fact that governments are eventually worn out with time, however, obliges the president to deal himself with an increasing number of policy issues. He is, in addition, pushed in this direction by the fact that individual ministers tend increasingly to appeal to him against the decisions made by the prime minister, and such appeals may even come from the prime minister himself in cases where it is not possible for a decision to be taken at the prime ministerial level. The prime minister is thus the instrument of his own dispossession of power. In general, all presidents of the Republic, whatever their own personal temperament, have felt themselves under an obligation to demonstrate to public opinion their ability to take charge of a policy, particularly as they have generally made concrete commitments in the course of their election campaigns. The most complete example of this is provided by the 110 'propositions' of Mitterrand's candidature.

This tendency of the Elysée to take control of a large number of the levers of power is reflected in a number of identifiable facts. First, the president's domination of the system of appointments, especially of senior office holders (top civil servants, prefects, ambassadors, or heads of nationalized industries), many of whom are drawn from among ministerial (or *cabinet*) general staffs. Second, the growing intervention of the president's advisers in the daily functioning of the governmental machine, without any previous contact with the prime minister's *cabinet*. Presidential advisers, who are regularly invited into departmental meetings and committees held at the Hôtel Matignon, seldom speak at these meetings, so as not to commit the president to the conclusions reached there. (The interventionism of the Elysée is thus shown in other ways, by the direct dealings of presidential advisers with ministerial *cabinets* and senior officials.) Third, the bodies responsible for providing expert advice, which are in theory under the political direction of the prime minister and the administrative authority of the General Secretariat of the Government (for instance the Service for Information and Documentation, the General Secretariat for National Defence, the Secretariat for Questions of European Economic Co-operation, etc.), in fact tend to find themselves placed under a double command. Fourth, the tendency towards presidentialism is expressed in the structure and working of the prime minister's general staff, which is now reduced in size and shows a tendency to give up any wish to exercise total control of all sectors of governmental activity.

Thus, the political change that took place in France in 1981 has not called into question the administrative developments that were already under way from the beginning of the Fifth Republic onwards. The practices followed during the first two years of François Mitterrand's term of presidential office have only brought about short-lived deviations from the established course.

Twenty-five years into the Fifth Republic, a number of tendencies can thus be clearly discerned. Successive presidents have increased their efforts to demonstrate their ability to evolve an autonomous line of policies. In this they have in large measure succeeded, but not without causing a significant development in the non-official circuits of decision-making. The general staffs of a more political nature have become much more substantial, but this has not in fact allowed them to take control of a governmental apparatus that has been constantly made more complex by the development of specialized structures not fully integrated into the traditional administration (this is known in France as '*l'administration de mission*'). Very little recourse is had, at any level, to advisers outside the public administration, in order to get expert opinions on questions of public policy. One should note, however, that there is a striking exception to this, as far as problems of communication with the public are concerned, precisely because recourse to the traditional administration for this sort of work does not appear proper. There is a symbiosis between advisory personnel and the personnel who occupy the leading positions in administrative management. This tendency accentuates the risk of isolation of the president and the prime minister from public opinion.

The Quasi-monopoly of Senior Civil Servants

Ministerial *cabinets* have confirmed their position under the Fifth Republic as the central locations of decision-making. This has reinforced the domination of the executive over the conduct of public business. The quasi-monopoly of senior officials in the composition of these *cabinets* has increased the weight of the public service in all the decision-making mechanisms.

Those whose function is in theory to put into practice political decisions made by others, have thus in fact provided most of the personnel who are in a position to take these decisions. A single statistic is very eloquent: from 1958 to 1981 87 per cent of members of ministerial *cabinets* were senior civil servants.

When the Left came to power, it was expected that there would be substantial changes in the situation. Throughout their years in opposition, the parties of the Left underlined their distrust of technocracy, and of government by an administrative élite, which they regarded as unable to take popular aspirations into account or even to be aware of them. Everything about these senior civil servants – their social origins, their way of life, their approach to problems – was offensive to left-wing sensibilities. There would therefore have to be a break with the traditional methods of recruitment to ministerial *cabinets*.

Before examining the present situation, let us look briefly at the way matters had been arranged previously.

The Cabinets *of the Fifth Republic up to May 1981*

Since the beginning of the Fifth Republic, presidents, prime ministers and ministers have, by a very large majority, placed their confidence in advisers recruited from the senior ranks of the civil service. A study published in 1973 on ministerial *cabinets*[16] gives no room to any category other than that of 'administration' in the tables devoted to the professional origin of their members. A further study of the *cabinets* of the different presidents and prime ministers[17] shows that the proportion of senior officials never fell below 58 per cent (in the presidential *cabinet* of Georges Pompidou) and rose as high as 77 per cent (in the prime ministerial *cabinet* of Pierre Messmer).

Table 3, taken from this latter study, is a clear indication of the domination of senior officials in all the presidential and prime ministerial *cabinets*. This is all the more striking as the category listed as 'economic sector: public' includes members of the public service or of the various state corps of engineers who have moved into the general staffs of public sector enterprises.

According to figures given in one study of presidential advisers,[18] 90 per cent of the entourage of General de Gaulle, and 85 per cent of that of Valéry Giscard d'Estaing, belonged, or had belonged, to the public service. The only

Table 3   Background of *cabinet* members

	Higher administrative civil service	Economic life			Others
		Public	Private	Total	
de Gaulle	76.0	7.4	1.6	9.0	15.0
Debre	69.0	0.0	0.0	0.0	31.0
Couve de Murville	76.0	4.0	0.0	4.0	20.0
G. Pompidou (PM)	66.0	10.0	7.5	17.5	16.5
G. Pompidou (president)	58.0	10.0	10.0	20.0	22.0
J. Chaban-Delmas	70.0	14.0	0.0	14.0	16.0
P. Messmer	77.0	6.7	2.3	9.0	14.0
V. Giscard d'Estaing	71.0	11.0	0.0	11.0	18.0
J. Chirac	68.0	8.0	0.0	8.0	24.0

president to have recruited non-civil servants into his personal staff to a significant degree, Georges Pompidou, did not, on the other hand, seek to obtain the services of businessmen, although some writers have said that he did so. A close analysis shows that the majority of the individuals concerned, even if their origins were not in the administration, had, a considerable time previously, left their first professional private careers and been recruited to the *cabinet* of the previous head of state, or to that of Pompidou during his period as prime minister. It was more their ability to 'serve the state' and the personal confidence of the president which led to their appointment than their remote past as lawyers or as businessmen.

Thus senior advisers, without any notable exceptions whatever, tended to be recruited from among the existing members of the state apparatus. One has to add, more precisely, that until 1981 the majority of appointees came from the ranks of the senior civil service. In the French administrative system there are also the so-called '*grands corps*': this designation is applied to the Inspectorate of Finances, the Council of State, and the Court of Audit, to which one should add the engineers of the *Corps de mines* and the engineers of *Ponts et Chaussées* (Bridges and Highways). Even though there is nothing in the regulations to prescribe this, the members of these *grands corps* tend to occupy the majority of the posts of director-general or director of administration in government departments. Until 1981, they were also the people who occupied the dominant positions in ministerial and presidential *cabinets*.

Tables 4 and 5, from a study by Ezra Suleiman[19] demonstrate this very clearly. It is true that these figures apply only to the year 1970, when Georges Pompidou was president and Jacques Chaban-Delmas was prime minister, but they are highly representative of the normal distribution of senior officials in all *cabinets* from 1958 to 1981.

If one includes the prefects, the *Corps préfectoral*, which Suleiman considers as belonging to the *grands corps*, it can be seen that there is generally a correlation between membership of an important *cabinet* and/or an important post in a *cabinet*, and membership of one of the *grands corps*.

The situation up to May 1981 can thus be summarized as follows: first, the entourage of ministers, prime ministers and presidents is essentially made up of civil servants; second, among these civil servants, very few belong to the research or teaching sectors, and almost all are so-called decision-making officials; third, the most important positions are monopolized by members of the *grands corps*, i.e. the administrative élite.

Up to 1981, then, the highest level of the public service appeared to set itself up as a closed system which also incorporated the advisory function. Some of its members, often those who had been marked out by their rank on graduating from the l'Ecole Nationale d'Administration (ENA) as the most brilliant, left their administrative functions for a time to take on advisory ones. They

Table 4 Representation of the *grand corps* in ministers' *cabinets* in 1970

Ministry	Total no. in cabinet	Corps of cabinet director	Representation of each corps						
			IF	CC	CE	CP	Mines	P&C	Total
President	19	CC	1	3	2	3	2	–	11
Prime minister	29	CP	4	–	2	4	1	1	12
Defence	9	IF	2	1	1	1	–	–	5
Cultural affairs	11	–	–	1	–	2	–	–	3
Relations with parliament	8	CP	–	–	–	3	–	–	3
Justice	10	–	–	–	1	–	–	–	1
Foreign affairs	11	IF	1	–	1	1	1	1	5
Interior	10	CP	–	–	–	4	–	–	4
Economics & finance	17	IF	5	2	–	1	1	–	9
Education	12	Mines	2	–	–	2	1	1	6
Industrial development	11	IF	1	1	1	1	2	1	7
Housing	9	CP	1	–	–	2	–	3	6
Post & telecommunications	10	IF	1	1	–	–	1	–	3
Agriculture	10	CE	1	–	1	–	–	–	2
Transport	10	–	–	–	–	2	1	1	4
Employment	9	IF	1	–	1	1	–	1	4
Public Health	10	CE	1	2	1	2	–	–	6
Ex-servicemen	8	CE	1	–	1	1	–	–	3
Regional reform	6	P&C	–	–	–	1	1	2	4
Overseas territories	10	CP	1	–	–	3	–	–	4
Total	229	–	23	11	12	34	11	11	103

IF: *Inspection des finances* (Inspectorate of Finances)
CC: *Cour des comptes* (Court of Audit)
CE: *Conseil d'Etat* (Council of State)
CP: *Corps préfectoral* (Corps of Prefects)
P & C: *Ponts et Chaussées* (Bridges and Highways).
Source: *La Documentation française*

generally did this at a relatively young age. The majority returned later to more traditional administrative functions. Spending a period of time in a ministerial *cabinet* simply served to accelerate their careers.

Already certain of reaching the best appointments because of their membership of the leading *grands corps*, those members of the public service who spent some time in a *cabinet* were certain of reaching the very summit of the state apparatus. Those who had graduated from ENA with a more modest grade saw in a period of service in a *cabinet* a way of a least partially catching up with their better-placed comrades. In all this, political affiliations played practically no role. Agreement on the essentials, and the ability to give good service to a

Table 5 Representation of the *grand corps* in the cabinets of secretaries of state (junior ministers) in 1970

Secretary of State	Total no. in cabinet	Corps of cabinet director	IF	CC	CE	CP	Mines	P&C	Total
African affairs	8	–	–	–	–	–	–	–	0
Prime minister	3	CE	–	–	1	–	–	–	1
Youth and sport	6	–	–	1	–	1	–	–	2
Public service	6	–	–	–	–	–	–	–	0
Prime minister	4	CC	–	1	–	–	–	–	1
Defence	4	CP	–	–	–	2	–	–	2
Relations with parliament	2	–	–	–	–	–	–	–	0
Relations with parliament	3	CP	–	–	–	1	–	–	1
Foreign affairs	4	–	–	–	–	1	–	–	1
Foreign affairs	6	–	–	–	–	1	–	–	1
Interior	5	CP	–	–	–	2	–	–	2
Economy and finance	9	–	1	–	1	1	–	–	3
Commerce	4	IF	1	–	1	1	–	–	3
Education	5	CE	–	–	1	1	–	–	2
Small and medium businesses	4	CC	–	1	–	–	1	–	2
Industrial development	4	–	–	–	–	–	–	–	0
Tourism	6	–	–	–	–	1	–	1	2
Housing	5	–	–	–	–	–	–	–	0
Agriculture	3	CP	–	–	–	1	–	–	1
Employment	4	–	–	–	–	–	–	–	0
Social affairs	6	–	–	–	–	1	–	–	1
Total	101		2	3	4	14	1	1	25

Abbreviations as for table 4.
Source: La Documentation française

member of the executive, would be enough. This would facilitate the re-entry of the adviser, at a more senior level, into a civil service that wanted to be regarded as politically neutral.

For a small number, however, things did not happen in this way. For them, the period of service in a *cabinet* was to be the point of departure for a public political career. It was very common in the parties of the majority up to 1981 for candidates for parliament or future ministers to be recruited from among the members of *cabinets*. To mention only the most famous examples, Georges Pompidou, Valéry Giscard d'Estaing and Jacques Chirac all began their political careers in this way. In this case, the osmosis – at least as far as the level of personnel was concerned – between administration and political leadership was complete.

On every one of these points it was possible to advance the hypothesis that the arrival in power in 1981 of the party of the Left would lead to profound changes in the situation.

Cabinets *since the Election of François Mitterrand*

Here we must distinguish the *cabinet* of the president from those of the members of the government, and for the latter, as for the prime minister, take account of a double evolution.

The Advisers of the President. It is at this level that changes in relation to the previous period have been the most clearly marked. If, as we have said, the internal functioning of the Elysée and the weight of the presidential apparatus have not been greatly changed, the presidential choice of individual advisers has been quite different. Valéry Giscard d'Estaing, who had surrounded himself with young members of the *grands corps*, saying 'technically, these must be the best', had now been succeeded by a president who was keen to make a different choice.

Table 6 indicates, on a percentage basis, the professional origins of the advisers of François Mitterrand, compared with those of previous presidents.[20] It will be noted that the number of state employees dropped from 90 to 53 per cent, and the number of senior civil servants from 63 to 28 per cent. It is also clear how far – apart from the Council of State – the public bodies that had

Table 6 The advisers of the president (May 1981)

Profession/corps	Elysée 1981[a] (%)	5th Republic[b] (%)
Inspectorate of Finances	0	10
Court of Audit	0	7
Council of State	16	10
Diplomatic Corps	3	13
Magistrature	6	6
Corps of Prefects	3	17
Other officials[c]	25	27
Nationalized industries	6	3
Private sector[d]	41	7

[a]Total number = 32.
[b]*Source:* Aline Coutrot 'Les membres des Cabinets du Premier ministre et du Président de la République, 1959–1974', in *Administration et Politique sous la Cinquième République* (Presse de la Fondation Nationale des Sciences Politiques, Paris, 1981)
[c]Including teachers.
[d]Including party staff.

additionally provided the essential part of the presidential staff were now under-represented. The Inspectorate of Finances, the most prestigious of the *grands corps*, no longer had a single representative on the presidential staff.

The new head of state recruited his collaborators in the first instance from among those who had worked with him for a long time, even friends of long standing, whether or not they were socialist leaders, and with even less account paid to the question of whether they were senior civil servants. The president's special adviser and his Secretary-General were political appointees, whereas the director of the presidential *cabinet*, the adviser for African affairs and the adviser responsible for the most delicate missions were personal friends. The team was completed by trade unionists, and only a limited number of senior civil servants.

One man was characteristic of this change: Pierre Beregovoy, the new Secretary-General of the Presidency. He was a self-taught man whose success came from his record as a long-time party militant.

Since May 1981 this situation has not changed greatly. Only nine members of the original team of 37 have left. The new arrivals and the internal reorganizations of the team have rejuvenated the group, and have slightly reinforced the position of members of the public service. For instance, Pierre Beregovoy, when he became a minister, was replaced by Jean-Louis Bianco, a member of the Council of State who had been a long-time collaborator of the president. One personal friend, an industrialist, who was director of the presidential *cabinet*, has been replaced by a professor of law, who until that time had been his deputy, and who had for a long time been a close collaborator of President Mitterrand.

The characteristics of the entourage of the president are that there are fewer members of the *grands corps*; there are more middle-ranking public officials and teachers; there is a general tone of greater political militancy; and there is a solidarity born from shared political combats linked with personal friendships, but in a less marked fashion than in the *cabinets* of the first government formed after the election victory.

The Mauroy Government of June 1981. Table 7 indicates the professional background of the members of the *cabinets* of the prime minister and other ministers in June 1981. The first point to be noted on examining this table is the very large increase in the total number of advisers.

If there were 280 official members of ministerial *cabinets* in June 1981 – which already marked an increase in comparison with the previous Barre government (244) – there were in reality nearly 600 people in the ministerial general staffs. (There is a tradition in France of not making official the complete list of advisers of members of the government.) By any standards, no previous government had arrived at such large numbers of advisers.

Table 7 Professional background of members of ministerial *cabinets* in the Mauroy government formed after the legislative election of June 1981

Profession	%	%
Administative *grand corps*	7	
Tax inspectorate		2
Council of State		3
Court of Audit		2
Other senior administration	19	
Prefects		3
Diplomats		3
Civil servants		13
Judges	3	
State engineers	5	
Mines		3
Bridges and Highways		1
Others		1
Armed forces	2	
Medium-rank administration	35	
Teaching and research	9	
Total public service staff	80	
Non-administrative background	20	

The total number for all posts = 595.
This table and tables 9 and 11 have been drawn up on the basis of the official and semi-offical documents available. The figures do not include those members of the *cabinets* responsible for relations with the press, who are by definition atypical.

The second conclusion one draws from table 7 is the success of new categories in providing members for the *cabinet* staffs. The permanent officials of political parties now appear. The individuals concerned were above all parliamentary assistants, who had been made available to members of parliament and to senators, and who now entered the *cabinets* in large numbers. Trade unionists and certain middle-ranking employees from the economic sector were also recruited. These are the three professional sources which make up the bulk of the 21 per cent of staff of 'non-administrative origin'.

There are also more teachers in the *cabinets* that in the past. With 9 per cent (almost 7 per cent of them university people), there are twice as many as in the government immediately preceding May 1981. This figure reflects the over-representation of teachers at ministerial level in the parties of the Left. Although they only represented 3 per cent of the working population, they constituted, for example, 25 per cent of the delegates at the socialist party's Valence Conference.

Lastly, and most importantly, the perennial presence of public servants will be noted. Seventy-nine per cent of *cabinet* staff came from the public service. This figure is comparable to those for previous periods. In contrast, what is new is the internal composition of the group of public servants who – as the traditional expression has it – 'rise up' to work with their ministers. The hierarchical structure of this category has been very clearly shifted downwards. No more than 10 per cent of *cabinet* staff are members of the *grands corps*, whereas the main line administrative ranks, who have generally graduated from ENA but with an inferior grade, are now more strongly represented, and as many as 35 per cent of the total have been recruited from the middle ranks of the administration. To take a single example – though a significant one – the main line administrative officials of the Finance Ministry have largely displaced inspectors of taxes in the ministerial *cabinets*. It is very much as if the less-favoured elements of the state service were taking their revenge against the previously dominant categories.

Very probably this situation of having been dominated both objectively and subjectively explains why these officials, as indeed the other members of the *cabinets* of left-wing ministers, should be much more political than their predecessors (see table 8).

In this connection we should note that even though the ministers themselves have often had leading positions in the party (for instance, 12 members of the executive committee and the directing committee of the socialist party are or have been ministers), the members of their *cabinets* have only in exceptional cases been political leaders. They have come rather from the 'study committees' of the left-wing parties, committees where the programmes had been prepared and during which many medium-rank officials found, in the period when the Left was in opposition, a compensation for their relative lack of responsibility in the state administration.

All these traits – the presence of a larger number of party officials, of

Table 8 Membership of a political party among members of *cabinets*

Political party	% Cabinet directors (n = 66)	% 'Chefs de cabinet' (n = 43)	% Specialist advisers (n = 294)	% Total (n = 403)
Socialist party	65	65	55	59
Communist party	5	7	7	6
Left radicals	1	2	1	2
Other parties	0	2	2	2
Without party affiliation	29	24	35	31

Source: M. Dagnaud and D. Mehl, *L'Elite Rose* (Ramsay, Paris, 1982), p. 350

Table 9 Professional background of members of the *cabinets* of the communist ministers in January 1984

Profession	%	%
Administrative *grands corps*	2	
Tax inspectorate		0
Council of State		2
Court of Audit		0
Other senior administration	7	
Prefects		0
Diplomats		0
Civil servants		7
Judges	0	
State engineers	16	
Mines		0
Bridges and Highways		2
Others		14
Armed forces	0	
Medium-rank administration	23	
Teaching and research	26	
Total public service staff	74	
Non-administrative background	26	

The total number for all posts = 43.
The communist ministers were those for transport, the public service, vocational training and employment.
Source: see table 7

teachers, and of middle-rank officials, and the weakening of the *grands corps* – are to be found in a more marked form in the *cabinets* of the communist ministers, as table 9 shows. One may ask, however, whether these special features of the entourage of today's ministers, and particularly that of the prime minister, are not in the process of being weakened. A recent development, begun by the last Mauroy government and accentuated by the Fabius government, has been the tendency to make the left-wing *cabinets* of today more similar to those of the years before 1981.

Ministerial Staffs in the Government of Laurent Fabius. Already, in Mauroy's last government, there had been a reduction in the number of advisers: there were 433 in this administration, as opposed to 595 in 1981. Furthermore, the number of places occupied by members of the *grands corps* was tending to grow (see table 10).

When Laurent Fabius became prime minister, a 'return to normal' could be observed, to a degree that could not be explained simply by the disappearance

Table 10 Increase in *grands corps* membership of *cabinet* staffs to January 1984

Grands corps representation	June 1981	January 1984
As percentage of all *cabinet* staffs recruited from the public service	8	12
As percentage of all *cabinet* staffs recruited from main line civil service[a]	10	15

[a]That is, excluding teachers and researchers.

of the communist ministers. As table 11 shows, civil servants now represented 83 per cent of the total, the middle ranks of the administration now accounted for 5 per cent of the staff, and the share of the higher administration and particularly of the *grands corps* was reinforced. Table 10 can thus be complemented by the figures given in table 12.

Table 11 Professional background of members of ministerial *cabinets* in the Fabius government formed in 1984

Profession	%	%
Administrative *grands corps*	11	
Tax inspectorate		3
Council of State		5
Court of Audit		3
Other senior administration	36	
Prefects		5
Diplomats		10
Civil servants		21
Judges	5	
State engineers	9	
Mines		3
Bridges and Highways		3
Others		3
Armed forces	2	
Medium-rank administration	5	
Teaching and research	15	
Total public service staff	83	
Non-administrative background	17	

The total number for all posts = 152.
Source: see table 7

Table 12   Increase in *grands corps* membership of *cabinet* staffs to July 1984

Grand corps representation	June 1981	January 1984	July 1984
As percentage of all *cabinet* staffs recruited from the public service	8	12	25
As percentage of all *cabinet* staffs recruited from main line civil service[a]	10	15	36

[a]That is, excluding teachers and researchers.

Without having returned to the sort of composition they had before 1981, ministerial *cabinets* are now tending in that direction. Technical competence and youth again seem to have become the criteria by which the majority of ministers' advisers are chosen. It is exactly as if the French conception of the state, and the relative power of those in charge of directing its administration, made any other choice practically impossible. What is more, ministerial posts are more and more frequently filled by people who have been recruited from the higher civil service. A quasi-monopoly of 'servants of the state' in public affairs is thus in the process of becoming a reality, which means that the presidency of François Mitterrand has not in fact produced any deep or durable reversal of this long-term tendency.

It has often been stated in France that Laurent Fabius himself is a perfect symbol of this new type of ruling élite. A graduate of the ENA, a member of the Council of State and 37 years of age, everything in his track record and his style make him a sort of paradigm. In this sense, he could be regarded as forming a contrast to Pierre Beregovoy, with his lack of university education and a career as a party militant.

In the internal life of the socialist party things are obviously less clearly marked, at least for the moment. We should not forget that Laurent Fabius has been for many years a close collaborator of François Mitterrand, that he has played an important role in the life of the party and that he has strong local political roots of his own. It should also be recalled that Pierre Beregovoy, now Minister of the Economy, of Finance and of Budget, has found a way to recruit for himself staff of a very high technical quality.

Paraphrasing Max Weber, one could say that the political vocation in France is evolving no longer from amateurs towards professional politicians, but from professionals in politics alone towards professionals in administration. Perhaps there is here a powerful mechanism leading to what might be called the 'autonomization' of the state in relation to civil society, the effects of which may, in the long term, be extremely important.

Notes

1 The presidency of the Republic is known as 'the Elysée', just as the term 'Hôtel Matignon' is often used in France to signify the place where the prime minister's functions are carried out.

2 Quoted by François Bloch-Lainé, *Profession Fonctionnaire* (Seuil, Paris, 1946).

3 Translator's note: the word *'cabinet'* is normally used here to mean the personal staff or private office of a minister or other office-holder; 'general staff' means a political or administrative team.

4 It is interesting to note that General Saulnier, Chief of the Personal Military Staff of President Mitterrand, occupies the second place in the presidential hierarchy, immediately after the Secretary-General.

5 Michael Jobert, who was director of the *cabinet* of Prime Minister Georges Pompidou, then Secretary-General of the Presidency when Pompidou became president, reflects this situation in his writings.

6 The term *'rateau'* is applied to the filtering system used by the close entourage of the president.

7 Jacques Attali's reputation of being the most faithful interpreter of Mitterrand's thinking is regarded by many as the explanation of his influence with the president, especially influence over the composition of his entourage.

8 Mitterrand's two successive directors of the *cabinet*, although they belong to different generations, can both be regarded as long-standing disciples.

9 This was justified by Giscard d'Estaing in the following way: 'We are heading towards an increased presidentialism and we must accept its consequences. The ruling groups will have to change with the man who is elected to executive office by the people.'

10 A notable exception to this rule is Jean-Louis Bianco, the present Secretary-General of the Presidency, who was brought into the Elysée on the personal recommendation of Jacques Attali to François Mitterrand, who had not previously known him.

11 Among these, the adviser for social affairs has always exercised a pre-eminent role. The very strong personality of the men who have held this post has often placed them in a position of direct competition with the director of the *cabinet*, and this explains why this post is periodically dropped from the organizational structure.

12 François de Baecque and Jean-Louis Quermone (eds), *Administration et Politique sous la Cinquième République* (Presses de la Fondation Nationale des Sciences Politiques, Paris, 1981), p. 153.

13 Jean-Louis Bodiguel and Jean-Louis Quermone, *La Haute Fonction Publique sous la Vème République* (PUF, Paris, 1983), p. 144.

14 Ibid., p. 206.

15 Thus the tax reductions expected for 1985, and the abandonment of the government's bill on private education were announced by President Mitterrand in a television programme and not after a meeting of the Council of Ministers.

16 J. Siwek-Pouydessau, 'Les cabinets ministériels', in *Les Superstructures des Administrations Centrales* (Cujas, Paris, 1973).

17 P. Birnbaum and B. Bodie, 'L'autonomie des institutions politico-administratives: le

rôle des cabinets des Présidents de la République et des Premiers Ministres sous la Vème République', *Revue Française de Science Politique*, April 1976.
18 S. Cohen, *Les Conseillers du Président, de De Gaulle à Giscard d'Estaing* (PUF, Paris, 1980).
19 E. M. Suleiman, *Les Hauts-Fonctionnaires et la Politique* (Seuil, Paris, 1976).
20 From M. Dagnaud and D. Mehl, *L'Elite Rose* (Ramsay, Paris, 1982), p. 336.

Marie-Ange Laumonier

The organization of the work of the government cannot be considered in isolation from the nature of political institutions and political life. The first questions to be asked are: 'What is the government?', 'What is its function?', 'What do we mean by the work of the government?' and 'What do we mean by the concept of "organization" as far as the government is concerned?'

The answers to these questions can be found in the constitution and in constitutional practice. Acting under the authority of the president of the Republic, who is responsible for the continuity of the state, the prime minister, who is appointed by the president, directs the activity of the government. The president chairs meetings of the Council of Ministers, which bring together the government as a whole. Two fundamental characteristics of the government of the Republic are thus its collegiate and its hierarchical elements.

The work of the government is to prepare for, and to take, the decisions which make up the totality of public policy. Governmental action has to be coherent and effective, and inter-ministerial coordination is a fundamental element in the organization of governmental work. There can be no governmental work without coordination, and it is to this end that there exists the General Secretariat of the Government. It is attached to the prime minister's offices and is essentially the instrument of the collective work of the government.

I intend to examine first the role of the General Secretariat and secondly its organizational structure.

Historical Development

It was quite natural that political leaders with responsibility for heading governments, even in the time of the Third Republic, should try to make sure that they had a suitable organization for carrying out the necessary tasks of coordination within the administrative structures of the state. After an initial attempt in 1924, under Edouard Herriot, the idea was taken up in a decisive form in 1934 by the then-president, Gaston Doumergue, with these words: 'The prime ministership [*la présidence du conseil*] should be provided with facilities and with a selected personnel of a permanent kind, and not too numerous, seconded from the great departments of state.' Thanks to these 'facilities', the prime ministers, or presidents of the council, of that period were able to supervise the activity of each government department, to ensure that they were not getting in each other's way and that the actions and initiatives taken by each were coordinated with a view to the general good. The national budget of 1935 included the necessary financial provision for the new institution. It was, indeed, at this period that the presidency of the council was installed at the Hôtel Matignon. The institution made only modest progress initially: its first Secretary-General was Léon Noel.

It was with the arrival in power of Léon Blum (1936) that the General Secretariat of the government became a really important organization. It was decided at this stage that the Secretary-General would now be present at the Council of the Cabinet (i.e. ministerial meetings chaired by the prime minister), as well as at the meetings of the Council of Ministers (under the chairmanship of the president). This has become a tradition, practised continuously since the time of Blum. It was also during this period, 1936–8, that the Matignon Conference took place, at which important decisions were taken in the field of social affairs (between the government and the representatives of employers and trade union organizations).

In 1943, as soon as the Committee of National Liberation had been established, General de Gaulle appointed Louis Joxe as Secretary-General: at the liberation, he became the first Secretary-General of liberated France. In 1947 a document entitled 'The internal organization of the work of the government' defined the role of the General Secretariat of the Government as far as the organization of the work of the Council of Ministers was concerned. However, this role is not one which is limited by definition in a single text, and the Secretariat has considerable flexibility. Under the Fourth Republic, the institution took on a definite form: something which had previously been no more than an enlarged version of a political *cabinet* now became a structured administrative unit.

Louis Joxe's successor was Segalat, who held the post for 12 years (1946–58), during which time 21 prime ministers and 21 administrations came and went. His successors were in turn Roger Belin (six years, 1958–64), Jean Donnedieu de Vabres (ten years, 1964–74) and Marceau Long (eight years, 1974–82).

The General Secretariat of the Government has thus taken on the function of a hinge between the government and the civil service.

The Role of the Prime Minister's *Cabinet*

The prime minister is aided by a *cabinet* made up of individuals chosen by himself or by the director of the *cabinet*, on the basis of their qualifications or of their personal expertise. (There are certain differences between the *cabinet* of Mauroy and that of Fabius.)

The Council of Ministers

The weekly meeting of the Council of Ministers is a meeting of the entire government (except for the junior ministers – Secretaries of State – who are only included on an *ad hoc* basis, according to the agenda of the meeting), under the chairmanship of the president. The draft agenda of the Council of Ministers is prepared by the General Secretariat of the Government, in liaison with the prime minister's *cabinet* and the Secretary-General of the Presidency. The weekly agenda is compiled on the basis of the programme of work expected for the week, to which any topical questions are added.

A closed meeting of the prime minister's *cabinet* takes place in advance of the preparation of the first draft of the agenda (this meeting takes place each Friday morning). When approved by the prime minister, the draft agenda is submitted to the president, on Monday, by the Secretary-General of the Government and the Secretary-General of the Presidency. The president makes the final decision on it, and it is then sent out to ministers.

The meeting of the Council of Ministers is preceded, on Wednesday morning, by a final conversation between the president and the prime minister. The Secretary-General of the Government and the Secretary-General of the Presidency are present at the Council meeting; they take notes and are available for consultation by the president and the prime minister. The notes taken by the Secretary-General of the Government are submitted to both the president and the prime minister; these notes are used for preparing the summary of decisions taken.

The agenda of the Council of Ministers always falls into three parts. Part A consists of items which are adopted without any debate. Each minister introduces the bills falling within his or her area of responsibility; the prime minister, for his part, presents drafts with inter-departmental implications, or matters of exceptional importance, for instance those providing for the nationalization of industries. Next come the items of Part B: these consist of appointments or other measures affecting individuals (the defence minister plays a prominent part in this section of the agenda). The heart of the meeting is Part C: this consists of ministerial presentations which may be followed by debate. During these meetings, the silences of certain ministers may be as important or significant as the speeches of others.

The president, chairing the meeting, insists on strict observance of the rule that only those ministers who really have something to say may speak. He himself presides over the discussions, but his own interventions are limited. Moreover, when a debate takes place, he always concludes it by giving the floor to the prime minister, who is thus able to arbitrate between the different points of view expressed.

Part C of the proceedings always begins with a presentation on the international situation by the minister for external relations. This tradition goes back to the monarchy, reflecting a characteristic of historic nations to take account, before debating any other subject, of the state of the world and of the international role of their own country. A procedural tradition lays down that, before he leaves for the Elysée on Wednesday morning, the prime minister's aide-de-camp hands him a sealed envelope containing a brief survey of the main trouble-spots of the world.

In organizing the work of the Council of Ministers, considerable preparation will have taken place inside the prime minister's *cabinet* in liaison with the General Secretariat of the Government. Each meeting of the Council of Ministers is followed by an official communiqué, although not every presentation made to the Council of Ministers is mentioned (for instance, questions of diplomacy or defence are omitted). The communiqué is transmitted to the press, shortly after the meeting has finished, by the spokesman for the president.

The Role of the General Secretariat of the Government

The Secretary-General of the Government helps the prime minister's *cabinet* in its collective role. He is responsible for the minutes of inter-departmental meetings chaired by the prime minister's advisers (*conseillers techniques*); he keeps a note of the results of these meetings, and later draws up a summary of the decisions taken.

These summaries are important both from an administrative and from a legal point of view. Thus, when an official draft (a legislative bill or draft decree) goes to the Council of State, it is the summary made by the Secretary-General of the Government which records ministers' agreement to a certain document, which gives it considerable weight throughout the civil service. At the moment all official texts have to be submitted to the various consultative bodies, and it is the General Secretariat of the Government which takes charge of circulating them in this way.

The Secretary-General of the Government is also responsible for collecting and recording the agreement of all concerned to any given document and then arranging for its publication in the official journals. This practice is most important as a text only becomes definitive once it has been published.

The General Secretariat of the Government thus plays the role of legal adviser to the prime minister's *cabinet*. It also acts as a transmission channel to and from parliament in legislative procedures, since it is responsible for the necessary formalities with regard to the tabling of bills, either before the Senate or before the National Assembly.

The General Secretariat of the Government is also involved in the procedure for transmitting legislative documents between one House and the other. Furthermore, it is responsible for convening meetings of special committees, and for emergency procedures.

Conclusion

The procedures described here reveal that the work of the government is a result of compromises: between a collegiate system and a hierarchy; between diversity and cohesion; between daily pressures and medium-term or long-term action; between the carrying out of a programme and reaction to external constraints; between discretion or even secrecy and an opening-up of public life; between firmness of decision and a range of possibilities of adaptation; between the need for principles on which to organize work and a reaction against the formalism that may result from excessive organizational constraints.

This balancing act between contradictory demands may give rise to doubts about the solidity or the quality of the organization of government work. It is certain that in the case of a conflict between organizational rules and precise political exigencies – which often win the upper hand – it is vital to find acceptable compromises. This offers a lesson in humility for believers in organization.

In the last resort, application of the best-tried organizational techniques may count for less than exploitation of the founts of individual psychology. This is hardly surprising, since the organization of governmental work is directly related to the very art of governing.

Appendix: the Composition of the *Cabinet* of Prime Minister Laurent Fabius, November 1984

Director of the *cabinet*
Louis Schweitzer (42)
Inspector of Finances
(Son of Pierre-Paul Schweitzer, former Permanent Secretary of the French Treasury and head of the IMF)

The structure of the *cabinet* was tightly formed and pyramid-shaped. It consisted of:

Five senior advisers (*conseillers*)
Christian Becle (42)
Senior Educational Administrator
Former Rector of Upper Normandy region (Rouen)
Responsible for educational policy

Hélène Ploix (39)
Managing Director of the Banque Industrielle et Mobilière
Responsible for the economic policy sector

Claude Silberzahn (49)
Prefect of the Region of French Guyana
Responsible for the policy area of home affairs and decentralization

Bernard Pecheur (33)
ENA
Adviser on social policy

François Gros (59)
Doctorate in Natural Science, Professor at the College of France, Director-
    General of the Institut Pasteur
Previously a member of the Mauroy Cabinet
Responsible for research policy

Eleven specialist advisers (*conseillers techniques*)
Jean-Pascal Beaufret (33)
ENA
Inspector of Finances
Responsible for economic policy

Daniel Bernard (42)
ENA
Counsellor, foreign affairs
Responsible for international affairs

Jean-Dominique Comolli (36)
ENA
Responsible for budgetary questions

Bernard Faivre d'Arcier (39)
ENA
Former Director of the Avignon Festival
Responsible for the cultural infrastructure

Yves Lyon-Caen (34)
ENA
Responsible for questions of agriculture and trade

Denis Verret (34)
ENA
Responsible for international economic relations

Jacques Nicolas Biot (31)
Polytechnician, engineer of the School of Mines
Responsible for industrial questions

François Blanchard (34)
Polytechnician and graduate of the National School of Bridges and
    Highways and of the University of California at Berkeley
Responsible for environment and transport

Louis Joinet (50)
Judge
Responsible for judicial questions

Jean-Marcel Bichat (37)
Graduate in literature and in political science
Responsible for relations with parliament

Jean-Gabriel Fredet (40)
Journalist
Responsible for relations with the press

Additional advisers
Thierry Lajoie (32)
Lawyer
Chef de cabinet

Solange Semeteys (48)
Head of the prime minister's personal secretarial staff

6

Canada

Colin Campbell

Canada has an exceedingly segmented society. As the world's second largest geographic entity, the country spans immensely diverse regions. In addition to encompassing the so-called 'two solitudes' – the English and the French – the nation has fitted other ethnic minorities into an increasingly intricate mosaic.[1]

Canada worked relatively well as a state until the 1960s. The maritime provinces and Newfoundland relied so much on 'equalization payments' from the federal government that they rarely stirred.[2] The west operated as a quasi-colonial jurisdiction. The approximate equality of Quebec and Ontario in economic power generated just enough wealth in the former to support the development of a monied francophone community concentrated in Montreal. Thus, a Canadian variant of consociational democracy emerged whereby the political leadership of the English and French linguistic groups could work out their differences amicably and, for the most part, in secret.[3] The Liberal Party best tapped this spirit of Canadian consociationalism, right down to its still-honoured tradition of alternating between English and French leaders. Liberal cabinets, with their larger-than-life Quebec contingents, provided the forum for the closed-door type of brokerage that has characterized the Canadian policy arena.[4]

However, separatist rumblings from Quebec and Alberta have already signalled the fact that the federal system has not operated adequately in the past 25 years. Part of the difficulty stems from the 'Quiet Revolution' in Quebec during the mid-1960s. Francophones simply will no longer tolerate leaders who set themselves up as mediators between the two solitudes;[5] they want their special claims brought directly to bear on their governance. This radical shift in the Quebecois view of confederation effectively spells the end of consociational democracy. Even historically, the Canadian parliament has bottled up regional protest. The appointive second chamber – although nominally intended to provide weighted representation for the four great regions – has never in the entire history of confederation fulfilled this role.[6] An exaggerated party discipline whereby Liberals very rarely vote against their party has made regional stances by MPs extremely risky. Thus, the strident character of regional protest has taken root in the years of pent-up frustration over finding effective outlets in Ottawa. It is a small wonder that Trudeau's last caucus only included two MPs from the western areas. Westerners concluded some 20 years ago that it was better to press their claims on the government from the opposition side of the House.

These points all serve to stress the fact that Canadian prime ministers and cabinets since the 1960s have had to alter substantially their ways of controlling and coordinating the executive. The fractiousness of Quebec and the western provinces has meant that cabinet no longer functions effectively as the central mechanism for federal–regional accommodation. An elaborate system of inter-governmental committees at both the official and ministerial level often eclipses entirely cabinet's integrative function.[7] Such executive federalism frequently enhances the influence of individual ministers and the prime minister when private negotiations actually result in viable agreements. However, the unwieldly character of the process preordains that many critical matters go untreated due to intractable federal–provincial discussions.

An Overloaded Omnibus

Canada's original constitutional document, the British North America (BNA) Act of 1867, stipulated that the governmental system would operate similarly to that of the United Kingdom and that a council would 'aid and advise' the government of Canada. From the outset, these provisions gave very great weight to the concept of collective responsibility for the affairs of state. Canadian cabinets, thus, have always met on a regular basis. Early on, they devised subgroups responsible for developing issues and/or enforcing decisions in key areas of executive responsibility. Exceptional among these is the Treasury Board. Responsible for financial management, this cabinet-level body dates back to pre-confederation times and has enjoyed a statutory life since 1869.

The regional and linguistic/cultural representational imperatives that bear on Canadian cabinets have historically tempted prime ministers to sacrifice manageability in favour of large size. When John Turner took office in June 1984 he reduced the size of the cabinet from 37 to 29. His was not the first recognition of the fact that representational imperatives can push cabinet to an unworkable inclusiveness. For example, efforts to streamline the cabinet through the creation of superdepartments actually predated and partially inspired similar moves in Britain under Lloyd George.[8] However, Turner's action attempted to roll back the greatest proliferation of portfolios ever to have taken place in Canada. (His efforts were negated, however, when Brian Mulroney presented a 40-member cabinet in September 1984.)

The burgeoning of cabinet from 19 to 37 ministers with portfolios occurred simultaneously with Trudeau's years as prime minister, that is, from 1968 to 1984, with a nine-month Progressive Conservative interlude during 1979–80. It fitted Trudeau's highly rationalistic mode of thought in two ways. First, it coincided with the view that portfolios should correspond to the dominant issues of the day. Thus, highly specialized ministries such as science and technology, urban affairs, consumer and corporate affairs, energy, mines and resources, regional economic expansion and even 'supply and services' as distinct from 'public works', played prominent roles in various squabbles with departments responsible for more conventional areas such as industry, trade and commerce, defence and health and welfare. Also, ministers of state without departments served as lightning conductors in contentious areas such as the Wheat Board, small business and tourism, youth, fitness and amateur sports – here the incumbent embodied as often as not the physical antithesis of all three – and women.

Second, cabinet's constant expansion fitted Trudeau's approach because it did not, in his mind, strain the capabilities of modern decision-making. That is, Trudeau and his key advisers – principally Michael Pitfield – believed implicitly in the capacity of proper organization of cabinet and supporting staffs to allow a high level of functional differentiation in operational departments, while optimizing central coordination and guidance.[9] Yet, unwieldiness at the level of operational departments simply wrought excessive complexity within central agencies. By the time Trudeau retired, a Federal–Provincial Relations Office (FPRO), an Office of the Comptroller General (OCG), and a Ministry of State for Economic and Regional Development (MSERD), and one for Social Development (MSSD) had joined the Prime Minister's Office (PMO), the Privy Council Office (PCO), the Department of Finance and the Treasury Board Secretariat (TBS) as agencies supporting the prime minister, the cabinet and its committees, or, in the case of Finance, enjoying a private reporting line between its minister and the prime minister. Significantly, John Turner announced the dismantling of MSERD and MSSD on the very day on which he appointed his cabinet. Brian Mulroney did not commute the death sentences.

A Highly Routinized Process

Even before Trudeau, collective decision-making in the cabinet as supported by secretariats had become considerably institutionalized. Indeed, the first 'clerk' of the Privy Council – a person who previously had served in the same capacity for the Executive Council of the United Province of Canada – assumed his post on the date of confederation in 1867. By the middle third of this century, it became increasingly the responsibility of the clerk of the Privy

Council to supervise the preparation – often through inter-departmental committees of officials – of major government initiatives for cabinet review and to monitor the implementation of key policy decisions.[10] This 'secretariat' dimension to the Privy Council Office, however, did not receive an official identity until 1940, when the clerk took on the additional title of secretary to the cabinet. An Act of Parliament gave his role statutory sanction in 1974.[11]

Most prime ministers, Trudeau included, have adhered religiously to the custom of weekly meetings of the full cabinet. However, Lester B. Pearson (1963–8) and Trudeau presided over vast improvements in the business management capacity of PCO. This is not to suggest that previous clerks failed to do their jobs adequately; in fact, Robert Bryce, the clerk/secretary under John Diefenbaker (1957–63), earned virtual canonization through his heroic efforts at neutral process management for a prime minister who relentlessly bullied his cabinet and openly scorned the bureaucracy's role in supporting collective decision-making.[12] However, Pearson and Trudeau created a managerial environment in which the Privy Council Office began to impose very strict order on the timing and form of departmental submissions to cabinet.[13]

Along with this increased institutionalization came added leverage whereby PCO officials involved themselves more directly in inter-departmental panels right down to rendering judgements as to which departments should participate, where the gestation process should take officials in each phase of the procedure and when they should present material to cabinet and its committees.[14] In short, routinization of procedures allowed PCO officials to use their expertise on timing and form as a vehicle for transmitting signals – even directions – as to what departments should do in order to optimize their chances of winning ministerial approval for their initiatives. Interestingly, John Turner moved to simplify significantly the cabinet committee structure, and to cut back on the number of cabinet submissions and the amount of supporting documentation. The Mulroney government has continued to apply these strictures.

PCO's strategic role regarding cabinet process is at the heart of one of the serious failures of the central agency complex in Canada. In 1962, the Royal Commission on Government Organization urged that the secretariat for the Treasury Board be moved from the Department of Finance to PCO. The commission argued that this move would expand the secretariat's perspective on financial management from narrow expenditure scrutiny to assisting 'ministers in discharging their collective responsibility for program priorities and administrative standards'.[15] By way of compromise, the government hived-off the secretariat from Finance and gave it a separate minister entitled the 'President' of the Treasury Board. This reform did have its desired effect in that the TBS greatly improved its capacity for assessing departmental expenditure proposals from the perspective of programme priorities and planning.[16] The more TBS succeeded in this regard, however, the more PCO became protective of its own prerogatives in assisting cabinet's identification of priorities and longer-term goals.

PCO – with no small staff enhancement in its own right – began to satisfy itself that it – not TBS – would take the lead in analysis-based planning. However, as we will see later on, PCO operated with an exceedingly eclectic staff largely unschooled in systematic approaches to policy analysis. One caustic assessment by a former TBS officials who locked horns with PCO often in the late 1960s and early 1970s asserts that, while TBS was no paragon, PCO became a haven for dilettantism:

> There were people at PCO with diverse backgrounds involved in what was euphemistically called 'planning'. This largely consisted of drawing up systems diagrams: pages of labeled boxes and arrows . . . The labels were idiosyncratic . . . The work was, in my view, at best simplistic discription and at worst fatuous nonsense.[17]

Notwithstanding the 'soft' nature of PCO's rival analyses, the agency so astutely exploited its direct access to the prime minister and the cabinet committee chairmen that TBS began to see its role wane. The key here was the practice whereby PCO would keep cabinet documents from TBS until their reference to full cabinet.[18] This procedural wrinkle allowed PCO to win 'approval in principal' from cabinet committees for favoured departmental initiatives even though the relevant expenditure implications had not been thoroughly considered. It also varied sharply from the current British practice whereby the Cabinet Office must automatically refer papers with expenditure implications to the Treasury and the chief secretary may attend any pertinent committee and exert a suspensory veto over proposals with expenditure implications deemed unacceptable by his department.[19] Stressing the role played by Pitfield, the former TBS official quoted previously puts very well just how PCO's ascendency in this period marked the triumph of positioning over substance:

> Those who did the work on PCO plans were not tied into the decision-making process except as they influenced Michael Pitfield's thinking . . . I never doubted that Pitfield had enormous influence with the prime minister but I saw little connection between these so-called PCO planning studies and the day-to-day specific decisions that actually emerged from cabinet committees.[20]

A former PCO official intimately conversant with the agency's approach during the same era echoes the same points:

The idiot fringe of chart-makers and systems diagrammers was probably harmless
. . . What is more important is that Michael Pitfield and some of his colleagues
had an important influence, from time to time on the substance, but most
frequently on the timing, framework and implicit priorities within which decisions
were taken. They had a crucial, if unobtrusive, power to determine what was and
was not an issue.[21]

How the Parts Relate to One Another

As already noted, eight separate central agencies operated from 1979 until John
Turner dismantled the MSERD and MSSD in June 1984. Three of these, the
Prime Minister's Office, PCO and the Federal–Provincial Relations Office fit
organizationally under the prime minister. That is, deputy minister level
officials in charge of the agencies report directly to the prime minister. In
adddition to providing policy advice to the prime minister, however, PCO and
FPRO support him in his capacity as chairman of the cabinet and its executive
committee on priorities and planning. Also, PCO supplies secretariats for the
various committees of cabinet.

TBS, of course, provides a free-standing secretariat for the Treasury Board.
Its sister agency – the Office of the Comptroller General – has worked since its
creation in 1976 at improving departments' financial management systems by
encouraging their adoption of advanced efficiency and effectiveness evaluation
procedures. The now defunct ministries of state reported directly to the
chairmen of the economic and regional development and social development
committees. Their efforts focused largely on assessment – from the standpoint
of the government's agreed priorities and plans – of the policy proposals and
expenditure plans of operational departments belonging to the respective
committees. Finally, the Department of Finance reports to the Minister of
Finance. It enjoys central agency status by virtue of the minister's direct and
private reporting line to the prime minister on matters relating to the annual
budget and his membership of every cabinet committee in which expenditure
issues touching on management of the economy are likely to arise.

The Prime Minister's Office

Although prime ministers have maintained small personal staffs since W. L.
Mackenzie King regained power in 1935, PMO greatly institutionalized its role
under Trudeau.[22] Trudeau's five principal secretaries all held deputy minister
rank. Each, however, was a partisan appointee – the near exception being Jacob
Austin who, notwithstanding an unsuccessful candidacy for Parliament under
the Liberal banner, became principal secretary after serving for four years in
the permanent civil service as deputy minister of energy, mines and resources.

PMO has not played a consistent role in the development of government policy. MPs, members of the media and attentive scholars have kept a weather eye out for the growth of a partisan staff assisting the prime minister. Their concerns reflect an exaggerated sense of the resources available in the US White House.[23] Their rallying call, 'we don't want a presidential system like the Americans have', tends to rank a large PMO with high murder rates, unsafe streets and all other aspects of life south of the border which any right-minded Canadian repudiates as a matter of national survival. Thus, the agency normally keeps its professional complement to around 30 – virtually all of whom are partisan appointees. Another 70 staff members serve in secretarial and clerical positions. As well, PMO had largely restricted itself to the 'switchboard' functions concerning the prime minister's schedule, legislative relations – including preparation for question time in Parliament, partisan appointments, correspondence and political liaison with the Liberal Party. In this respect, it had even fallen short of arrangements at No. 10 in the United Kingdom, where five career officials in the private office give the prime minister alternative lines into Whitehall to those available through the Cabinet Office and a similar number of personal advisers – usually from outside government – working in the Policy Unit provide independent briefing notes on the key issues the prime minister faces.

Under Trudeau, PMO attempted to review systematically major policy decisions during two periods. First, while Marc Lalonde – who subsequently became an MP and held several key cabinet posts – was principal secretary (1968–72), PMO began to link fairly effectively into the bureaucratic apparatus. Although never a permanent civil servant, Lalonde had held a number of important advisory positions in Ottawa. Along with Michael Pitfield in PCO, Trudeau looked to Lalonde at the outset of his prime ministership to teach him how to operate the machinery of government. Other officials in PMO began to benefit from Lalonde's strong personal ties to the prime minister.

A more elaborate PMO effort towards greater influence on policy decisions occurred under Jacob Austin. As a former deputy minister, Austin knew exactly what he faced in trying to earn a more significant place for PMO in the central agency community. He recruited four appointees with clear partisan credentials whose training and career experience suggested that they would work extremely well at highly advanced process management. He chose a political adviser to the premier of Nova Scotia with a PhD in systems theory, Michael Kirby, to head the 'policy unit'. Kirby set out a rigorous organizational format whereby he and his staff – assisted by Austin and two other senior PMO officials – would personally monitor the activities of every cabinet committee. In its elaborately worked out memorandum advocating a stronger partisan input in the policy process, Kirby styled the group as seeking to realize the government's plans 'within the timeframe which is most politically advantageous' and to ensure that 'the desired goals and objectives are achieved by the time the next election is called'.[24] All this had not anticipated adequately the very severe economic strains that inundated the planners by 1975, resulting eventually in the highly unpopular anti-inflation programme. Indeed, Austin left his post in 1975, while Kirby resigned the following summer.

A number of ways have been identified in which officials in PMO differed substantially in their orientations and backgrounds from other central agents.[25] PMO staff much more than others characterized their roles as involving to a very significant degree communication with individuals and groups outside of government. They said much less frequently than others that they monitored departments' implementation of policies. PMO recruited disproportionately from Montreal – Trudeau's home city. Its members, more than any other agency's, had earned advanced degrees in business administration. The average age of PMO officials, 39 years, fell six years short of that for PCO and FPRO and reflected the non-career character of the office. Owing no doubt to their close proximity to the prime minister, PMO staff interacted personally with the prime minister much more than did other officials. Even in comparison with PCO and FPRO officials, PMO officials found more numerous opportunities for informal contacts with departmental ministers as well as the prime minister. Their attendance level at committees, both at cabinet and officials' level, was relatively low.

PCO and FPRO

The Privy Council Office occupies essentially the same sector of responsibilities as the Cabinet Office in the United Kingdom. Created in 1974, the Federal–Provinical Relations Office simply performs certain functions formerly carried out by PCO under a separate secretary to the cabinet. In the fiscal year 1981–2, the two agencies employed more than 400 staff, of whom some 50 were senior officials.[26] If we include the now defunct UK Central Policy Review Staff, the British Cabinet Office in a comparable period kept a complement of around 350 staff of whom just over 60 were from senior ranks. When we consider the fact that Canada has about half the population of Britain and the federal government spends about half as much as the UK, the combined PCO and FPRO resources stand up very strongly indeed. When we add the fact that, between 1979 and when Turner took office in 1984, separate ministries of state supported the cabinet committees on economic regional development and social development, the PCO and FPRO appear almost lavish by UK standards.

PCO units divide into three categories. The two units in the first category work directly to the clerk of the Privy Council and secretary to the cabinet in his capacity as the prime minister's principal adviser on issues spanning the breadth of the bureaucratic establishment. The first unit, consisting of nearly 15 professionals, operates as the nerve centre for and key source of advice on the operations of the security and intelligence community in various parts of the federal government. The second unit, taking in some ten professionals, supports the clerk/secretary in his role as the premier career civil servant. That is, it carries out work connected with his chairmanship of the committee of senior officials. This body reviews for the prime minister appointments at the assistant deputy minister level and above, and assesses for him policies governing personnel issues for all senior ranks. While broad interpretations of prime ministerial prerogative often permit the two units in this first category to skirt collective bodies, including ministers, they do act as the secretariats for the security and intelligence and public service cabinet committees respectively.

The next two units function under the direction of the deputy secretary for plans. Each has around five professionals. The first forms the secretariat for the priorities and planning committee of the cabinet. This body, chaired by the prime minister and comprised of every cabinet committee chairman, essentially operates as the steering group for the cabinet. The secretariat, aided at the time by a 'planning projects' unit, played an especially significant role during Trudeau's 1974–9 government. That is, it backed up the deputy secretary in his direction of the annual priorities exercises whereby PCO would require departments to submit in detail how their plans for a Parliamentary session met the principal objectives established each autumn by the cabinet. The secretariat continued in this role during Trudeau's 1980–4 government. However, the ageing prime minister's increasingly selective engagement in the affairs of state – along with the constraining effects of battles over Quebec separatism, the protracted process whereby the constitution was finally patriated in 1982 and the inauspicious economic conditions connected with the world recession – sharply curtailed the complexity and expansiveness of annual priorities exercises.

The other unit largely working to the deputy secretary for plans is 'Machinery of Government'. With a staff of six, this secretariat prepares advice to the prime minister on major reorganizations of portfolios and all matters relating to cabinet's decision-making systems and processes. Trudeau's highly experimental approach to the creation and revamping of ministries and the proclivity of PCO towards fine-tuning central coordination have kept the Machinery of Government secretariat in a pivotal position since the mid-1970s.

The PCO deputy secretary for operations supervises four units, each of which supports one of the 'policy' committees of cabinet. These committees – economic and regional development, social development, foreign and defence affairs and government operations – wield greater power than other specialized cabinet-level bodies through their authority over eight of the ten 'envelopes' in which cabinet establishes policy priorities and allocates expenditure resources between programmes. Under the system, the priorities and planning committee assumes the same role regarding fiscal transfers to provinces and the public debt.

The expenditure envelope system emerged in 1979 on the theory that individual ministers might be more willing to point to possible cuts in their departments' programmes if the funds stayed within the same broad category of expenditure rather than returning to the general treasury. As we will see, the new system dove-tailed with the creation of the MSERD and MSSD as central agencies dedicated entirely to support of their respective committees. Only very astute bureaucratic politics on the part of the under-secretary for external affairs, Allan Gotlieb, prevented the creation of a similar ministry of state for foreign and defence affairs. Gotlieb agreed, however, to set up a secretariat within his department designed to back up his minister in the latter's capacity as chairman of cabinet's foreign and defence affairs committee. Meanwhile, the TBS took on double duty as the agency monitoring the aggregate figures under the so-called Policy and Expenditure Management System (PEMS) with special responsibility towards the envelopes falling under the cabinet's government operations committee.

All these developments might lead one to expect that PCO's operations side has seen its role eclipsed considerably in the past five years. In practice, the two secretariats that had to coordinate with the ministries of state, economic and regional development and social development, greatly enhanced their staffs to eight professionals each, while the foreign and defence affairs secretariat reached a staff of seven professionals. Thus, only government operations remained at a pre-1979 level of four professionals. It seems that for a central agency with such a strong prime ministerial mandate as PCO's, staffing expands in proportion to the increased complexity of bureaucratic gamesmanship.

There remain five additional units which only sporadically play vital roles in the grander scheme of PCO activities. Three of these operate as secretariats for, respectively, the legislation and House planning committee, the special committee of council and the communications committee. As the titles imply, the first body manages the processing of government legislation through Parliament, the second approves – on cabinet's behalf – emergency orders-in-council and the third coordinates departments' communications policies and strategies as well as monitoring their compliance with the freedom of information legislation. The final two secretariats work, respectively, to cabinet's security and intelligence committee on matters relating to 'emergency planning', and to its labour relations committee in instances where strikes threaten government services and/or commerce.

The Federal–Provincial Relations Office evolved in 1974 from a PCO secretariat assigned to a separate cabinet committee reviewing policies concerning inter-governmental affairs. With the 1976 separatist election victory in Quebec, federal–provincial relations so preoccupied the priorities and planning committee that the federal–provincial relations committee of cabinet disbanded. Nevertheless, FPRO soon experienced an aggrandizement of its role whereby no fewer than three officials, in addition to the secretary, filled positions at the assistant deputy minister level or above. Two or these, the consitutional adviser and the deputy secretary for coordination – with special responsibility for Quebec separatism – even enjoyed the privilege of reporting to the prime minister without going through the secretary to the cabinet for federal–provincial relations. The third deputy secretary headed three units handling, respectively, support for the priorities and planning committee on federal issues and analyses of regional politics, review of all departmental policies and programmes with major federal–provincial components, and long-term strategies.

FPRO gained notoriety in this era through its housing a unit of highly questionable constitutional repute. Styled the 'Canadian Unity Information Office', this organization disseminated pro-federal progaganda, mostly in Quebec. Only two FPRO secretariats, strategic and constitutional planning and provincial analysis and liaison, have survived the easing of separatist threats over the past few years.

Both PCO and FPRO are career-orientated organizations. The clerk/secretary during Trudeau's first six years, Gordon Robertson, was every inch a permanent civil servant and the unrivalled dean of the deputy minister community. While he presided over the enhancement of PCO's role during the early Trudeau years, Robertson took pains to assure critics that his agency would avoid becoming a haven for superbureaucrats. Along the lines of the British Cabinet Office, PCO would staff itself by secondments from operational departments:

> There are virtually no officers making a career within the Privy Council Office . . .
> The term of appointment is purposely kept short: three to five years with personnel on loan from all departments. Vigor and integrity are maintained, but an elite with any sense of separateness or difference is not permitted to form.[27]

Robertson became the first secretary to the cabinet for federal–provincial relations when he left PCO in 1974.

At this point Michael Pitfield entered the equation as clerk/secretary. A high-flyer *par excellence*. Pitfield came across as the antithesis of Robertson. In the first place, he knew the prime minister intimately. Indeed, as a young lawyer Pitfield had distinguished himself as one of the only anglophones involved in the *cité libre* movement through which Trudeau and several francophone intellectuals had spawned Quebec's Quiet Revolution in the late 1950s and early 1960s. Even before Trudeau came to Ottawa, Pitfield had started his meteoric rise in PCO, whereby he would become clerk/secretary at the age of 37. However, Trudeau's implicit trust of Pitfield accelerated the latter's advancement through the ranks after 1968. Moreover, Pitfield became associated in the critical mind as precisely the aloof PCO man that Robertson had argued would never be allowed to emerge. Only a two-year stint as a deputy minister for consumer and corporate affairs immediately before he became clerk/secretary and nine months out of office during the Clark government broke the near 14 years during which Pitfield served as Trudeau's organizational architect and most-consulted bureaucratic confidant.

During Pitfield's years as clerk-secretary, PCO staffing took a different shape from that anticipated by Robertson. For example, notwithstanding two changes of government, 36 of 86 professional-level officials listed in PCO at the end of 1977 remained in the agency in December 1980. Of those still in PCO, nine had received promotions. In fact, PCO has often created new ranks in its hierarchy in order to provide its officials with an opportunity for advancement that does not require transfer to another department.

Surely the most flagrant abuse of the career orientation of PCO and FPRO occurred in 1980, when Trudeau replaced Gordon Robertson as head of FPRO with Michael Kirby, the former director of the ill-fated PMO policy unit discussed above. The débâcle surrounding efforts to patriate the constitution without provincial approval was very largely due to this move. Kirby had learned little from the failure of the policy unit. In an exhaustive memorandum to cabinet, he mapped out a strategy whereby the federal government would provoke a stalemated federal–provincial conference in September 1980.[28] Armed with clear evidence of provincial intransigence, the federal government would run a unilateral bill through the House of Commons and the Senate on the grounds that national survival required immediate action. This strategy, which ministers accepted with scarcely a whimper, failed to anticipate a number of pitfalls. Most dramatically, the leaking of the entire document to the government of Quebec – which in turn released its contents just before the September convention – made sheer mockery of the federal government's claim that it alone was negotiating in good faith. Moreover Kirby's memorandum had scarcely considered the possibility that Margaret Thatcher might be loath to introduce to the UK Parliament a constitution overwhelmingly repudiated by the provinces. Finally, it had not anticipated the emphasis placed on constitutional convention by the Supreme Court when it shamed Trudeau back to the bargaining table by noting in a September 1981 opinion that the federal government's unilateral resolution, while adhering to the letter of the British North America Act, had violated its spirit.

A number of ways have been noted in which PCO and FPRO officials differed from their counterparts in other central agencies.[29] They believed more than other officials that they should work to improve the quality of government and, interestingly, to analyse issues independently. They tended strongly to have received their education at one of the nation's most prestigious universities – Toronto, Queens, McGill and Dalhousie. They earned the highest percentage of PhDs, and, next to PMO, claimed the highest proportion of law degrees. Much more than the other groups, they had worked in a central agency before joining PCO. Although the average length of their careers in government fell just between those for Finance and TBS, they tended much more than others to attribute their expertise at least partially to experience in government. Their interaction with the prime minister and ministers, while less personal and direct than among members of PMO, proved more robust by far than for officials from Finance and TBS. As might be expected, such contacts centered on PCO officials' involvement with cabinet committees. In almost every respect, PCO officials appeared less open than their opposite numbers in other agencies to interactions with legislators and representatives of interest groups.

TBS, OCG, MSERD and MSSD

Earlier we saw how PCO used its control of cabinet processes to prevent the Treasury Board Secretariat (TBS) from assessing the expenditure implications of proposals before cabinet until the eleventh hour. A 1976 agreement between PCO and TBS sought to provide the latter with better access to cabinet documents. It gave the president of the Treasury Board the option of commenting on cabinet documents when they first entered the PCO process.

At the time, TBS incorporated five branches, each headed by a deputy secretary. However, three of these – administrative policy, personnel policy and official languages – focused their efforts on public service management issues that fitted clearly within the statutory power of the Treasury Board. That is, the three branches operated relatively unencumbered by fear of conflicts with PCO. Thus, the two remaining branches, programme and planning, operated in the eye of the storm. The first, consisting of eight divisions each containing more than ten professionals, advised the Treasury Board on aggregate and programmatic issues arising from review of departments' expenditure budgets. The second, consisting of 45 professionals, including a deputy secretary and five directors, conducted in a modular format in-depth effectiveness studies of various governmental programmes. As most of its projects were inter-departmental, the planning branch would usually assign a team of professionals headed by a director to serve as the secretariat for what normally amounted to assessment by committee.

The first cracks in TBS's arrangement with PCO appeared later in 1976 when the auditor-general released perhaps the most damning report ever on the adequacy of financial management in the federal government. Arguing from the premise that departments should adopt comprehensive auditing, the auditor-general advocated much more rapid and thorough dissemination by central agencies of advanced techniques for routine evaluations of the efficiency and effectiveness of departmental programmes. The outcry forced Michael Pitfield and the secretary of the Treasury Board, Gordon Osbaldeston, to recommend the dramatic step of creating separate deputy minister level agency reporting to the Treasury Board. The resulting Office of the Comptroller General (OCG) began to undermine the *raison d'être* of the TBS planning branch, especially through its overlapping interest in evaluations of effectiveness.

From the time of its 1976 concession to TBS, PCO was drafting plans for radical reforms of the cabinet system. Very much enamoured of the superdepartment concept, Pitfield became especially fascinated by the idea that ministries of state serving the cabinet's policy committees might act as halfway points in the gradual aggregation of portfolios into umbrella agencies. Under the scheme, devolution of TBS's responsibility for review of departments' expenditure proposals to ministries of state would result in assessments more sensitive to balancing claims within 'envelopes' of governmental functions.

A number of favourable circumstances resulted in PCO's plans catching fire very rapidly. The serious economic turn in 1978 resulted in a stringency programme that would require a great deal of voluntary cost cutting on the part of ministers. A complex regional and sectional consultation process on industrial development had foundered largely through mismanagement by its lead department – that of industry, trade and commerce. As Trudeau's government faltered in the polls, it seized upon economic development as the central element to its recovery programme. Finally, PCO banked on the openness of new governments to reorganization and prepared to press its full range of plans on the Progressive Conservatives even before their cabinet was sworn in. By mid-1979, two ministries of state were well under way.

Before Turner disbanded them, the MSERD and MSSD had acquired, respectively, 55 and 35 professional-level positions. Taken together, the three ministers and deputy heads, seven assistant deputy heads, three assistant secretaries, 25 directors and 143 other professionals in TBS, MSERD and MSSD in 1982 exceeded both in 'brass' and numbers the US Office of Management and Budget's commitment to review of departments' expenditure plans. This truly vast assignment of resources for a nation with one-tenth the budget of the United States corresponded with a government whose expenditures grew so large that they exceeded revenues by more than 50 per cent in the fiscal year 1982–3. Moreover, the accompanying new processes proved – if anything – less suited than the previous ones to bringing ministers to adopt policies that mitigate the most intractable elements of economic, regional and social development.[30]

Now that MSERD and MSSD have fallen by the wayside, one might expect TBS to regain full status as the chief agency for expenditure review. One study found that TBS officials revealed by far the strongest orientation towards working for a specific cabinet committee.[31] As the thorniest expenditure issues in various envelopes return more to formal review by the Treasury Board, the planning branch will again rival PCO as an agent for review of aggregate policy and expenditure plans for the cabinet.

Finance

Our discussion takes us last, but certainly not least, to the Department of Finance. This department controls the principal analytic and fiscal tools for macromanagement of the economy. That is, it takes the lead in preparing economic forecasts, including those informing the fiscal framework for the budgets presented annually by the finance minister. Responsibility for developing the fiscal framework extends to recommendations to the minister about the types of spending programmes and tax measures most likely to foster the desired level of economic activity. As noted earlier, the minister stands apart from his cabinet colleagues by virtue both of his private reporting line to the prime minister on the annual budget and his free access to all cabinet committees considering issues touching on management of the economy.

The department maintains a complement somewhat smaller than the United Kingdom Treasury's. Whereas the latter has over 1,000 staff, of whom some 140 are senior officials, the Department of Finance comprises around 560 staff, including 35 at senior ranks. The discrepancy makes especially good sense if we keep in mind the fact that units from the department formerly responsible for expenditure review and management policy, similar to those that still largely reside in the UK Treasury, provided the nucleus of TBS when it emerged as a separate secretariat in 1966.

Finance officials were found to have the highest degree of departmental ésprit found among the central agencies.[32] They believed more than other officials that they developed policy and monitored its implementation. They based their roles on professional training in economics and related fields, such as tax law and accounting. The department tends to recruit disproportionately candidates from outside government. Once inside what several officials termed 'the best economics department in the country', many obtain virtual tenure on the grounds that someone good enough to land a post in the department cannot be easily replaced.

Finance officials ply their trade in committees. A procedural peculiarity makes these forums especially potent vehicles for the department. In Canada, ministers rarely attend committees without an accompanying official. They also frequently deputize officials to cover meetings which they are unable to attend. Here the finance minister's exceptionally wide access to committees comes into play. As he could not possibly fulfil all his obligations personality, finance officials gain considerable exposure to cabinet-level bodies as surrogates for their minister. In fact, as becomes clear in two finance officials' explanations of their roles in cabinet committees, senior members of the department readily accommodate themselves to the role of full discussants with cabinet ministers.[33]

> If my own minister is present at the meeting, then I will speak only when called upon for advice. If my minister is not present, then I become the representative of the department and involve myself fully in the discussion.

> I'm the one in the department on top of issues which come up before that committee. If I go, it's because Finance has something specific to say about a matter. I'm not there as an observer, I'm there because I have a viewpoint and something to say.

All has not been plain sailing for the department during the Trudeau years. Increasingly, the priorities and planning committee has probed the department's plans for the fiscal framework before release of the budget. In 1975, the department failed for months to lead business and labour to an agreement on voluntary price and wage controls. Eventually, PMO and PCO forced the department's hand towards a mandatory programme. During the remainder of Trudeau's third term, the prime minister began to rely very heavily upon his PCO economic adviser – Ian Stewart – to the detriment of the Department of Finance. TBS's primacy in matters concerning the details of departments' expenditure budgets also somewhat eclipsed the finance department's role regarding microeconomic policies. However, the emergence of the two ministries of state – along with periodic prominence, induced by an energy crisis, for the Department of Energy, Mines and Resources – confronted Finance with so many challenges to its area of authority in the early 1980s that its morale visibly declined. Now, especially with the failure of the ministries of state, the department seems destined for a resurgence.[34] It has held on to the principal economic levers and its minister still possesses a key to the court that opens more doors than do those of any of his colleagues.

Conclusion

A near-cyclical process has overlapped with a proliferation of ministries during the past two decades to produce a highly unstable central agency community in

Canada. The former factor stems from the Department of Finance's inability to operate creatively in the expenditure control field during the expansionary 1960s, PCO's short-circuiting the tentative steps of TBS towards paring cabinet's wishlists at the onset of economic difficulties in the mid-1970s, and the emergence of the ministries of state – MSERD and MSSD – by 1979 as part of a desperate attempt to force ministers into radical cuts on the grounds that the freed funds would go to programmes more essential to the umbrella objectives of the various expenditure envelopes. The proliferation of ministries – which only complicated priority-setting during the expansionary period, the move towards fiscal contraction and the era of economic crisis – took root in the severe fragmentation of Canadian society.

John Turner's decision to cut the size of the cabinet and eliminate MSERD and MSSD took Canada back at least as far as the mid-1970s. Although his successor – Brian Mulroney – has expanded cabinet's size again beyond its previous high, he might still negotiate the cyclical and representational pressures bearing down on the central agency system better than did Trudeau. First, PMO must develop continuing capability within decision-making areas. Most essentially, it must provide the prime minister with a small corps of career civil servants – such as is found in the British prime minister's private office – who can provide lines into the permanent bureaucracy independent of those available through PCO. PMO must develop as well a tradition whereby a small group of partisan appointees with impeccable credentials in several key issue areas *monitor* development and implementation of the policies most essential to the platform. The stress on monitoring appears to be crucial in the light of the Kirby experiment. A policy unit will simply repeat the 1974–6 failure if it attempts to involve itself comprehensively in priority-setting exercises.

Second, PCO must fall into line as a career-orientated cabinet secretariat. Michael Pitfield's departure to the appointive Senate and succession by Gordon Osbaldeston – the latter being as guarded about partisan association with the Liberals as was Gordon Robertson – helped greatly towards rehabilitation of PCO's image as the agent of neutral brokerage. It remains to be seen whether Osbaldeston will follow through by turning PCO into the secondment-based staff necessary to break down its superbureaucratic nature.

Third, the finance department will be likely to continue to land on its feet in the macroeconomic policy field. TBS, however, will require a great deal of help with its remit. Most centrally, it must report to a more prestigious Treasury Board. Although the president has normally ranked among the senior members of cabinet, other board members – apart from the finance minister, who rarely if ever attends – have usually come from the least prestigious portfolios. The Treasury Board will not be able to enforce the government's guidelines for expenditure envelopes – let alone engage itself effectively in the highest level of cabinet gamesmanship necessary for creative allocation of contracting resources

– unless it achieves a standing among cabinet committees rivalled only by priorities and planning. Actual practice over the past two decades has seen only relatively junior ministers serve on the Treasury Board in addition to the president and the finance minister. Morever, the latter minister has rarely involved himself directly in Treasury Board proceedings. While Brian Mulroney has adhered to these conventions, he created an entirely senior body – also supported by the TBS – and launched it on a comprehensive search for uneconomic and undesirable programmes. Entitled 'the ministerial task force', the committee is chaired by the deputy prime minister and includes, as well the president of the Treasury Board, the minister of finance and the minister of justice.

Notes

1 John Porter, *The Vertical Mosaic: an Analysis of Social Class and Power in Canada* (University of Toronto Press, Toronto, 1965).
2 T. N. Brewis, *Regional Economic Policies in Canada* (Macmillan, Toronto, 1969).
3 Arend Lijphart, *Democracy in Plural Societies: a Comparative Exploration* (Yale University Press, New Haven, Conn., 1977), pp. 119–29; S. J. R. Noel, 'The Prime Minister's role in a consociational democracy', in Thomas A. Hockin (ed.), *Apex of Power: the Prime Minister and Political Leadership in Canada* (Prentice-Hall, Scarborough, Ontario, 1977).
4 R. M. Punnett, *The Prime Minister in Canadian Government and Politics* (Macmillan, Toronto, 1977); W. A. Matheson, *The Prime Minister and the Cabinet* (Methuen, Toronto, 1976).
5 Kenneth McRoberts and Dale Posgate, *Quebec: Social Change and Political Crisis* (McClelland and Stewart, Toronto, 1980).
6 Colin Campbell, *Governments under Stress: Political Executives and Key Bureaucrats in Washington, London and Ottawa* (University of Toronto Press, Toronto, 1983).
7 Richard Simeon, *Federal–Provincial Diplomacy: the Making of Recent Policy in Canada* (University of Toronto Press, Toronto, 1972); D. V. Smiley, *Canada in Question: Federalism in the Eighties* (McGraw-Hill Ryerson, Toronto, 1980).
8 Richard A. Chapman and J. R. Greenaway, *The Dynamics of Administrative Reform* (Croom Helm, London, 1980), pp. 78, 81; V. Seymour Wilson, *Canadian Public Policy and Administration: Theory and Environment* (McGraw-Hill Ryerson, Toronto, 1981), p. 321.
9 Laurent Dobischinski, 'Rational policy-making: policy, politics and political science', in Hockin (ed.), *Apex of Power*; G. Bruce Doern, 'Recent changes in the philosophy of policy-making in Canada', *Canadian Journal of Political Science*, 4 (1971), pp. 243–64; Michael Pitfield, 'The shape of government in the 1980s: techniques and instruments for policy formation at the federal level', *Canadian Public Administration*, 19 (1976), pp. 8–20; George J. Szablowski, 'The optimal policy-making system: implications for the Canadian political process', in Hockin (ed.), *Apex of Power*.
10 J. L. Granastein, *A Man of Influence: Norman A. Robertson and Canadian Statecraft,*

1926–68 (Deneau, Ottawa, 1981); Granastein, *The Ottawa Men: the Civil Service Mandarins, 1935–57* (Oxford University Press, Toronto, 1982).

11 J. R. Mallory, 'The two clerks: Parliamentary discussion of the role of the Privy Council Office', *Canadian Journal of Political Sciences*, 10 (1977), pp. 3–19.

12 Granastein, *The Ottawa Men*, pp. 267–72.

13 Richard D. French, 'The Privy Council Office: support for cabinet decision-making', in Richard A. Schultz, Orest M. Kruhlak and John C. Terry (eds), *The Canadian Political Process* (Holt, Reinhart and Winston, Toronto, 1979).

14 Colin Campbell and George J. Szablowski, *The Superbureaucrats: Structure and Behaviour in Central Agencies* (Macmillan, Toronto, 1979).

15 Glassco Commission (Royal Commission on Government Organization), *Management of the Public Service* (Queen's Printer, Ottawa, 1962), p. 55.

16 Richard D. French, *How Ottawa Decides: Planning and Industrial Policy-Making, 1968–1980* (Lorimer, Toronto, 1980).

17 Douglas Hartle, 'An open letter to Richard Van Loon (with a copy to Richard French)', *Canadian Public Administration*, 26 (1983), pp. 84–94.

18 Campbell, *Governments under Stress*, p. 193.

19 Ibid., pp. 183, 193.

20 Hartle, 'An open letter', p. 86.

21 Richard D. French, 'Did Ottawa plan? Reflections on my critics', *Canadian Public Administration*, 26 (1983), pp. 100–4.

22 Thomas d'Aquino, 'The Prime Minister's Office: catalyst or cabal?', *Canadian Public Administration*, 17 (1974), pp. 55–79.

23 Campbell, *Governments under Stress*, p. 19.

24 Ibid., p. 81.

25 Campbell and Szablowski, *The Superbureaucrats*, pp. 256–73.

26 Campbell, *Governments under Stress*, p. 19.

27 Gordon Robertson, 'The changing role of the Privy Council Office', in Paul W. Fox (ed.), *Politics: Canada* (McGraw-Hill Ryerson, Toronto, 1977), p. 384.

28 Campbell, *Governments under Stress*, pp. 96, 97.

29 Campbell and Szablowski, *The Superbureaucrats*, pp. 256–73.

30 G. Bruce Doern, 'The mega-project episode and the formulation of Canadian economic development policy', *Canadian Public Administration*, 26 (1983), pp. 219–38; Doern, 'Energy expenditures and the NEP: controlling the energy leviathian', in Allan M. Maslove (ed.), *How Ottawa Spends, 1984: the New Agenda* (Methuen, Toronto, 1984); N. Harvey Lithwick and John Devlin, 'Economic development policy: a case study in underdeveloped policy-making', in Maslove (ed.), *How Ottawa Spends*; Michael J. Prince, 'Whatever happened to compassion? Liberal social policy, 1980–4', in Maslove (ed.), *How Ottawa Spends*.

31 Campbell and Szablowski, *The Superbureaucrats*, pp. 256–73.

32 Ibid.

33 Ibid., pp. 167, 169.

34 W. Irwin Gillespie, 'The Department of Finance and PEMS: increased influence or reduced monopoly', in Maslove (ed.), *How Ottawa Spends*.

Michael Pitfield

[The remarks made by Senator Michael Pitfield are reported here by William Plowden.]

Senator Pitfield said he felt, with regret, that Colin Campbell's paper gave a misleading description of the Canadian case. It had several defects. First, the basic data was often wrong, or misinterpreted. It was wrong, for example, on the size of the Trudeau cabinets and the list of departments established by Trudeau. Again, it spoke of a 'highly unpopular' anti-inflation programme, when, to his own knowledge, the anti-inflation programme had enjoyed overwhelming popular support from beginning to end. In considering Professor Campbell's figures for the number of PMO, PCO and FPRO senior officials, it was important to bear in mind that the only way of arriving at his totals was by including the staffs of the President of the Privy Council, the staffs of all ministers without portfolio, all travel officers, all catering staff, the entire central messenger service, Royal Commission managers, building security managers, the staff of the three official residences and so on. Most of these people were far removed from what might be thought of as the Cabinet Office or the Federal–Provincial Relations Office staff.

Second, Senator Pitfield said Professor Campbell was ill informed on matters of government organization and process. In Canada all deputy ministers had a right of access to the prime minister. There was an enormous difference between the Treasury Board, by which was meant Treasury Board ministers, and Treasury Board staff. There had never been any connection between PCO planning studies and day-to-day specific decisions in an immediate sense. The central agency status of the Department of Finance depended on its role as the macroeconomic manager and only little on any private reporting relationship to the prime minister: this relationship had been a great deal less close, under the five prime ministers for whom he had worked, than was suggested in the paper. The Department of Finance recruited disproportionately from outside government because it was, by definition, a direct entry department. The role of the special committee of Council had only to do with the approval on behalf of Cabinet of very routine Orders in Council. The Canadian Unity Information Officer was, significantly, not in the FPRO or the Cabinet Office, but reported to the partisan office, namely the PMO.

Third, Senator Pitfield suggested that certain events described in the paper either had not happened or had been misconstrued. It was a cardinal principle that the Cabinet Office could not prevent and should not prevent ministers from getting to cabinet or cabinet committees if they wanted to. There were manifold procedures to ensure that they were not so prevented. The paper also attributed the creation of the ministries of state to an effort to enforce radical cuts. But the dates showed that this was wrong; the ministries of state had in fact come into existence after the budget-cutting events. As Professor Campbell had said in his remarks, the aim of the ministries had been to rationalize the decision-making process, not to enforce cuts.

Because, he said, this was the first time since leaving the public service that he was able to talk about these things, he would take the opportunity to set the record straight in stating that the PMO and the PCO had not forced prices and incomes controls on the Department of Finance; the Department of Finance had forced them on the other departments. In so doing they had probably been right. The establishment of a ministry of state for external affairs and defence had never been seriously considered, quite possibly because when the matter came up he had himself just returned from Harvard where he had been working with Roger Porter, among other things on the National Security Council; he could guarantee that anyone who had studied that subject would never consider establishing a ministry of state for external affairs and defence. As for the delayed distribution of cabinet documents to Treasury Board staff (a much accentuated point in Professor Campbell's papers), the reasons for this were not those indicated in the paper. The real reason was that the Treasury Board's staff wanted an absolute veto on ministerial discussion in committee on spending proposals. This problem was later dealt with by passing ministers' decisions, once arrived at, to the Treasury Board ministers for comment before they went on to the full cabinet. Professor Campbell had also mentioned the Treasury Board staff's attempt to establish a reporting relationship for effectiveness studies whereby they would go direct to their own minister on such studies rather than to the departmental minister concerned. The important issue in both these cases was the need to preserve ministerial responsibility from the central agencies, a continuing preoccupation of the PCO at that time. It had caused them a lot of trouble with the Treasury Board staff.

The application of PCO staffing policy had never varied from the period chosen by Professor Campbell as a period of transition of governance. One or two people might have been kept on as the result of the government being unfamiliar with how to govern; but basically the figures had always abided by the guidelines. As for disproportionate levels of recruitment from Montreal, this always happened for the simple reason that Canada was a bilingual country and Montreal was by far its biggest francophone city. There had never been a PCO 'conspiracy' to establish ministries of state; it had been a recommendation in which both the Deputy Minister of Finance and the Secretary of the Treasury Board had fully participated and fully concurred, that led to their establishment.

Senator Pitfield said he objected to the degree of personalization in Professor Campbell's paper, not only with respect to himself – the paper did not indicate that he had been away for four out of the ten years between 1970 and 1980 –

but more particularly with respect to Michael Kirby. The Kirby memorandum had been misrepresented: one of the options in it had been as described, but it had also put forward several others. One would not know from Professor Campbell's paper that when Mr Kirby had left the job he had been tendered a dinner by the provincial representatives with whom he had negotiated.

More basically, Senator Pitfield said that he objected to the methodology of the paper, including the composition of the sample on which it was based; for example, a great deal was made of the profile of the public service as professionals and career civil servants and yet into the sample upon which that profile was based was imported the PMO staff, which was an entirely partisan, short-term, appointed staff. What distortions this gave rise to he could only imagine. There were also problems with the assumptions upon which the paper was built, including for example the 'size of country' factor: should a country which has a population one-tenth of that of the United States have one-tenth the number of central agencies? He regretted the omission of any mention of the Congressional facilities for budget control and so forth that existed in the United States, the failure to examine the Canadian federal factor and, more particularly, the fact that presidents and prime ministers and British prime ministers really did work differently. The more he saw of the British system the more he realized that in Canada – perhaps because of its federal nature – collective responsibility was extremely important; he had remarked earlier that when talking about government 'at the top' Canadians thought automatically of the cabinet rather than of the prime minister.

Professor Campbell's paper had three main conclusions. First, the PMO must develop a decision-making capacity, and it must have a small core of career civil servants. He could say only that this had been tried in the past, and it had not worked. The public servants who were involved came out very politicized, and the cabinet as a whole had not been well served. The Canadian model had been consciously adopted and no reasons were given in the paper as to why it should be abandoned. Second, that the PCO should be career-orientated and secondment-based. To this his response was that Professor Campbell's paper had itself acknowledged that the PCO was already career-orientated, and he himself had said the evidence showed that it was overwhelmingly secondment-based. Third, that the Treasury Board should meet less, should include chairmen of all committees and should be rivalled only by the priorities and planning committee. In other words, that ministers should be made even more subject to a very powerful staff, that the Treasury Board should be a committee of the spending departments and should lose even the powers it now had over priorities and planning. This proposal displayed ignorance of the Treasury Board's actual workload and the process and political realities among ministers.

It was a pity, he said, that Professor Campbell's paper missed the real and larger story. Briefly, this was as follows. The modern transition to a large and pro-active government had given rise to a desperate need for ways to deal with multi-department problems, ways to handle federal–provincial coordination, ways to control bureaucracy – including control of the guards who guard the guards – and ways to control expenditure: in short, ways to put ministers under control. (Putting Parliament in control of ministers was another story.)

To this end, prime ministers and senior officials since Diefenbaker and Glassco had increased the number of ministers and developed the organization and process of decision-making. They had discarded the model of super-departments. They had found a tiered cabinet impossible to create out of the fabric of a federal parliamentary system. They had felt they had to break the power of inter-departmental committees. All this had led to a system of an executive committee or 'inner' cabinet and specialized cabinet committees attended by a few officials as needed. The old 'cabinet meeting' had been turned into parliamentary tactics and monitoring. Colin Campbell has made the point that representational imperatives can push cabinet to unworkable inclusiveness. In fact this had not happened. Mulroney and his colleagues seemed happy with present arrangements; disaster had followed Turner's efforts to abandon 'due process'. The process had been one of evolution, not of revolution. It was of critical importance to adhere to constitutional principles even while developing them. This could be illustrated by the role of ministers in effectiveness studies, or the question of 'suspensory veto' for Treasury Board staff. Also important were better definition of government objectives, of organization, departmental mandates and process and of public service (particularly senior service) personnel policy (always the weaker sister of public administration).

Senator Pitfield said Trudeau had never been 'consumed' or 'fascinated' by these matters. He saw them as means to do his job better – and they had played some role in his being able to govern for 16 years. The real story was an interesting one, he said. It was far from perfect, and did not always reflect well on the players. It was still not complete; but it was worth telling for the benefit of others passing or deciding not to pass the same way.

Editor's Note

Further discussion of the points raised in this chapter can be found in Richard Van Loon, 'A revisionist history of planning processes in Ottawa? An open letter to Colin Campbell S. J.' and Colin Campbell, 'The pitfalls of a revisionism too eager by half: an open reply to Richard Van Loon', *Canadian Public Administration*, 28 (1985), 2.

PART II

Systems of Advice

7

Types of Advice

Patrick Weller

Advice to top decision-makers has often been categorized in ways that are analytically useful even if they are not always descriptively accurate or precise. The most frequent distinction is between political advice and policy advice. By 'policy' is usually meant technical and professional alternatives or the outcome of 'objective' or rational analysis. 'Political' is taken to refer to consideration of the likely electoral or media consequences of a course of action. The former is seen as substantive while the other is often regarded as more self-interested. A further distinction can be drawn between political advice and party-political advice, which is concerned with the likely reactions of the backbenchers and the outside party activists. That these divisions are essentially artificial is acknowledged, but in some systems they have been notionally institutionalized in the distinction between those who are non-partisan career civil servants, who provide policy advice, and those who are seen to be partisan and committed, and who provide political advice.

A second division is concerned with the time horizon of the advice. Should it be short-term advice, looking at the immediate consequences and outcomes and reacting to the inevitable crises that affect leaders, or should it have longer perspectives and examine the long-term eventual implications of the government's actions? Should that advice be couched in such a way that it helps the government stay on course to achieve its main objectives? Another related way of asking the same question is to draw a distinction between the capacities of advisers to assist in the setting of priorities (however that concept is defined) and their need to act as firefighters and policy analysts in short-term areas.

Within that general area lies the question of who ought to be receiving the advice. In a system where there is a single elected leader, such as a president, such doubts need not arise, but when there is a cabinet and a prime minister or chancellor some ambiguity about who does and who ought to get that advice is likely to occur. If the advice is to be directed towards the collectivity rather than the individual, then the detail and the content might be different.

In this summary, therefore, each of these three notional distinctions will be considered to determine whether there is a difference in the advice that leaders do receive in either political sensitivity or in time horizon.

Policy or Partisanship?

In Britain and the other countries that have adopted variations of its system of government there is a clear distinction between those advisers who are seen as partisan and temporary and those who are non-partisan and permanent. The latter have always been predominant in Britain; the prime minister's chief advisers have been the Cabinet Secretary and the Principal Private Secretary at No. 10, while the prime minister also has regular access to the permanent secretaries of the Treasury, the Foreign Office and, while it survived, the Civil Service Department.

For a long time it was argued that that was all the prime minister needed. At times it still is. But significantly, some very senior civil servants now believe that a prime minister needs more assistance to be able to keep up with the demands of modern government. He or she needs to be the guardian of the strategy, to steer the government, to be kept informed and to initiate policy. The prime minister needs advice to judge the proposals that his or her ministers are presenting. With an effective staff of only about 35, the support for Mrs Thatcher barely seemed adequate. There is, of course, a long tradition of additional partisan support that can be traced back at least to Lloyd George's 'garden suburb'. Nevertheless, the establishment of a well-publicized set of partisans at No. 10 did not occur until it was developed by Harold Wilson in a random way in the 1964-70 government and then institutionalized in the Policy Unit in 1974. Mrs Thatcher formally abolished the Policy Unit when she came to power in 1979 but she has maintained the reality if not the form and many of the duties and policy areas are now divided up among her advisers in a more systematic way than ever before. The partisan adviser is clearly a permanent part of the British political scene. The majority of them are seen as temporary and committed to the objectives and the continued existence of the government.

But the question remains as to what difference that distinction makes in the content of the advice that the prime minister gets. Two points have emerged. First it is necessary not to overstate the degree to which civil servants avoid politics. To suggest that they are non-partisan is to say no more than that they will serve any elected government to the best of their ability and not that they will refuse to discuss the sensitive political questions with their ministers. It may be true that the more crude political advice is kept to private conversations and that the written advice is more measured, but even then the political lessons are implicit in the analysis. Besides, policy advice will always take account of political sensitivities; if the government wants to cut expenditure then care has to be taken in the type of recommendations that are made. When the advice of the Central Policy Review Staff (CPRS) suggesting that cuts in welfare were an option was leaked, it created such a furore that such cuts were ruled out immediately and one possible line of action was closed. It is therefore impossible in the provision of real advice to distinguish between the policy itself and the political aspects, because they are bound to be mixed.

Second, the political advisers are still likely to judge issues on their technical merits, but from a particular set of assumptions about objectives. One adviser at No. 10 commented that he asked the same questions and gave the same advice in No. 10 as he had done previously in the CPRS; the main change was that he felt greater freedom to indulge his political judgement and give it full rein because his instincts supported those of the prime minister. The important thing was to get the policy right and he felt it easier to assist in that at No. 10. For policy analysts, therefore, the change of position did not lead to change in the nature of their advice because the role they had to play – commenting on policy proposals to assist the prime minister and making her aware of the environment in which decisions had to be reached – had not altered. But the change in position was significant because of the freedom it gave them and possibly because the prime minister had greater confidence in the knowledge that they were now working exclusively for her. There was no longer any ambiguity about the position of the policy analysts.

In other countries, the process of institutionalization has developed to a much greater extent. In Canada and Australia the Prime Minister's Offices (PMOs) are accepted to be entirely political and to serve exclusively the interests of the prime minister. Even where some of the members of the Australian PMO were public servants, it was acknowledged that they were on secondment and no longer bound by the normal public service constraints (although they did shy away from some of the dealings with faction bosses that were required of the office). In both countries the members of the PMOs serve during the prime minister's pleasure. By contrast, in both countries, the civil service advisers are kept distinct; the Privy Council Office and the Department of Prime Minister and Cabinet in Canada and Australia respectively, are staffed by civil servants. Despite the fact that they give frequent advice on policy issues and may second-guess departments at times, and despite the fact that both have been accused of being over-powerful bodies and excessively politicized, they have remained largely free from formal political ties.

Indeed the existence of the PMOs clearly indicates that there are perceived to be some roles that the civil servants should not play. In practice both bodies are likely to give advice on the same topics, that is, the problems that concern the prime minister; they will do it from the same data base but from different assumptions, thus providing the prime minister with a range of ideas. The extent to which the PMO will challenge departmental policy may depend on the priority which the prime minister gives to that topic. Further, these bodies not only give advice, they also order and sieve the advice that comes from other sources to ensure that the prime minister receives only what is important.

However, they also argue that they try to ensure that no one gains a monopoly of advice on any subject and that the prime minister has a right to get advice from as many sources as is necessary; they therefore both order advice and comment on it. The policy advice and the political advice will always overlap – both bodies comment, hopefully sensitively, on proposals, albeit from different perspectives – but they are seen to be distinct.

This distinction, however, may be peculiar to the 'Westminster' systems. The mixture of career and political advisers is not found in other places. In the United States, for example, all the president's senior advisers are partisan appointments; even those Senior Executive Service members who reach high ranks are given the position as a political choice. The White House staff have to pull together advice from all sources that want to have an impact on the president. These may include several departments with interests in any matter, the Congress, particular states, labour unions and industry, and electoral bodies; in all there may be up to a dozen streams of advice competing to influence the president. The White House staff have to sift these proposals and pool them to help the president, while accepting that it would be inappropriate for him to be prevented from knowing what various people are individually suggesting. In these cases it is, of course, impossible to distinguish any boundary between the political and the technical nature of the advice because they must be intertwined.

By contrast, in West Germany and France the distinction does not operate for different reasons. In both countries there is little scope for political leaders to draw partisan advisers into the official structure on a long-term (rather than a consultancy) basis from the universities or the parties. It is assumed that the French prime ministerial *cabinet* or the German Chancellor's Office will have developed the political sensitivity to be conscious of political needs.

In West Germany, the assistant secretaries of the 'mirror-image sections' in the Chancellor's Office are expected to keep an eye on the political scene and to keep in mind what will make the government look good. However, an incoming chancellor has limited scope to introduce partisans into the advisory structure, although he may remove a small number of 'political' public servants in whom he has no faith. Further, there is little capacity for policy analysis in the Chancellor's Office, in part because its function is seen more as managing the policy process and in part because in West Germany the chancellor may be able to formulate policy guidelines but is not responsible for the detailed formulation of policy. The system is more closed and complete; whether there is some mobility into other sections of the civil service or not, there is virtually none with outside bodies.

A distinction also needs to be made in all instances between those civil servants who are politically very sensitive (usually those who are working close to the centre of government) and those who are further away and who may be more interested in the smooth procedure of policy. It is not true to argue that all public servants are equally sensitive.

The French situation is similar to that in West Germany. There, the ministerial *cabinets* are responsible for keeping a check on both the long- and the short-term issue, but they are staffed almost exclusively by civil servants. For a time after the Mitterand government took power it seemed possible that this stranglehold might be broken but the influence of members of the *grands corps* and of graduates of the Ecole Nationale d'Administration was quickly reasserted.

What differences do these arrangements of the partisan and non-partisan advisers make? The most obvious distinction may be that their terms of analysis are different; they bring diverse skills to the same problems. Partisans share the leader's view of the world; civil servants provide more technical advice, based on an awareness of likely consequences and public reactions. There is a need to accept that distinction and appreciate that not all advisers are equally competent in both aspects. As far as personnel are concerned, the main difference is between those whose *public* commitment leads to temporary appointment as potentially powerful advisers close to the leader and those whose careers are notionally unaffected by changes of government. In the United States all senior positions are so affected whereas in West Germany this applies to almost none.

It is not clear that the actual advice eventually received on policy matters is very different; or that the nature of the recommendations could be forecast accurately on the basis of who was giving it. The reality is more complex. In Britain it was suggested that the prime minister gets advice from six different sources:

1 departmental policy advice (with the political dimension coming from the minister);
2 broader view from the Cabinet Office, dealing particularly with procedure;
3 political advice from the Policy Unit;
4 party-political advice from the political staff;
5 presentational advice from the press office;
6 outside advice from bodies such as the Centre for Policy Studies.

These multiple sources of advice are not necessarily contradictory; indeed they may be usefully complementary as different parts of the system provide alternative perspectives.

In other systems, the same range of advice may be available, but not necessarily from the same side of the partisan/non-partisan fence. In Canada and Australia the policy analysis may come as easily from the PCO or the PMC, where there is an explicit policy capacity to analyse and if necessary to second-guess departments. The PMOs in both countries were also capable of giving both policy, political and presentational advice.

In those countries where the advice is almost exclusively from civil servants, there may be the same range of policy analysis if it is required by the leader because the expectations are naturally there.

Of course it is also true that leaders are by no means limited to their official advisers. Although there are always claims that leaders are too cosseted and protected by their private offices, much of their advice will still come from their ministers and party contacts. In West Germany, for example, Chancellor Kohl is chairman of his party and still relies on the party officials with whom he built up a rapport when the party was in opposition. Further, the process of cabinet government remains very real in Westminster and in European countries, and leaders therefore have regular interaction with their leading political colleagues.

If it is not possible to draw clear distinctions between the type of advice that is given, some lessons do seem to be generally accepted as important. First, most participants at this conference have agreed that all advisers should try to ensure that they do not prevent access to the leader. It is seen to be of crucial importance that the leader continues to get as wide a range of advice as is needed to understand the problems. Close advisers should order and integrate that advice but not restrict it.

Second, there is a feeling that the disapproval with which the term 'political advice' is met is a misunderstanding of reality, as the political is not necessarily shabby, nor is technical advice somehow pure. Fears have been expressed here that the advisory process might be 'polluted' if the most pressing or persuasive advice were concerned with symbolic or cosmetic matters because this might detract from answers that were technically better. But it has been pointed out that political life is quite properly about survival and the art of making the necessary appear to be the possible. As one participant put it, 'politics is your rival's policy'.

Third, there seems to be an acceptance that, however essential close advisers are (and they are regarded as having a role to play), they cannot act successfully without ensuring that those who have to implement the policy have been involved in its making.

The difference in the content of the advice that people get has not been perceived to be great, whether the close advisers are partisan or not; it is the track record of the individual, rather than the status or formal position, that matters. But it does seem to be accepted by participants that leaders require policy support in some form if their duties are to be fully and adequately performed in the modern world.

Whose Priority? Whose Strategy?

The second area of dispute in the politics of advice is concerned with the time horizons of that advice. Who is responsible for determining strategy and for setting priorities? Who is best suited to give government a sense of direction? In some systems the answer may seem simpler than in others. An individual leader, like a president, is better placed to provide authoritative directions than a prime minister or a chancellor who must at least nominally share that responsibility with a cabinet. Nevertheless, there are always two parts of the process: determining what the strategy is and maintaining some adherence to it.

Two points have stood out in discussion. The first is a firm belief that all governments have a need for broad and long-term objectives. Professor Dror's contribution speaks of the necessity to ensure that advisers and policy analysts are not too easily distracted from the analysis of longer trends by the need to advise leaders on problems of immediate concern. He emphasizes the importance of longer horizons if policy analysis is to serve a useful role.

Practitioners have seen similar advantages. The CPRS had been created partly to act as policy grist in the policy-making mill but also to maintain an overview of the government's strategy. After it was abolished, some civil servants argued that it should be restored because it might provide a means of institutionalized access for the presentation of longer-term views; in the existing situation there was no one to play that important role. In Canada, the 'priorities' exercise of 1975–6 sought to identify and rank the most pressing problems. In Australia, the Royal Commission on Australian Government Administration recommended in 1976 a sophisticated system of forward estimates and the Economic Planning Advisory Committee, created in 1983, was designed to assist the government in medium-range planning. President Reagan established an Office of Planning and Evaluation to develop strategic plans and provide six-monthly blueprints for action. In West Germany, the planning division of the Chancellor's Office was created to assist in the setting of priorities and bodies like the Economic Advisory Council were designed to provide some picture of likely economic conditions. In France, the Economic Planning Commissariat was to take a long look at the economy. The belief in the importance of assessing the long-term impact of policies was clearly widespread.

But the second point is that these bodies have rarely been seen as successful in that role. Their existence has been subverted, or the exercise was doomed to the stating of the obvious, or they became only marginally relevant institutions. The CPRS was abolished in 1983 but its most successful work had been discrete policy analysis rather than strategic thinking. The Canadian priorities exercise was overtaken by events. The Australian forward estimates were never implemented and EPAC became a forum for an exchange of views rather than serious discussion. President Reagan's Office of Planning was soon diverted to more immediate issues while the German chancellor's planning division was diverted to problem-solving. Attempts at grand strategy seem to have failed.

However, it is necessary to be clear about the meaning of terms like 'strategy' or 'priorities'. In the grand sense of a comprehensive set of interlocking plans that determine how the parts of a government's objectives relate to one another it may indeed be impossible to achieve. Some still thought that it was an objective that should be sought. However, less grandiose meanings may be equally useful. For instance, a leader might provide a list of objectives, or one overriding objective, to be achieved in the first term – reducing the deficit, tackling unemployment, maintaining a trade union accord. President Reagan, for instance, listed budget and tax reform, a recruitment freeze and deregulation. Or the leader may provide a measuring stick against which all policies are to be judged, such as a determination to return powers to the federal states. In the latter case all other policies are to be subordinate to it, however important they may seem. Always assuming that the leader is serious about the implementation of the policy (and of course not all always are), contradictory policies are thrown back for further consideration.

In these circumstances, the priorities are politically inspired and often presented in general terms. Because they appear clear, however, they can provide a focus for action. The role of the adviser is then to judge policies in terms of these ideas or to maintain momentum in the right direction. As one contributor put it, Mrs Thatcher knows where she is going; the advisers are employed to help her get there. And in this process of keeping the long term in view, the best tactic was to connect the longer view with the proposals for short-term action.

The implication is, of course, that the advisers may help to formulate these priorities but they need the maintained support of the leader. The analyst is concerned to show where proposals are drifting away rather than to determine the strategy itself.

Advice to Whom?

Who then are the leaders who need advice? In the United States it is obviously the president, but in parliamentary systems it is less clear. What is certain is that more help is needed. One participant identified seven problems created by modern government; he saw a pressing need for better ways:

1 to deal with information overload on decision-makers;
2 to deal with multi-department problems;
3 to handle coordination with other levels of government;
4 to control bureaucracy (including controlling the guards);
5 to control expenditure;
6 to secure a longer-term perspective in decision-making;
7 to offset the trend towards centralization of decision-making on to the prime minister.

He argued that greater assistance was needed for the ministers in a collective government if they were to reassert political control over the direction of government.

One option that has been widely discussed is indeed the provision of advice to ministers as a group. Collective responsibility has been retained, but at times without the cabinet as a group having the ability to impose it. Therefore, it is argued, there is a need to boost the capacity of the collectivity to give it a greater chance of developing a sense of cohesion. The CPRS, it is suggested, was not given a fair try or adequate resources. If any long-term policy is to be developed, it is argued, it will require the broad involvement of all the cabinet.

An alternative is to accept that collective priority-setting has not worked and that advisers are needed to allow the leader to assert *de jure* what the pressures of modern government have already created *de facto*, that is, the policy direction of the government. Only there can the short and the long term be best connected because all leaders already have the responsibility for controlling the policy process.

A neat way of looking at the same problem is to examine one impressive formulation of the leader's role in modern times. It is mainly concerned with providing direction and cohesion. A leader should:

1 devise strategy to avoid being driven by day-to-day winds;
2 maintain a skilled early warning system;
3 have honest brokers to mobilize information, analyse alternatives and dispense quality control;
4 insist on a map of the substantive and political reality of alternative consequences;
5 have advisers to monitor and implement his decisions.

In this formulation political advice and policy advice, the short and the long term, are inevitably mixed. That must be so if leaders are to get the rounded and sensitive advice they need. In different systems both partisan and non-partisan advisers may be able to help in meeting that objective.

8

Advice on Economic and Foreign Policy

Howard Machin

All policy advisers to a president or prime minister are not equal. Some are 'more equal' than others, and the degree of inequality does not simply depend on the ruler's personality and interests. Almost invariably, the 'inner circle' includes the top advisers in both economic and foreign affairs. These are the most important policy areas for all governments. Almost everywhere, the prime minister or president is increasingly involved in decision-making in those domains. Indeed, economic and foreign policy advisers merit special attention, as their role is both an indicator of, and a key element in, the apparently universal trend towards centralization within governmental decision-making, whether presidential or prime ministerial. Hence, a study of economic and foreign policy advice to rulers reveals a great deal about the dynamics of this intra-governmental centralization process. What are the systemic factors which push or pull heads of government into decision-making in these fields? What are the structural constraints checking the growth of the rulers' power in economics and foreign affairs? What kind of advice is wanted and what is provided? Who provides the advice and to whom does it go?

The answers to these questions illustrate that the common trend towards intra-governmental centralization is not totally unchecked. Indeed, there are a number of factors limiting this trend, but they vary considerably in importance from country to country.

Factors Leading to Greater Ruler Involvement

Here it is useful to distinguish between traditional factors and more recent developments, although the two are closely interlinked. The defence of the realm against foreign aggression and the promotion of the economic prosperity of its citizens, along with the maintenance of law and order, are not only the oldest functions of government, but also, with the development of liberal democracy, have become two of the most electorally significant. Obviously, public perceptions of the personality of the head of government (whether president or prime minister), or his challengers, do affect electoral behaviour, as the careers of Ronald Reagan and Michael Foot exemplify in very different ways. But, in general, economic policy performances and promises are the makers and breakers of victories at the polls and, in exceptional circumstances, foreign policy may share this role (as in Britain, in the general election following the Falklands conflict). In more normal times also, the voters' perceptions of their ruler's weight in international affairs and his or her stance on defence, the European Community or other international questions may well influence their choices.

Hence, whatever their personal preferences, actual and would-be heads of governments in liberal democracies, by electoral inevitability, are concerned with economic and foreign policy-making. In practice, four traditional economic and foreign policy roles can be identified: policy initiation; policy coordination and arbitration; party and coalition leadership and liaison in parliament and elsewhere within the political structures; and social coalition building and maintenance of contacts with interest groups and the media.

Before the massive transformations of the post-war era the second and third of these roles were probably the most significant. Arbitration and coordination have always been needed in both policy areas. Clearly economics, like foreign affairs, is not so much one policy area as a group of policy areas. Just as 'foreign affairs' involves not merely diplomacy, defence, intelligence and international trade, but also tourism, monetary and fiscal policies, technological collaboration and even cultural exchanges, so too 'economic policy-making' concerns money supply, taxation, industry, agriculture, commerce, employment, housing, transport and regional policy. Indeed ultimately all government activities interlink in economic and foreign affairs.

Both economic and foreign policy-making involve several different and distinct institutional actors: ministries, state agencies or advisory boards. For all these bodies to act together, presidential or prime ministerial coordination and arbitration are constantly required if efficient policy-making is to take place. This is especially true when two or more large, powerful and prestigious departments – the State and Defense Departments in the United States are good examples – are permanent rivals in the same policy area. Clearly, the head of government wishes to avoid 'capture' by one of the protagonists, or endless, time-wasting negotiations.

Furthermore, the annual budget has always required some kind of integration of and coherence between all the different areas of governmental action. Although the basic work is normally performed by the finance ministry or department, making the big, final decisions has long been the task of heads of government. Increasingly, however, in recent years, presidents and prime ministers have also been drawn into the preparatory negotiations.

This kind or arbitration and coordination is at the centre of political coalition building and maintenance. As party or coalition leader, each president (or prime minister) seeks not only the desirable within the limits of the possible, but above all the expedient in terms of immediate success in the legislature and electoral gain in the longer term. Hence the political importance of these policy areas has always meant that the head of government was directly involved in decision-making.

This political importance has been markedly increased by post-war developments and the role of the head of government has grown accordingly. The biggest development has been the growth of the state and the massive widening of the scope of governmental intervention. Through social security and welfare schemes, by huge involvement in the provision of health and education services, by direct economic action regulating competition, providing infrastructure, protecting the environment and the consumer, or directly owning and managing industries, the governments of almost all advanced liberal democracies have become massively interventionist. They are concerned with distorting the market by social transfers (revenue redistribution) and replacing it by public resource allocation, and doing both on an unparalleled scale. Keynesian doctrines have passed into, and out of, fashion, but the economy as a whole remains of crucial concern to *all* governments simply to avoid reducing existing and expected levels of services, or massive, politically unacceptable, and economically damaging, tax increases. Moreover, whatever the pro-private sector public protestations of the Thatchers, Reagans and Kohls, the expansion of public services over many years cannot be swiftly or easily reversed.

Even the forecasts on which governments base their economic policies have become subjects of considerable political controversy between ministers and ministries, within governing parties or coalitions, and between governments and oppositions, for complete strategies depend on these forecasts. Inevitably, rulings from the president or prime minister are often called for by their colleagues.

Economic difficulties since the oil crises have only exacerbated the trend for the head of government to be drawn into arbitration and coordination, if not policy initiation. At times when national income remains constant or even diminishes, automatic annual increases for spending ministries are replaced by bitter battles to maintain funding levels. In this way, the annual budgetary process becomes much more conflictual, and presidential or prime ministerial arbitration much more frequent, even when, as in Britain, a cabinet committee (the 'Star Chamber') does the dirty work.

This post-war growth of 'big government' has been accompanied by the continued growth of 'big business', with the result that the success of certain corporations may become crucial concerns for national governments. When problems arise, governmental intervention may be essential for the firm to survive. Serious financial difficulties of nationally important firms – Rolls–Royce in Britain, Lockheed in the United States and the big steel companies in France – have drawn heads of governments not known for their strong beliefs in state interventionism, including Richard Nixon, Edward Heath and Raymond Barre, into 'firefighting' operations, which in two cases led to nationalizations. In such crises the policy implications may be very broad indeed – employment, foreign trade, industrial strategy or even defence may be involved – and hence, at such times, decision-making is almost inevitably the task of the head of government.

International economic dependence and western political cooperation have also grown in the post-war era, and this, too, affects intra-government centralization, for economic and foreign affairs are increasingly inter-linked. This is especially true for Britain, France, Italy, and West Germany, which, as members of the European Community, are committed to joint policy-making in many economic domains and to cooperation in determining their foreign policies towards the rest of the world. The debates in 1985 about the joint construction of a European fighter plane amply illustrate the complexity of this inter-linking. This connection is also very familiar in the United States, where the debate on the 'pork barrel' politics of defence contracts long predates the discovery of a 'military–industrial complex' in the 1960s. The major oil price rises of the 1970s, the row over the Russian pipeline construction, the disputes over the rescheduling of the overseas debts of Poland and several Latin American countries, and the introduction of sanctions against South Africa have all been both economic and foreign problems, demanding integrated policy responses from the countries involved. In short, growing economic internationalization and interdependence mean that many economic problems are international and many aspects of foreign relations are economic. It is almost always the head of government who must integrate policies to ensure some minimal level of coherence and who must ultimately reach agreements with heads of other governments.

Reflecting and encouraging this trend to greater internationalization has been the growth of summit meetings, where presidents and prime ministers meet their peers to discuss, negotiate, and very occasionally solve the problems of the day. Whatever the reality at home, a coherent presentation of each nation's economic and foreign policies is certainly expected from the head of government at all international summit meetings. Whether at GATT (General Agreement on Tariffs and Trade) negotiations, meetings of the Western economic powers, or bilateral talks, it is the heads of governments who inevitably lead the discussions about both economic and foreign issues. For members of the European Community such summits have become frequent, normal parts of the decision-making and crisis-resolving mechanisms, for only the heads of government can take responsibility for the wide-ranging political and economic package deals.

Clearly all these developments have not affected all heads of governments in the same ways or to the same extent. None the less, everywhere there has been the same kind of trend, to involve the head of government in more and more economic and foreign policy decisions. To respond to this trend presidents and prime ministers have sought – and obtained – advice in many different ways.

Structural Constraints on Rulers' Power

Four major types of constraint on the economic and foreign policy roles of rulers can be identified: constitutional, institutional, political and practical. They vary considerably in importance from country to country.

In some countries with written constitutions there are real limitations on what governments can do in these areas. Nowhere is this problem so acute as in the United States. Outside the federal administration there are such powerful bodies as the states' governments, the Supreme Court and Congress itself which may modify, check or reverse presidential policies. Congress can rely on the expert advice of its own advisers in the Congressional Budget Office, with a highly trained staff numbering over 400. The president cannot make treaties, declare war or even pay civil servants without Congressional approval. Hence one of Washington's strangest spectacles – even under Ronald Reagan – is the sending home of vast armies of bureaucrats when the government structures of the world's richest nation fail to produce a budget on time.

At least in France this eventuality is precluded (by constitutional provision) and there is no federal system, but there is a Constitutional Council which rejected one budget (and created problems over European integration and nationalization) and even the enfeebled French parliament sometimes causes trouble. West Germany, however, has both a Constitutional Tribunal and a federal system. It also has an independent second chamber, the Bundesrat, which can make considerable difficulties for a government with a clear majority in the Bundestag (the lower house). In theory, these constraints limit the powers of the government as a whole, rather than those of its head. None the less, in countries like Britain where no such constitutional obstacles exist, the policy-making role of the head of government can develop more easily.

Institutional checks are provided within all systems by those institutions with whom the president or prime minister must act to make economic or foreign policy. These may be big, prestigious, independent bodies, with skilled staffs, massive information and research staffs and 'house views' of their own. In the United States, for example, to make economic policy the Executive Office of the President must work with major departments, such as the Treasury, the

Department of Commerce and Agriculture, and the Federal Reserve Bank system, the federal agencies and commissions, which often have considerable autonomy in practice. France too has an executive of byzantine proportions. Not only is there a prime minister's office but also a powerful finance ministry. And it is sometimes matched by other economic ministries (a ministry of the budget, or a ministry of the economy, or a ministry of industry, or even a ministry of economic and regional planning in recent years). Within the prime minister's services there are a number of semi-autonomous economic fiefdoms, of which the Planning Commissariat and the Regional Action Delegation (DATAR) are well-known examples. There is also the Banque de France, whose governor has often seemed unaware of his theoretical subordination to the finance minister. Even in Britain the 'Treasury view' and the Bank of England provide weighty institutional checks. In West Germany, the president of the Bundesbank, attends meetings of the cabinet for budget and all key economic discussions; he has no vote, but may have an important influence on decisions, and certainly has an opportunity to voice his views, or those of his institution. In countries like West Germany and the United States, where the central bank has considerable constitutional autonomy, it is both a source of advice and a weighty constraint on policy-making.

There is also a variety of *political* constraints. As both economics and foreign affairs are the central concerns of public policy-making, the heads of the major government departments concerned are often the senior, most respected members of their governments. In coalition governments, these posts may be given to leaders of junior coalition partners, as is frequently the case in West Germany. These ministers may be old rivals of, or potential successors to, the present head of government. Hence whilst leadership in these policy areas by the head of government has become more essential, it has not been made any easier. Clearly, the people appointed by a US president as his secretary of the Treasury and his director of the Office of Management and Budget expect to be the main economic policy-makers in normal times and the key economic advisers at times when presidential arbitration is necessary. In France (from 1958 to 1986) the *de facto* head of government (the president) faced the *de jure* head (the prime minister) who was at least a close political ally, but also a potential rival or successor. Giscard d'Estaing's failure to recognize that Prime Minister Chirac needed some kind of respectability contributed significantly to his own downfall.

In most countries the political weight of ministers (or secretaries in the United States) varies considerably. Some ministers have considerable independence – either as representatives of coalition partners (or factions within a party), or as senior authority figures, or as symbols of a particular policy option. The minister's length of tenure of office, his expertise and tactics and his conception of his role (technical, managerial and executive or reforming, even politically crusading), all influence his ability to resist presidential or prime ministerial interventions.

In West Germany, a further political factor is the quasi-permanence of coalition government. The coalition parties are powerful, well-organized forces and expect to have a say in policy formation. No sooner has the financial year begun (1 January) than negotiations start in preparation for next year's budget, coordinated by the finance minister. In June there is a major coalition negotiation and as a result the government only then decides the 'cornerstones' – the main lines – of the budget for the next year.

There are practical constraints on rulers, not the least of which is the personality and style of the head of government himself. The contrast between the approaches of Presidents Carter and Reagan, as described in Stephen Wayne's article, is very striking in this respect. In France, de Gaulle was fascinated by foreign affairs but generally bored by economics and content to leave it in the hands of lesser mortals such as the prime minister (Pompidou) or finance minister (Giscard d'Estaing). A second important practical constraint is simply the size of the head of government's own staff, which in the short term may be limited by law, convention or party considerations. Clearly Mrs Thatcher, with a mere handful of policy advisers, has a more difficult task than President Mitterrand (with a staff of 40 advisers) or President Reagan (whose Executive Office is vast).

Finally, the non-policy-making roles played by the head of government – in state and military ceremonials, on visits abroad, or in political campaigning – may severely restrict the time and energy he has available for decision-making. The French and US presidents are in constant demand to open public buildings, preside over patriotic occasions and carry out state visits. In May 1968, for example, President de Gaulle was away on a state visit to Rumania whilst the students rioted and industry ground to a halt in a national strike. Many rulers may envy the British prime minister, who has a monarch to perform much of the tedious work of ceremonial representation.

The overall result of these structural constraints is that whilst most rulers are increasingly the ultimate decision-takers in economic and foreign affairs – either as arbitrators or coordinators – the parameters of their decision-making are almost always rather limited. They are constantly bombarded with information, expert evaluations and policy proposals and have little time in which to read, let alone digest, the mountains of papers proffered by colleagues, friends and subordinates. One of the clear similarities between countries which has emerged during discussions at this conference is that the adviser has an important role to play in helping the ruler to digest all the information and advice available.

Rulers' Requirements from Top Advisers

What is often required by rulers from their economic and foreign policy advisers is imaginative aid in assessing expert advice from below. Basic policy research is the responsibility of others, and especially of the aides of the ministers. The ruler often wants advice on his other advisers' reports. Moreover, this advice should essentially have four qualities: it should be expert, loyal, imaginative and fast.

Expertise is certainly required: the adviser should be at least as competent as the minister whose work he follows, or whose projects he is asked to evaluate. Loyalty here means both an appropriate partisan approach and a strong sense of discretion, or at least sensitivity to a ruler's constant probem of facing hypersensitive colleagues, a hyperactive press and a hostile opposition, all ever ready to exploit any opportunity. Imagination is equally essential: clearly the adviser is of no value if he merely reiterates what civil servants have already said; a fresh approach is wanted. Equally he must work fast. Very frequently his advice is most wanted when there is least time available to consider the issue. Economic crises and summit meetings are both good examples of cases where almost instant advice may be demanded.

Over and above these qualities, it is clear that there is a good deal of diversity in other requirements from country to country and from ruler to ruler. In Greece, for example, we are told, the current [1984] economic adviser was more often asked for advice on the long-term and socio-political implications of policies than on short-term economic decisions themselves.[1] This situation was hardly surprising under a prime minister who was a professional economist himself, and whose working relations with the finance minister were extremely close. The economic adviser also considered foreign economic policy issues, notably those arising from membership of the European Community.

The Portuguese situation in 1984 was apparently somewhat similar, with the finance minister as the real economic adviser to the prime minister. Here, however, the prime minister's staff adviser came from the private sector and often saw problems in a rather different way from the finance minister. The prime minister also sought advice on specific issues from many other sources: bankers, other ministers and party leaders.[2]

In Israel the prime minister's economic adviser was a relatively new post, as previously the finance minister had dominated this policy area. The economic crisis and galloping inflation had led to a wide search for advice – from professors, journalists and bureaucrats as well as from politicians – and the task of the prime minister's adviser now was to help him choose from amongst all the different views available.[3]

To some extent the ruler's use of advisers depends on his own career and experience. Hence in Britain, Mrs Thatcher, with little knowledge or experience of foreign policy-making or of the Foreign and Commonwealth Office, needed expert advice, but Lord Carrington's presence as Foreign Secretary meant that great discretion was required. After the Falklands crisis had confirmed the prime minister's suspicions and Lord Carrington had resigned, this advisory role grew considerably as the prime minister expanded her own foreign policy role.

In all these varied cases, the precise role of economic and foreign advisers is never the same, but it is almost always distinctive. It involves assisting the ruler to make decisions in the two policy areas where the results may be crucial to the ruler's own political future, where the departmental ministers or heads may be relatively independent and where the departmental staffs are often the most professional and hostile to 'political interference'. Hence, the methods chosen by the ruler within the many constraints of his or her system are very personal and very political. The adviser may often be involved in choosing between reports and recommendations from below. He or she may be involved in discreet contacts with private businessmen or overseas bankers. The work always depends on the personal work methods of the ruler. To have the confidence of the ruler and the ability to communicate easily and clearly with the ruler are obviously essential qualities.

The Producers and Consumers of Advice

One of the frequent fears of the political consumers of policy advice is that of becoming the prisoners of their suppliers. This could arise either from the existence of permanent closed advice circuits, or from the shared approaches and values of advisers in competing advice supply channels, or from both. Who are the rulers' advisers, and what are these advisers' sources of information and expert analysis?

The United States' foreign policy advisers in particular have been widely criticized for the 'groupthink syndrome'[4] and recent administrations have attempted to avoid it. Hence there has been a marked preference for 'multiple advocacy', especially since the Vietnam War. Mrs Thatcher's suspicions of the Foreign Office as a monopoly supplier of foreign policy advice, noted above, shows a similar fear. In France, criticisms of the Quai d'Orsay[5] have been less frequent, perhaps because of the independence of the president's personal foreign advisers on his own staff in the Elysée Palace (Mitterrand, for example, appointed a professor of dentistry as his African adviser). It is in France, however, that the 'groupthink' criticism has been especially strong against the economic advisers. Here the argument has been that the *grands corps*, and especially the Inspectorate of Finances, recruited from the Parisian bourgeoisie and trained at the same school, the Ecole Nationale d'Administration (ENA), have been the unique suppliers of presidential, prime ministerial and finance ministry advisers, with the result that rulers have had few real choices in economic policy. In Britain criticisms of the Treasury in particular or the civil service in general (the 'Yes, Minister' school) have taken a similar approach. None the less, there is considerable evidence that at most times and in most places it is less a question of concentration of supply than one of failure of the rulers to exploit the many and diverse sources available.

In most countries, there is an excessive and diverse supply of advice, so many and varied are the sources and approaches of the policy advisory networks and research units. It should be noted, however, that not all these bodies provide the same kinds of advice. Some are concerned with the presentation and analysis of data. Others are highly partisan agencies, advocating the ideas of particular groups or parties. In almost all states, there are many producers of many different kinds of advice, especially on economics and foreign policy. For the rulers, as consumers, the difficulty may be that of coordinating, say, long-term and short-term views, or that of choosing between different options, or that of obtaining precisely the information or ideas required.

The producers of information and advice for the policy advisers in the United States are perhaps more numerous and varied than in other countries. Today, Washington is swamped with groups and individuals offering expertise and advice to the president and his staff. In economic affairs, the president has his own people at the heads of the Office of Management and the Budget (OMB) and the Office of Policy Development (in the White House) and generally sympathetic professional economists at the Council of Economic Advisers. President Reagan has also called in a group of 13 'outside' economists for policy discussions with himself and his policy and OMB staff every three months. There are also numerous 'think-tanks', of which Brookings, the American Enterprise Institute and the Heritage Foundation are perhaps the best known, ever ready and willing to provide additional outside advice. In foreign affairs, the field is smaller. Even here, however, there are the heads of the State and Defense Departments, the Director of the CIA, the National Security Adviser and the Ambassador to the United Nations all at hand to provide the president with information, advice or evaluations of each others' advice. Furthermore, the 'spoils system' may not facilitate smooth and continuous policy-making, but it does bring in a new group of heads of departments with the possibility of a fresh approach each time a new administration takes over.

In West Germany there is a similar diversity of advice sources. The two main economics ministries both have research teams, as has the foreign ministry. The Chancellor's Office, analysed so clearly by Professor Mayntz, is subdivided into specialist divisions, and one of these deals with economic and fiscal policies. The political parties have their own groups of experts. The 'five wise men' of the *Sachverstandigenrat* (Committee of Experts), despite their formal link to the Chancellor's Office, are largely autonomous. This committee produces annual reports analysing economic performance, but does not make specific policy recommendations. The federal government also funds five university research institutes to make reports on economic policy and performance. Each year, in November and December, these institutes publish separate and often very different reports, usually based on different economic and political assumptions. In short, there is a generous supply of information and expertise, even if the reports avoid formulating precise recommendations.

In France, the criticisms noted above provoked a number of different attempts to diversify the supply of economic advice. One device used by Pompidou was to employ his own staff adviser as a kind of *advocatus diaboli* each time he discussed policy with the finance minister. Under Giscard d'Estaing, state funds were provided for the creation of an autonomous research institute, the *Observatoire français des conjonctures économiques*, and encouragement and assistance were given to a number of independent research centres. Mitterrand has often employed several staff members to work separately and in competition on the same project. Like Reagan, Mitterrand has shown a penchant for consulting businessmen, including the managing directors of Club Mediterranée and Schlumberger. In France (as in Britain under Margaret Thatcher) academic economists have also been brought in as advisers, and in one case, that of Professor Barre, as prime minister.

Despite the existence of these varied sources, problems still remain for the rulers as advice consumers. One such problem, stressed by Lord Hunt, is the fact that decisions are frequently taken rapidly and under pressure, so that there is little time to read or listen to much advice, however good or varied. In practice, the diversity of sources may have little effect because there remains one dominant supplier or group of suppliers with a virtual monopoly at key moments.

A second and very different problem was raised by Roger Porter's contribution. This is the difficulty of getting the two groups of policy advisers, those concerned with economic policy and those who specialized in foreign affairs, to work – or even to talk – together. Porter noted the lack of success under President Reagan of attempts to persuade foreign and economic advisors to coordinate their efforts. This problem is familiar to rulers of states in the European Community, but the solution is not simple. In France, several ministries, including finance and agriculture, have created specialist units to deal with European questions. In Germany, however, it is the foreign ministry which has set up its own services to inform and advise on European economic, agricultural and technical issues. In all cases it remains the task of the head of government to ensure the coherence of economic and foreign policies and this involves integrating the advice from the different groups concerned.

Conclusions

It is clear that economics and foreign affairs are of primary importance to almost all rulers of modern states. The two policy areas are increasingly closely linked and together they impose an integration of and coherence between all other government policies. They are directly important in electoral terms. They are also the most difficult to coordinate and control, as the ministers are often the most senior and independent of the ruler's colleagues and their ministries are usually the largest, most powerful, most prestigious and autonomous. Almost invariably rulers require personal advisers in these areas even when they place their top advisers in positions of political responsibility (as Richard Nixon did with Kissinger and Valéry Giscard d'Estaing did with Barre). In these circumstances the advisers have a task which is of great importance but also presents enormous difficulties. To assist the ruler in challenging or even changing the official lines taken by the foreign affairs or economics ministry, the adviser requires very special abilities, not just as an expert but also as a political animal. Not the least of the ruler's difficulties is choosing advisers who will not themselves wish to move into 'open' politics, to claim the praise for their policy decisions and to pursue independent political careers. In these policy areas, more than in most others, discretion and the ability to retain the ruler's confidence are the foremost qualities for the successful adviser.

Notes

1 Based on the conference contribution of Dr Yanni Papanicolaou.
2 Based on the conference contribution of Pedro Salgado.
3 Based on the conference contribution of Yossi Beilin.
4 On 'groupthink' see Irving L. Janis, *Groupthink* (Houghton Mifflin, Boston, 1982).
5 The French foreign affairs department is often referred to thus by its location.

9

Relationships between Advisers and Departmental Civil Servants

William Plowden

Two sorts of relationship are crucial to the effectiveness of advisers: those with their 'clients', the rulers, and those with all the other actors in the policy process (including actors outside government altogether). Two general comments can be made on this complex of relationships. First, that whatever the formal institutional arrangements, working relationships will largely be determined pragmatically by the corporate and personal characters of the actors involved. Second, and consequently, it is hard to make any general prescriptions about relationships: they will largely be country- and culture-specific.

Perhaps the most fundamental point to be made about relationships is the importance of a high degree of 'empathy', to put it no more specifically, between advisers and rulers. In the absence of this, all sorts of other problems arise. The closeness of relationships, and the effectiveness of communications within relationships, are connected; the further the adviser is from the ruler, the less impact he is likely to have. In addition, since the attention of the ruler is an extremely scarce resource, it seems to follow that 'closeness' is an element in a zero-sum game: the closer the adviser is to the ruler, the further – relatively – others will be. Lack of this essential rapport seems to have been one reason for the short life of the Australian Priorities Review Staff, set up by Gough Whitlam in 1973, headed by a man whom Whitlam barely knew, and abolished only a few years later.

But once the questions of personal rapport have been answered, the institutional issues remain. From where should advisers be drawn? Should they be 'career advisers' or seconded from elsewhere for limited periods? How should they be structured or organized? What skills and disciplines should be represented among them and how, in practice, can a reasonable balance be struck between different disciplines and the influence of each on the advice that is given? How – to ask perhaps the most basic question of all – can advisers ensure that their advice reaches their clients? And what should be the intrinsic relationship between their advice and that reaching their clients from other sources? Should they aim simply to order and provide a neutrally analytical commentary on the latter? Should they synthesize it into a limited number of themes, so as to reduce its diversity and the confusion that this might cause? Should they attempt to impose their own distinctive set of prescriptions, over and above all others? Finally, what advice do they themselves need, and where should they seek it – for example, in universities or research institutions?

The basic background and identity of advisers seems to vary widely. In Britain 'advisory' posts, whether in the Prime Minister's Office, the Cabinet Office or the now-defunct Central Policy Review Staff, have almost always been filled by people on secondment, whether from the permanent civil service or from outside. The prime minister's official private secretariat has been composed exclusively of civil servants; the recently created advisory unit has consisted – under both Labour prime ministers and Mrs Thatcher – almost exclusively of outsiders. The CPRS was approximately half civil servants and half outsiders; few of either group stayed for more than two years. In Canada, most of the staff of the Privy Council Office are on three- to five-year secondments from departments. In Australia, the practice is long established of moving people, including political advisers, between the the Prime Minister's Office, the Cabinet Office and departments.

In other countries, for example West Germany, central offices are by contrast staffed mainly by people who make their careers there. It is argued that if the ruler is to have complete confidence in his advisers, they must be close to him in every sense; and that they cannot, therefore, be officials on secondment since on returning to their departments they would be felt to have lost their proper neutrality. There can be 're-entry' problems when officials, having been seconded to positions of glamour and some real influence at the centre, are subsequently returned to the relatively humble levels in departments from which they originally came. On the other hand, there can be disadvantages in creating a cadre of 'central specialists', with no knowledge of life and its problems as experienced in the line departments. This can inhibit the development of effective working relationships between centre and line.

The importance of this point is increased if it is accepted that a large proportion of an adviser's activities – as much as half, it was suggested in the German case – is concerned with policy implementation. This can in principle include direct responsibility for carrying out decisions as well as oversight of those doing so. Views at the conference differed as to how far advisers should even monitor decisions, let alone help to implement them: it could be argued that to do so blurred the proper distinction between line and staff. On the other hand, some blurring of functions is desirable, as well as probably inevitable; problems are less likely to emerge at the implementation stage if those responsible have been involved in the policy-formulation stage as well.

In general, conference contributors thought it important to avoid too distant a relationship between advisers and departmental officials. One government represented at the conference found, on first taking office, that many new ministers were extremely suspicious of the permanent officials who had advised their predecessors – with some apparent reason, since most senior officials were believed to have supported or to have been even more directly involved with the previous governing party. Some ministers, as a result, had consulted their advisers privately, excluding officials from this process. The consequence of this, we learned, had been unfortunate; working relationships between these ministers and their departments had deteriorated. In general, those ministers who had come to trust, rely on and consult their officials had been more effective; others had had much more difficulty in mobilizing and motivating their departments.

A more extreme version of the view implicit in this account was expressed by a practitioner from another country. He suggested that the status of advisers was, as a whole, disproportionately greater than their practical significance. The simple reason for this was that in practice advisers found it hard to gain access to rulers – and thus to make their advice heard. This was inevitable: the time scale for most major decisions was so compressed that any adviser not directly integrated into the bureaucratic chain of command had little chance even of seeing the papers on their way to the ruler, let alone of producing and delivering considered analysis and advice. In general, rulers' time was so precious that it was often impossible for advisers to secure even ten minutes to discuss issues unrelated to immediate decisions. The only significant exceptions to this pattern were institutionalized advisory mechanisms such as the British CPRS or French *cabinets* which had developed recognized procedures and virtual rights of involvement. But in general, advisers were likely to be more effective (and less disruptive) if, instead of trying to influence rulers directly, they aimed to insert their views into the departmental mainstreams in the hope of influencing the content of these as they flowed upwards to the rulers. (All this was in contrast with the situation when rulers, and advisers, were in opposition. Then rulers had time for reading and for conferring with their advisers; when they came to office, their views might well have been influenced by this.)

The above is, of course, a highly conservative view of the policy process of a kind often put forward by departmental officials. Ostensibly descriptive – rulers *have* little time to confer with advisers – it has a concealed prescriptive content – rulers *ought* not to let themselves be distracted or, still worse, deflected by the heterodoxies of outsiders.

However, like other views of the proper relationship of advisers to rulers and to the policy process, this one implies some assumptions about the activities of advisers within this framework. Are they, in fact, peddling their own heterodoxies? And if so, is this a legitimate function? It can be argued that an adviser is failing in his principal duty if he does not offer advice. If he does so, he is in effect trying to guide the ruler towards a particular conclusion, whether or not this be favoured by the bureaucracy. But others maintain that it is no indication of the quality of an adviser that he necessarily have a view of his own; his main task should be to ensure that all (realistic) alternative options are presented to the ruler. A third option for the adviser is to help to make the ruler's task as simple as possible by synthesizing into the least complex form feasible the different lines of advice reaching the ruler from different quarters – once again, without necessarily imposing on these, or contrasting with them, a distinctive view of his own.

The antithesis that underlies these different views seems to be between process and substance: some feel that the adviser's contribution should be to help the ruler cope with the advice reaching him from other sources; others, that the adviser should add something distinctive of his own. Practitioners, like the one quoted above, often maintain that the task of the ruler and of his line staff is difficult enough without being further complicated by advisers' attempts to insert their own views into the process, and that at the top of government the need for speed in decision-making is so great that the costs incurred by delays caused by advisers are usually unacceptable. From this follows the view that the adviser's task should mainly be to reduce to the smallest feasible number the various viewpoints and options confronting the ruler. In West Germany, Chancellor Schmidt had inherited from his predecessor an advisory structure which more or less precisely mirrored the line departments, and which generated a second separate and often distinct stream of advice. After some months, Schmidt insisted on being given only a single consolidated stream of advice. He indicated that he saw the job of his staff as being to offer views that did not conflict with, but rather complemented, those of departments. In effect, they should help the latter to do things that they could not do by themselves.

Others at the conference felt that the adviser's role should go well beyond that of simply orchestrating, in neutral mode, advice coming from other sources. Advisers should indeed do this where feasible, but where necessary should go further and express positive views of their own. A weakness of the British CPRS was its propensity to ask too many questions and to supply too few answers.

This raised the question of whether analysis impeded decision-making. Even if it were accepted that decision-making should be preceded by analysis, and by a stage in which a large number of options were posed and considered, rulers have to be capable of moving from the analytical to the decision-making mode. They also have to be capable of moving in the other direction: to recognize when a particular course of action has failed and the time has come to begin an analytical process and to confront other options. A celebrated case of a ruler's inability to do this occurred in British government in the 1960s, when the option of devaluing sterling had been so totally ruled out by the prime minister that it was not allowed even to be discussed. Advisers could help rulers to recognize the need for such a change of mode. They could and should also occasionally help by preventing rulers from taking decisions or becoming personally involved in situations from which they could not be extricated without damage; some rulers have shown a dangerous propensity to play a leading part in completely inappropriate activities, such as negotiating with terrorists.

A final set of relationships discussed at the conference were those between rulers and their advisers on the one hand, and external sources of advice, such as universities, on the other. Two different questions seemed to arise here. First, could such external advisers be an adequate substitute for internal advisers, including civil servants? Second, were there in any case adequate channels of communication between governments and external sources? The answers to both questions would seem as so often, to be country-specific. In some countries the 'external' advisory community is relatively small or under-developed, and governments correspondingly rely heavily on internal advisers and on the civil service in particular. (A variant of this is where a particular political party does not have close links with, or strong support among, the academic community: in opposition or in office it thus has to find other sources of advice.) Elsewhere the crucial variable is the relative status of the different groups. A contrast might be made here between France and the United States: in France the status of civil servants is in general very high, much higher than that of academics, and as a result governments rely relatively little on the latter. In the United States the positions are reversed, in all respects.

Whatever the status of external sources of advice, a perennial problem is ensuring that their advice is timely and relevant to the needs of rulers. Academics and governments do not share a common culture. Few academics see it as their responsibility to support governments: rather, it is to criticize them. Briefing external advisers can be expensive in resources, and there is always the risk that when their advice is available it will be leaked to the media. In countries with a powerful culture of official secrecy even consulting academics can create problems. For all these reasons, it is often more satisfactory to change their status, and to bring them into government, as internal advisers, on short-term contracts.

10

Institutionalization and Informality in Advisory Systems

Colin Seymour-Ure

Do advisory systems work better when institutionalized or when left informal? Of the two, informality strikes at first the happier chord; it connotes easiness, responsiveness, adaptability. Institutionalization, however, should not be confused with the opposites. Institutions do not have to be unresponsive and inflexible. Equally, 'informal' arrangements may in fact be a shambles.

The key to institutionalization is that relationships are made explicit. An institutional system of advice will involve the explicit, formal definition and regulation of tasks, procedures and responsibilities for the advisers, and of their relationships with each other and with those whom they advise. Of course, the definitions may be poor and the system is most unlikely to work in practice exactly as it is prescribed. Even so, the basic recognition of a distinct advisory function is unlikely to be lost, whereas under informal arrangements, the distinction can be lost easily. 'Advice' may become inseparable from decision-taking; advisers may nominally have other functions. Informality means an implicit downgrading of the notion of advice as a distinct function; it is the friend of secretiveness, of the *éminence grise*, and of government which blurs political, non-partisan and specialist advice.

The problems and advantages of institutionalization in principle affect every aspect of advice. In practice, argument can be focused on five headings: the range of advice; the scale of advisory systems; the status of advisers; continuity of advice; and adaptation and flexibility.

The Range of Advice

Some types of advice lend themselves better to institutionalization than others. Advice given by central coordinating bodies such as the British Cabinet Office, the PMC in Australia, the PCO in Canada and the Chancellor's Office in West Germany, is an integral part of their function of 'facilitating' decisions. One would expect advice coming up from the departments to be more easily accommodated than external advice. External advice may be limited by constraints on short-term secondment of outsiders to government, as in West Germany and Britain. Or where it is the advice rather than the adviser that is wanted, there may be problems of selection and mediation. Forecasts by the Council of Economic Advisers in the United States used virtually to have the field to themselves in the early 1960s. Now nearly every department or agency is equipped to challenge them and there is a welter of outside economic advisers besides. On a different scale of magnitude, the Israeli prime minister is faced with an equally bewildering range of academics and journalists offering economic advice – and with the task of deciding how to choose an official adviser to act as a filter. In West Germany the government supports five university institutes to provide sources of outside advice.

Science policy is another area in which external advice can be institutionalized by a variety of methods. At one end are government-funded research bodies such as the French CNRS. At the other are networks of consultative committees and individual advisers. In a field such as this, involving matters of great potential long-term significance, the status of an individual adviser may be valuable in itself as an important symbol lending legitimacy to a policy decision.

But even where external advice can be smoothly incorporated into a routine, the problem will still in principle have arisen about how to organize the advice so that the 'right questions' get asked. In science this is a familiar dilemma, since research about the 'unknown' has to be organized on the basis only of the known. Put more generally, the problem is of institutionalizing advice without eliminating spontaneity. Leaders tend to like the idea of spontaneous advice: it implies open-mindedness and fresh ideas. Although it seems intrinsically associated with informality, it can be provided for in formal structures too. Particular individuals can be guaranteed rights of access, for instance. One of the conventional measures of a US president is whether he has an 'open door' policy like Franklin Roosevelt and J. F. Kennedy, or whether he restricts access through a chief of staff, as did Richard Nixon. In Canada the rule for some years has been that cabinet ministers are assured an appointment with the prime minister on the day they request it. In West Germany the President of the Central Bank (a statutorily independent body) takes part in certain cabinet business, though without a vote. Spontaneity can be built in on a collective basis, too, by highly formal initiatives such as Australian premier Hawke's economic summit, held in the Canberra Parliament House shortly after he took office, and by *ad hoc* meetings or brain-storming sessions. (The latter, if timetabled, are likely to be jettisoned – in Downing Street at least – if more practical issues arise.)

But there is an inescapable element of unpredictability – randomness even – in the idea of spontaneity, which defies complete institutionalization. It blurs functional boundaries and formal procedures. It links with the psychology of leadership and the personality of particular leaders. 'Let me have men about me that are fat', says Julius Caesar. At the court of a modern ruler (about which George Reedy, for instance, wrote revealingly for Lyndon Johnson's presidency in *The Twilight of the Presidency*) the preferences of different personalities will determine the occasions for spontaneous advice, and 'advice' itself will dissolve into a swirl of other activities that vary, no doubt, with the issues of the moment. Not least, the kind of adviser who is personally close to the ruler, and with whom the ruler likes to unwind, must be a good listener – someone who receives confidences as well as gives them, and to whom anything, indeed, can be said. Even notoriously isolated rulers such as Richard Nixon have retained confidants in their retinue.

A special case of spontaneous advice is that which is required in an emergency. Crises are defined less by events than by governments' reactions to them. In their nature, though, their course is uncertain, even if sometimes their occurrence is not. The formalization of advice in advance is almost bound to be of limited value. The Treasury War Book in Britain used to contain (and perhaps still does) a sentence on these lines: 'In the event of an outbreak of hostilities, expenditure divisions will immediately inform the Estimates Clerk of the likely cost of the war.' The instruction epitomizes the problem. Crisis management almost by definition requires expediency. In the five most critical decisions of the Trudeau years, Professor Dror has suggested, the formal decision-making machinery was not substantially involved at all. Having said that, however, it is irrational for government not to try to learn from experience. After the 1977 terrorism in West Germany, for instance, the Chancellor's Office set up a crisis management system. The War Cabinet machinery during the Falklands crisis showed signs of learning from the experience of the Suez Crisis of 1956, including the provision for long-term analysis by the recently retired head of the Foreign Office, Sir Michael Palliser.

Long-term advice of all kinds is inherently difficult to build into the machinery. Government at the centre is a 'pressure cooker environment'. Senior civil servants in the British Cabinet Office operate within a two- or three-month time span. No elected chief executive can be expected to think far beyond the next election – if that far. (A US president, of course, is constitutionally limited anyway to two terms.) The British Central Policy Review Staff tried long-term thinking, and its establishment was an unusually premeditated piece of planning – but one of the difficulties that led to its abolition was precisely the clash between dispassionate long-term analysis and the political realities of the short-run context in which its advice was received. The report on long-term public expenditure options which occasioned its abolition arguably made Mrs Thatcher's government afraid of being locked in to positions that were intended purely for discussion.

Although there are exceptions, such as some of the work done in the French foreign ministry or the Commissariat du Plan, long-term advice thus tends to be informal or, more probably, left to outside organizations. In this way, issues may be put on the agenda without prejudicing outcomes. Apart from that, opposition, it can be argued, is surely the place where parliamentary politicians do their long-term thinking. A government might also perhaps set up a Royal Commission, but the fact that these, historically, have been used in most Westminster models as a means of procrastination, shows exactly how ill adjusted governments are to long-term thinking.

If types of advice lend themselves differentially to institutionalization, some advice is unlikely to reach its target at all unless it is institutionalized. Broadly, this may be defined as 'non-establishment' advice. At the centre, government is always most likely to be exposed to conventional wisdom. Today's heresy is tomorrow's orthodoxy: but the trouble is, not *all* of today's heresies are, and the problem is to spot which. This is as much a problem about expert as about partisan and political advice. At the extreme, it is a problem of ensuring that rulers do not hear only the advice they want to hear. An apt analogy here, as Professor Dror points out, is that of Ulysses and the Sirens. Like Ulysses, rulers ought to bind themselves to ensure that they do not give way to temptation – in this case, to shut out unwelcome advice. Such exclusion may lead to what Janis, in a study of presidential policy-making about Cuba, styled 'groupthink'[1] the kind of tunnel vision that reduces a government's range of perceived options. In a stronger form it may mean the deliberate suppression of currently unfashionable ideas, rather as Harold Wilson imposed a taboo in 1966 upon Whitehall discussion of sterling devaluation as a policy option. While the heretical idea may indeed be implanted informally in just such 'spontaneous' circumstances as have been described as like a kingly court, this must depend on the court containing someone with both the necessary opinion and the authority to voice it. (In many societies this has been a function of the court jester, who in reality was often nobody's fool.) To rely on informal arrangements for the tendering of discordant advice is to take a risk: better that it should come from an established institution.

The Scale of Advisory Systems

The relation between the institutionalization and the scale of advice necessarily features in a discussion of governments of differing size and complexity. In the smallest government, arguably some degree of institutionalization is unavoidable, especially if a broad view of the nature of advice is taken. There is almost bound to be a coordinating role, of a chief of staff or cabinet secretary kind, which will involve routines and procedures for a leader's conduct of business in which advice will form a part. What starts informally may generally become formalized, as may be said of the developing arrangements during the incumbency of a US president or the evolution of the Cabinet Office and, most recently, the idea of the prime minister's Policy Unit in Downing Street.

If the system is large enough, the coordinating function will involve the presence of an intermediate level of organization between leader and advisers. This is commonly in the form of a mirror system, in which the structure of departments is reflected in the structure of the coordinating body. The interplay between a department and its mirror representative is likely to be extremely subtle, and formal arrangements – such as the practice in Canada of having the officials in the PCO at a rank at least one level below those with whom they deal in the departments – are no doubt only a partial guide to actual working relationships. In West Germany, for instance, the mirror units are small, accumulate considerable experience and have the last word to the chancellor about departmental matters. So although they have no constitutional power to make departments do what the chancellor wants, they have great leverage.

As that example shows, in the process of predigesting and orchestrating advice, a coordinating body acts as a gatekeeper to the leader. Beyond that, there is a tendency for it to share – some would say usurp – the leader's decision-making role. This allegedly happens with presidential decisions in France, where the Secretary-General of the Cabinet is a key figure. In the United States the chiefs of staff of Eisenhower (Sherman Adams), Nixon (H. R. Haldeman) and Reagan (James Baker), for instance, clearly pre-empted or shaped decisions by their regulation of the form and flow of business.

A large system is likely to face, too, the traditional problems of scale. To some outsiders the elaborate system of advice built up at the centre in Canada during the Trudeau years seemed over-elaborate, an example of 'hyper-organization'. In Britain, the system of Policy Analysis and Review (PAR) arguably became a victim of the same tendency: it made too much work with too few results. The US presidency is notorious for its difficulties in constructing effective agencies for liaison with the bureaucracy (in particular, say, the State Department). In addition to over-organization, central bodies may develop the bureaucratic vices of serving their self-interest (the CPRS was thought to have been 'captured' by the civil service, for example), and of loss of direction and control.

The Status of Advisers

To say advisers 'usurp' decision-making implies impropriety. A chief feature of the institutionalization of advice is that such matters are made explicit and the intentions of working arrangements are clear.

How far, for example, should advisers be involved in decision-making and, beyond that, in implementation? If advising and deciding tend in practice to become blurred, then the only way of keeping them separate may be to construct institutions for that purpose. In Australia, Britain and Canada, to take three parliamentary models, partisan and non-partisan advice are sharply differentiated by different structures, and each can be kept out of decisions for which they are not required. The chief arguments for letting advice mingle with decision-taking are, first, the claim that the distinction between the two is arbitrary: the process of decision is a seamless web or continuum – a claim which assertions about 'usurping' serve to support. Second, responsibility for executing decisions based on their advice helps advisers to keep in touch with the issues concerned; it improves their motivation and commitment (an important consideration in the United States, where power, in the conventional phrase, is the power to persuade); and it helps to reduce the risk of decisions being diluted further along the line. Against that, it may be argued that advice is a staff not a line function; that advisers should be involved in establishing criteria for implementation but not in the implementation itself; and that they should, in effect, stick to their specialities (technical, partisan, procedural and so on) rather than muddy their advice through participation in some process of synthesis.

Institutionalizing advice enables other distinctions and relationships to be kept similarly clear. One is the crucial matter of access – be it to the leader or, almost as important, to papers. The institution of an advisory body necessarily requires some indication of its authority – or an indication that it will be left to sink or swim. The authority of the CPRS, when it was established, was signalled by its director's right of access to the prime minister. The institution has an advantage over the individual adviser here. However much the individual may in theory enjoy an explicit right of access, in practice he is more likely to be shunted into a siding than the representatives of an institutional part of the advisory process. Thus, the prestige attached to ministers' individual political advisers in Britain has probably been rather greater than their access and impact on events. In office, the political adviser can easily become just a speech-writer.

Jockeying for access is an important part of the game in the White House; and from the United States no doubt comes the imagery of the 'turf' which is often used to describe the importance of institutionalization in establishing another key element in an effective advisory system – the definition of a sense of identity and of the ground within which advisers work. If there is tension between line administrators and advisers, for example, a clear definition of their territory at least gives the advisers a minimum basis of authority. It was thus important that the CPRS was not seen simply to be 'second-guessing' the departments in its particular studies; and that Mrs Thatcher's Policy Unit emerged, clearly, in the words of one member, as 'custodian of the strategy', with a distinct, political (though not strictly partisan) orientation that was quite different from the Whitehall bias of the CPRS.

On a larger scale, the claim that Britain should institute a Prime Minister's Department can be based on the argument that the functional boundaries of the Cabinet Office have become unclear and should be newly delineated, for it acts both as processor of business for the cabinet and adviser to the prime minister – yet presently as a somewhat half-baked version of the PCO in Canada or the PMC in Australia. In the United States, again, the establishment of an office in the White House for the vice president, an intrinsically weak post, can be seen as a modest accretion of authority. In West Germany, Chancellor Brandt strengthened the advice of social scientists in a system traditionally dominated by lawyers when he set up in 1969 a planning division (chiefly staffed by social scientists) which subsequently increased its leverage by developing its own 'mirror organization' of the departments, paralleling the existing arrangements within the Chancellor's Office. (Chancellor Schmidt later brought the two into line.)

Beyond this, institutionalization can improve the effectiveness of a system of advice in a number of other ways. It may help to secure 'multiple advocacy', for instance, by defining proper spheres for different sources of advice. Thus the staffs of some American presidents have acted as brokers in a competition of ideas. 'Never be the captive of a single system' is an axiom widely shared, and institutionalization facilitates the accountability of advisers, at least in the sense that their activity is to some extent openly defined and acknowledged. Even apparently trivial matters are affected, such as advice being more likely to be written down in an institutionalized system than given orally. Predictably this idea appeals most to those with experience of such complex arrangements as those prevailing in Canada and America, where commitment to paper is seen as imposing clarity and saving time.

In general, then, institutionalization of their status appears to be a source of strength to advisers in all but the most simple systems. But two notes of warning might be sounded. First, the practice can arouse exaggerated expectations of what advisers may achieve. Second, it may focus hostility, jealousy and suspicion. The latter may be roused by the very prospect of setting up an advisory system, as may perhaps have happened in Greece or Portugal. The idea of a Prime Minister's Department in Britain creates equal suspicion in some minds. In Washington both tendencies have been present over the years in attitudes to the expansion of the Executive Office of the President. This has both helped fuel expectations of what the president can do and in many areas has produced tensions between the White House and the departments.

Continuity of Advice

To one particular function, the continuity of advice – widely regarded as extremely important – institutionalization is clearly crucial. While the same leader remains in office, the problems are those of swings and roundabouts. Is it best ensured by a permanent cadre of staff, or by a system of secondment? If the latter, should outsiders be brought in?

A permanent staff acquires the advantages of experience, institutional memory, know-how and *esprit de corps*. But of course it may develop a departmental point of view, if not a complacent or 'ivory tower' mentality about its competence. The lack of opportunities for secondment out of the Chancellor's Office in West Germany is a source of stress, both to individuals and to the capacity of the system to adapt to changes of party control. Equally, the arrangement whereby tours of duty in the British Cabinet Office rarely last more than four years, if that, is regarded by all concerned as a strength both to the secretariat and to the departments, who are replenished by people with experience at the centre. The embodiment of continuity, in nearly all cabinet systems, including the hybrid French, is the cabinet secretary (however named), who tends to stay in post a long time. In Britain there have been five in more than 40 years, in France, six in 40 years and in Australia, four in 26 years.

Secondment from within a unified civil service, such as the British Service, may minimize the problems of someone joining an advisory unit, but even if he fits in quickly, his temporary status is likely to be a severe brake on his authority. Outsiders, by definition, are a pressure against continuity.

The greatest importance of continuity, however, is its relation to periods of leadership transition. It is an irony that the American president is potentially most powerful at the time when he is least organized – at the start of his incumbency. In many countries the degree of discontinuity is less great because of a career civil service. Prime Ministers in Britain invariably benefit from finding a going concern in the cabinet secretariat when they take office – as do their counterparts in other parliamentary systems. They need, of course, to adapt their system of political advice to office; but the processing of decisions and the more administrative kinds of advice are assured. The same applies for individual ministers. In West Germany, similarly, there is substantial continuity in the staff of the Chancellor's Office after changes of incumbent. The impact of the new person upon staffing may not start to be felt for a year or more. In France, the extent of continuity varies. When the prime minister changes without all his colleagues changing, those who stay may take the opportunity to make changes in the composition of their *cabinets* to reflect the shifts that will probably be taking place in the government's general outlook. When a minister leaves office, the members of his *cabinet* leave with him. Given the scale of the *cabinet* system, with five hundred or more people involved, there is a great deal of change overall. The effect is lessened somewhat when an entire new government takes office by the fact that so many of the senior members, politicians and civil servants alike, and regardless of political colour, share the common background of an *haut-fonctionnaire* and a training in the ENA. This was less true at the start of the Mitterrand administration but was seen to be reverting with the passage of time.

It is worth noting, lastly, that quite apart from its substantive value for a new leader, continuity of advisers can be a convenient way of signalling continuity of methods or goals. This is especially true in the United States and applies to relationships between offices – and even to their physical location – as well as to persons. It applies, too, to the use of outsiders, whether 'wise old men' who have spent a lifetime as in-and-outers in Washington, or to the research institutions and think-tanks that have poliferated there.

Adaptation and Flexibility

Lastly, whenever functions are institutionalized, questions of adaptability arise. Institutions remain long after the forces that created them have disappeared. It is tempting to infer that institutions are unadaptable and that informal arrangements for advice are adaptable because of their very informality. This is probably a false inference, especially if the term 'informality' simply cloaks ill-thought-out or inappropriate practices. Even so, an institutionalized system needs, so to speak, to incorporate criteria for reorganization, if it is to avoid atrophy or loss of purpose. Failure to adjust – to changing techniques or to changing needs for advice – is the obvious danger. But adjusting unnecessarily may be just as inefficient, for 'when we reorganize we bleed', as a British civil servant put it. Reorganization has costs, such as loss of institutional memory and adverse impact on morale. On the analogy of spending money to save money, reorganization is positively harmful if its object is not fulfilled.

What, then, are the warning signals? Practitioners offer rules of thumb. For example, 'It is time to reorganize when those involved are becoming more concerned with procedures than with substance'; or (in West Germany) when comparable advisory units acquire highly uneven workloads. These may be fair comments on particular cases. More generally the practice of secondment, from within or outside the bureaucracy, is an obvious source of flexibility, especially in matters of technique. Above all, though, the measure of an advisory system's need to adapt must be its relevance to the leader's role. One reason why advice machinery is continually adapted in the United States is that each new president, to use the textbook phrase, writes his own job description.

For the advisory system, the difficulty comes if the leadership role changes unwittingly. It can be argued, for instance, that in Britain the role of the prime minister has changed in this way. The cabinet retains collective responsibility for policy but lacks a collective capacity because of overload and inadequate briefing. The prime minister is increasingly the guardian of the cabinet's strategy, responsible for steering it in the direction his or her colleagues want. Regardless of personality, a prime minister could no longer expect to be able to just hold the ring and act as a neutral chairman.

For such a role the present advisory system is arguably ill suited; it serves the cabinet efficiently, but advice – whether from ministers or political advisers – reaches the prime minister too thin and too late. Within the Downing Street system it has certainly been possible for a Cabinet Secretary himself to devote an increasing proportion of his time to the prime minister as distinct from the cabinet, but the logic of the shifting role requires, on this analysis, a more formal adaptation. The difficulties of doing so would certainly include the sort of factors mentioned above, such as morale. Prime ministers have indeed considered the idea of a Prime Minister's Department but have shied away for fear of the reactions. Relations with colleagues might well be affected; and the relations of its civil servants with the departments would undoubtedly change. Prime Ministers have preferred to leave the system to evolve, adding bits on, such as the (political) Policy Unit, and taking them off, such as the CPRS; so that if a Prime Minister's Department is created, it will be in everything but name.

The danger for advisory systems, then, is that they may fail to adapt not only to internal needs of expertise, technique and the like, but – more seriously – to changing needs of leadership. In systems where the leader's role is subject to frequent fluctuation, advisory systems seem bound to fluctuate too.

Conclusion

There can be no general guidelines about institutionalization and informality. The two should be seen in practice as a continuum. For a government as a whole, some degree of institutionalization is inevitable, whether as a result of scale or the crystallization of informal relations over time. Equally, there is always room for the spontaneous or random element – perhaps even the maverick individual – and for experiment. Machinery of government evolves, as well as being deliberately constructed. In advisory systems, just as in other parts of the fairground, it seems that there will always be swings and roundabouts.

Note

1 Irving L. Janis, *Groupthink* (Houghton Mifflin, Boston, 1982).

11
Conclusions

Yehezkel Dror

As if someone were to buy several copies of the morning paper to assure himself that what it said was true.[1]

Introduction

The contributions collected in this book well reflect some of the main problems and practices encountered in advising heads of state in selected democracies. But to appreciate fully the problems underlying various advisory arrangements as adopted in different countries, the problematic nature of advising rulers must be put into a broad, theoretical perspective. Otherwise, emphasis on acutely perceived needs may result merely in pseudo-treatments of the effect expressed by Wittgenstein in the epigraph that opens this paper. Accordingly, this discussion is devoted to a preliminary examination of some of the fundamental issues involved in providing advisory support for rulers, by considering first a basic dialectic tension inbuilt into rulership, which poses the main problem advisers face, and then considering some of the many dilemmas faced by those who advise rulers.

The term 'ruler' is anathema to contemporary linguistic preferences, as shaped by humanistic values and liberal hopes. Still, I prefer to call those who rule 'rulers', so as to emphasize a main institution of human governance, which is pivotal to this discussion. Many of the characteristics of an oriental despot differ significantly from those of democratic heads of government. In particular, hereditary rulers are a fundamental institution throughout most of history that has nearly disappeared in the contemporary world. Nevertheless, basic features are shared by all 'rulers' and these are made more explicit by frank use of that term.[2] This chapter focuses on advisers to 'top public rulers', that is heads of government; but its analysis applies, *mutatis mutandis*, to advisory supports for lesser public rulers, such as ministers, governors of provinces, mayors of cities etc. With some further adjustments, the analysis also applies to top level decision-makers in other organizations, such as business corporations.[3]

The concept of 'adviser' is a complex one and includes quite different positions and roles. Historically, the people who later became ministers and heads of departments started as advisers to rulers. In contemporary regimes, ministers serve in a triple governmental capacity (with variations, especially between presidential and parliamentary–cabinet regimes), namely: as line heads of departments; as members of a collective top-level decision-making body; and as advisers to the head of government. To move from formal to informal dimensions, every ruler is advised by many people outside his formal office, ranging from party officials to friends and various kinds of family members, not to mention the mass media, self-annointed prophets etc. I am dealing here with a delimited kind of adviser, namely the officials in the office of the ruler, whose main function is to serve as advisers to the head of government. Despite significant differences between countries and changes with time in each country, I have adopted a general theoretical approach to the subject, rejecting historicism and trying to identify and analyse basic features shared by all structures of advisers to rulers.[4]

Methodologically, in addition to historical and comparative studies, this study is based on consultative field investigations of 35 offices of heads of governments, on close work with advisers to rulers in intense workshops on policy analysis and policy planning conducted in 16 countries, on intensive interviews with a large number of advisers and a limited number of rulers in different countries, and on serving as a long-term 'authentic adviser cum ethnograph'[5] in proximity to rulers and their advisers in two countries.[6]

Rulers and advisers belong to the Ur-core-components of human governance, as developed some 5,000 years ago or perhaps earlier. The very fact that key features of relations between rulers and advisers have not changed very much during that period[7] despite their many inadequacies, indicates that this is a rigid relationship with limited plasticity, unless some breakthrough occurs in the materials and ideas out of which this relationship is formed. The limited variety of contemporary arrangements for advising heads of governments, the instability of such advisory relations and the serious difficulties faced by all presently known options for structuring advisory supports for top decision-makers[8], further reinforce the conjecture that structural weaknesses are inherent in advisory relations with rulers and that a way to eliminate them is neither known nor applied. Indeed, ruler–adviser relations can serve as a paradigmatic illustration of fundamental reasons for incapacity to govern, which are, to speak metaphorically, 'congenital' to institutions of governance as human artefacts in their present phase of evolution.[9]

As already stated, I have adopted a broad theoretical approach. This discussion tries to go beyond institutional realities, as described in other contributions to this volume, and to explore deep factors that shape advisory realities and pose a challenge for their improvement. First, I shall provide the setting by exploring the fundamental dialectic relationship between the crucial need for rulers on the one hand and their inherent defects on the other, with advisers serving as one of the attempts to overcome this dilemma. The second section then looks at some of the main inbuilt contradictions and paradoxes of the advisory relationship itself and examines their nature and implications as well as some of the efforts to overcome them. Finally, some principles for the redesign of advisory systems for rulers are briefly outlined.[10] It is hoped that the theoretical perspective thus provided may serve to supplement the papers collected in this volume and provide an additional framework of appreciation[11] for considering the realities and dilemmas they have discussed.

The Fundamental Dialectics of Rulership

Any attempt at a deep analysis of the workings of advisers to rulers must be embedded within a broad and comprehensive theory of rulership. Despite continuous fascination with the subject and proliferating literature dealing with it, modern social sciences are still far from understanding the facts of political leadership and their real dynamics. Therefore, an essential basis for a sound theory of advisorship to rulers remains underdeveloped.

To overcome this handicap somewhat and provide a basis for in-depth treatment of advisers to rulers, at least one dimension of a general theory of rulership must first be worked out, namely the fundamental contradiction inbuilt into rulership which poses the main challenge to advising rulers. This contradiction can be conveniently and sharply presented with the help of a dialectic schema, without any of the metaphysical assumptions that often accompany it. The fundamental dialectics of rulership presents the thesis that rulers are important and, often, crucial while the antithesis is that rulers are defective. Advisers themselves are an important attempt at synthesis.

Rulers are Important

Without going into the philosophical debate on the role of individual rulers in history,[12] within a study-of-government perspective rulers are clearly important. In the contemporary scene, the least that can be said reliably is that no tendency for rulers to become less important can be discerned. This is the case not only in Third World and Communist countries, but also in democracies, where I think rulers tend to become more rather than less important. Rulers make a difference, even though they are constrained by many forces and institutions.[13]

A number of factors seem to be at work to build up the importance of rulers in Western democracies, as a general trend subject to local variations and individual accidents. These include, among others: the effects of the mass media, which focus attention on heads of governments; features of political culture, which increase the role of rulers in fulfilling mass psychological needs[14] and increase their electoral impact, which in turn strengthens their intra-party and public power; the growing role of summit meetings; and increasing problems of power politics which make rulers more important as power brokers. When the pivotal importance of rulers during crisis decision-making is added to the picture, their importance seems beyond doubt.[15]

These reasons for the very importance of rulers are accompanied by a growing functional necessity for relatively strong rulers in democracies.[16] The inter-departmental and pan-governmental nature of modern-day problems augment the essential coordination and integration functions of heads of government; the necessity for structural adjustments up to 'creative destruction'[17] requires power concentrations; and requirements for innovation and necessary policy entrepreneurship demand centres of government not caught in departmental interests.

These are only some illustrations of functional needs tending to increase the importance of rulers in democracies.[18] This is an important conclusion, to jump ahead to a later argument, because it limits the usefulness of reducing the importance of rulers as a main strategy for reducing the impact of their inbuilt defects. Rather, it increases the importance of upgrading the performance of advisers to rulers as a means of improving the production function of rulership in respect of expanding essential and desirable functions.

The causal and functional causes combine to make rulers very important in democracies, both as a matter of fact and as an unavoidable functional requirement of the adequate capacity to govern.

Rulers are Defective

The full and disturbing ramifications of the thesis that rulers are significant and are seeming to become more so are revealed by juxtaposing it with the antithesis that rulership suffers from serious inbuilt defects. This is a very important conjecture for our subject, because advisers can largely be analysed in terms of their function to counterbalance and offset the defects and limitations of their bosses. Therefore, the idea of 'inherent defects' of rulers needs clarification and demonstration.

The conjecture is that rulership as a role suffers from 'congenital defects' and inbuilt 'professional deformations'. Different individual rulers are more or less susceptible to various defects, within a statistical range, but no human being is completely immune to the error-producing effects of rulership. Weaknesses of reason shared by all human beings provide fertile ground for the development of the defect-producing effects of rulership. Moreover, typical career patterns of rulers may further increase their vulnerability to role-inherent defects.[19]

These inherent defects include the following:[20]

1   Quantitative work overload, with many ritual activities taking up a great deal of time and energy and super-saturated decision agendas producing great fatigue.

2   Qualitative overload, with perplexing quandaries combining with time pressures to result in stress. Such stress tends to cause decay in decision quality, leading to confused policy behaviour and policy convulsions.[21]

3   Strain and stress, which produce particularly dangerous defects in crisis decision-making, where important and sometimes momentous choices have to be made under extreme stress and distress.[22] The exigency of possible nuclear conflict is an extreme, but potentially fateful illustration of nearly impossible demands being made on human rulers under crisis conditions.[23]

4   Court politics and the 'corridors of power' syndrome, with a constant struggle for access to the ruler and for gate-control, which easily becomes mind-control. As time and attention are among the scarcest of the ruler's resources, court politics significantly influence and often distort his world pictures and options. The tendency of rulers to mismanage their time and attention resources further aggravates this defect.[24]

5   A preponderance of positive feedback. Deference to the ruler and often fear of him, as well as court politics and competition for his support, result unavoidably in the ruler's being surrounded by 'mirrors on the wall' which tend constantly to tell him how wise he is and how well realities fit his biases and prejudices. People who tell an emperor that he is without clothes have a very short survival expectancy at most courts! As a result, world pictures held by rulers tend to become increasingly distorted, while rulers tend to become increasingly estranged from reality and their self-esteem becomes over-inflated.

6   Option manipulation, which can involve overly limited options being presented to rulers, often with 'railroading', such as presenting a number of options in such a way as to support a single favoured one.

7   The pomp and ritual surrounding rulers, which also occurs in many democratic countries,[25] cannot but further distort perception of reality and augment ego-hypertrophy.

The impact of such defects of rulership are enhanced by the decision modes prevalent near rulers, such as 'groupthink'.[26] More fundamentally, the defects of rulership are based on decision-making weaknesses of human beings in general, which are brought to the fore and exacerbated by the situations of rulership and interact with the latter synergistically.

Three types of weakness in human decision-making in relation to the special situation of rulers[27] may serve to illustrate their effects on rulership defects.

1   Incompetence, in the sense of lacking knowledge and skills needed for good performance, even though these in principle are available and learnable. For instance, knowledge of economics, of social issues and of defence matters is essential for most rulers. Similarly, some knowledge of correct protocols for decision-making in the face of uncertainty is needed.[28] But the background of many rulers makes it unlikely that they bring with them more than at best partial knowledge of such matters;[29] and pressures of time as well as 'closed minds',[30] trained incapacities and predispositions make it difficult for many rulers to acquire such knowledge during their period in office. All these barriers to the reduction of incompetence are reinforced by the whole situation of rulership as discussed above, which reduces incentives for learning and makes correct learning difficult.[31]

2   'Motivated irrationality', in the sense of 'hot' reasoning, in which rationality is impaired by strong feelings, wishes, desires, emotions, hopes, fears and similar affective forces. As the activities of rulers are loaded with such 'hot' elements, motivated irrationality can be assumed to play an important role in downgrading the quality of rulers' performance.

3   'Perversions of reason', with the human mind and human reasoning suffering from many inbuilt propensities for error which assure mistakes. Over-reliance on salient but weak pieces of evidence, reverting to early 'framing' of issues as conditioning the search for solutions, and stubborn clinging to a solution once decided upon despite the emergence of rationally overwhelming counter-evidence, are but three perversions of reason. Dependence on subjective and doubtful 'attribution theories',[32] 'operational code beliefs'[33] and rigid 'cognitive maps'[34] constitute other types of perversion of reason. The propensities for error of the human mind when facing uncertainty are particularly malignant for rulers.[35] As nearly all situations handled by rulers are loaded with uncertainties, and as 'policy-gambling' is a main task of rulers,[36] perversions of reason in processing and coping with uncertainty illustrate well the extremely grave impacts on rulers' performance of universal perversions of reason. Another relevant illustration is the use and misuse of historical metaphors,[37] which is an insidious weakness of rulers, who frequently deal with situations where historical analogues are much relied upon.

Human beings differ in their susceptibility to the various kinds of irrationalities and propensities for error. Therefore, it is relevant to ponder whether the career patterns of rulers demonstrate that people who are relatively immune to the congenital defects of rulership are brought to the top, or rather those who are especially prone to all the dejects just discussed.

Present knowledge provides no answer, and does not support more than preliminary hypotheses. Simplistic notions on the characteristics of 'high-performance' rulers are very doubtful,[38] while 'common sense' psychological assumptions on 'normality' as desirable for rulers and similar 'humanistic' views of 'suitable' rulers[39] are contradicted by clear-cut cases of 'abnormal' rulers who have performed well[40] as well as by some theory.[41] No realistic profile of rulers and their recruitment has provided reasons to expect much hardening against most of the defects of rulership. A greater immunity against some weaknesses may assure increased susceptibility to others. Thus, charismatic capacities[42] may contradict 'cold' rational reasoning. Different leadership types fit various conditions,[43] but all are very susceptible to many of the defects inbuilt into rulership.

It is doubtful whether the typical career patterns of rulers prepare them for the rulership position. The nature of political competition in democracies emphasizes criteria that have little correlation with qualities needed for some of the main tasks of rulers, especially policy-making.[44] The very success in climbing up the political ladder and reaching the top may further increase susceptibility to the defects of rulership, for instance by strengthening self-assurance and by reinforcing world pictures and making the ruler a captive of autobiographical realities that do not meet rulership requirements and which reduce learning abilities.[45]

However weak such 'daring' conjectures may be,[46] they put the burden of refutation onto any contrary claim. There seems to be no basis for assuming that typical career patterns of rulers bring to the fore persons unusually endowed and equipped to withstand the performance-corrupting factors inbuilt into rulership. Unless and until the contrary is at least convincingly claimed, the safer assumption is to operate as if persons becoming rulers are quite susceptible to all the defects inherent in that role.

The conjecture that continuous occupation of a rulership position may increase defects, because of the accumulative effects of the inbuilt error-producing factors, further aggravates the emerging assessment. Reality pictures may become more and more distorted, self-criticism may be increasingly stifled, inputs may become more manipulated to fit the likes and dislikes of the ruler and so on.

Even if each of the above conjectures is open to debate, their aggregation strongly supports the conclusion that rulership suffers from serious inbuilt defects. True, an exaggerated image of the inherent defects of rulership and the consequent incompetence of rulers should be avoided. History shows many rulers who, all in all, have been very successful because of the quality of their performance, as distinct from chance. Also, a number of studies do indicate that human beings can develop skills, intuitions and tacit knowledge which permit them to overcome error-propensities and to perform well in the face of complexity and uncertainty.[47] But, empirical data on the behaviour of many rulers supports the analytical finding that errors are endemic to rulership.[48]

Even if sometimes the net performance of rulers is very positive, all rulers still make many errors that should be reduced. The growing potential costs of errors by rulers, errors that are now implemented with more powerful policy instruments, the social aspirations for high achievements by governments despite adverse conditions, the increasing difficulties of the challenges faced by governments and their rulers, and the intensified competition between Western democracy and other forms of regime and culture on their role in the future of humanity, all these give added importance and urgency to the search for improvements in the performance of democratic rulers.

Attempts at Synthesis

Improvement of the performance of rulers in ways that reduce their errors while not impairing their important functions: this is the task of synthesis aimed at overcoming the dynamic contradiction between the thesis and the antithesis, as discussed above. This difficult task is at the centre of human endeavours to improve governance.

The repertory of designs for improving the performance of rulers, as developed and tried throughout the history of governance, in various combinations, is quite diverse, but limited in its success. It includes constitutional limits on the power of rulers, changes in the selection mechanism of rulers, efforts to prepare future rulers better for their tasks, attempts to do away with rulers by substituting various collective decision-making bodies, multiple forms of accountability and incentive systems for rulers, moral guardians institutionalized at the courts of rulers, codes of ethics and visions to guide rulers, learning opportunities for rulers and the 'mirror-of-the-prince' genre of books. An additional main approach to improving the performance of rulers is the restructuring of their advisory supports.

Within efforts to upgrade the performance of rulers a distinction can be made between external 'bridles'[49] imposed on rulers, such as the 'rule of law', on the one hand, and attempts to enhance their performance by changing as it were the internal wiring of the 'rulership black box' on the other. Much of constitutional history and contemporary political theory alike concentrates on bridling rulers. But the end of this road may well have been reached in democracies because essential functions of rulers must not be impaired by further limitations on the authority and power of heads of governments. On the contrary, some strengthening of heads of government may be necessary in some democracies with relatively weak power centres, so as to meet present and expected policy predicaments, as already discussed. Therefore, upgrading rulers' performance in ways that deal directly with their operations and augment their capacity to fulfil their functions less defectively are all the more important. Hence, the importance of advisers to rulers as a main avenue for coping with the dialectic contradiction of rulership and for improving the quality of rulership performance without impairing its necessary power and authority and unduly inhibiting its perhaps expanding essential functions.[50]

The restructuring or redesign, perhaps even the design from new of structures of advisory support to rulers should be engaged in within a comprehensive approach to the improvement of rulership, with attention to all its dimensions. This, in turn, should be done within a broad perspective of upgrading the central minds of governments as a whole, and indeed all of governance.[51] But, given the special importance of rulership, improvement efforts focusing on improving advisory staffs to rulers are worthwhile and feasible, as long as a broader view is kept in mind.

Conflicts Facing Advisers to Rulers

Some of the necessary perspective for going beyond mere tinkering is provided, it is to be hoped, by the functional view of advisers to rulers as artefacts for overcoming the dialectic contradiction between the importance of rulership on one hand and the inherent defects of rulership on the other. But in order to improve systems of advice in a significant way, another set of deep factors must be examined, namely the inherent conflicts within the advisory function. It would be interesting to consider the psychological dimensions of these role conflicts, but lack of empirical material would make this too speculative an endeavour.[52] Instead, eight main areas of possible conflict will be looked at in a structural–functional way, with some comments on the possibilities for handling them.

'Cold' Inputs versus Emotional Support

Rulers are in great need of emotional support, because of the loneliness and dilemma of their situation[53] and the pressures to which they are subjected. Emotional support is not only a subjective need, but is objectively necessary to permit rulers to perform well. Therefore, a main function of advisers is to serve as 'friends' to rulers and to provide such support.[54] The absence of tension-reducing and support-providing historical court positions, such as court jesters and court priests, from the entourage of modern rulers[55] makes supply of emotional support all the more important a function for advisers to rulers. A possible variation is for advisers to fulfil a clinical function, in the psychological and psychoanalytical senses of that term.[56]

As against emotional support, however, advisers are charged with providing 'cold' inputs, in the sense of objective estimates and professional analysis, the content of which is not adjusted to the emotional needs of the recipient or to his possible emotional reaction. Some of the dilemmas posed by this seeming paradox are brought out by the following questions.

1   Should advisers provide inputs that are correct but will cause emotional damage to the ruler, reducing his overall performance?

2   Should advisers provide inputs that are correct but will make the adviser and his future inputs less acceptable to the ruler?

3   What about situations where the ruler is better left with an incorrect world picture, for instance in order to increase his efforts to achieve the improbable aided by self-fulfilling prophecy dynamics?

4   Should advisers to rulers engage in clinical and educational efforts to upgrade the capacity of a ruler to accept unpleasant inputs, to 'exit the system' and to cool his hot reactions?

5   To pursue the last question a little further, should advisers explicitly or implicitly sensitize a ruler to motivated irrationalities and thus try to reduce their hold over the ruler?

These issues condition the advisory role as an institution: the advisory system has to be structured and operated so as to handle the contradiction between providing emotional support and proffering cold inputs, both of which are needed for enhancing the performance of rulers.

Actual efforts to handle this dilemma are diverse and, largely, informal. Highly structured decision preparation procedures and formalized inputs, such as intelligence reports, are mainly 'cold' in their nature, even if known preferences of rulers are often taken into account, whether to spare his emotions or for reasons of 'court politics'. This applies mainly to the outer circle of advisers. The inner circle has to face the ruler and his personality needs from close up and probably tends to avoid 'cold' inputs when they may cause negative impacts and reactions.

Provision of emotional support is often a matter of personal accident, as well as the realm of individual advisers who build up close personal relations with the ruler. The habit of rulers to bring in as advisers some friends with whom they feel comfortable and who provide emotional support is often an inadequate solution and one carrying the risk of serious dangers if such persons serve too much as 'mind-keepers' of the ruler.

The history of court priests demonstrates that institutional efforts to provide necessary emotional support to rulers are conceivable, such as the inclusion of psychological advisers in the ruler's staff, perhaps in a camouflaged way. But at present such ideas are seldom acceptable. This is a domain where innovations in advisory systems are required, so as to meet rulers' needs for emotional support without over-diluting the 'cold' input functions of the advisory system as a whole.

Politics and Policy, Ideology and Morals, the Ruler's Career and Image

The conflict of interest between policy and politics in advice-giving is a well-known one, often handled structurally by differentiating between a larger outer office, mainly or entirely staffed by civil servants, and an inner office, mainly or entirely staffed by advisers chosen by the ruler because of their political and personal loyalty. But this arrangement does not solve the problem, as 'policy' and 'politics' cannot be isolated from one another[57] and have to be integrated in different mixes. As a matter of fact, outer offices of rulers do take political considerations into account, even if some civil servants loudly deny it; and many inner cicles engage in some fusion between politics and policy.

Another function of advisers to rulers, which adds a further dimension to this discussion, is to have regard to the personal career of the ruler and, which is not exactly the same, to his public relations and mass-media image. The latter, in turn, has important emotional impacts, as advice on handling the mass media often constitutes a 'hot' input to rulers, going far beyond any possible real impact on the career of the ruler, or on policy feasibility etc.[58]

All rulers in Western democracies have public relations advisers and this function tends to grow.[59] Its introduction into advisory structures causes many difficulties and tensions.[60] Conflict between mass-media advisers and other advisers is unavoidable, unless mass-media and public image considerations dominate the thinking of all advisers. The policy-creating effects of public relations activities, such as the shaping of policies and the influencing of the ruler's mind through speech-writing, further complicate this area of conflict.

We should add here mention of the function of advisers to serve as the 'conscience' of the ruler. Opinions will differ on whether and how advisers should offer views on the ethical aspects of the ruler's activities, but the question needs to be asked. The inclusion of moral philosophers on the staff of rulers may be worth considering,[61] as a modern substitute for those court priests and other parallel institutions of historical courts.[62]

A related function of advisers is to look after 'ideology'. The inner circle of advisers is sometimes supposed to oversee policy strategy and make sure it fits the ideology and to review policy proposals in the light of the ideology. This function is usually fused with 'politics', but follows a line different from political analysis, which is more pragmatic and power-orientated.

Altogether, the frictions between policy and politics, ideology and morals, a ruler's career and his image are very real. Some are well recognized and coped with by some advisory systems; others are quite ignored.

The ethical aspects of the performance of rulers, are in particular need of more attention, all the more so because of the growing importance of rulers in Western democracies. Reliance on external controls alone, such as the law and political accountability reinforced by investigatory journalism, may be inadequate – particularly with the improvement in political marketing tools at the disposal of rulers. Ideological commitment by rulers may not make matters much better, because of the dangers of dogmatism and possible justification of unethical acts in terms of ideological necessity. The game of politics certainly does not assure the high moral fibre of people who reach the top. Therefore, the danger of 'wanton' behaviour of rulers,[63] including those of democracies, should be taken seriously. Innovations within the offices of rulers as well as in external controls may be needed to meet this problem.

Mentors, Decision Process Management and Substantive Decision Inputs

A main function of advisers is to serve as mentors to rulers, so as to provide knowledge, overcome incompetence, counteract perverse casts of mind, cool down motivated irrationality and much more. Substantive knowledge inputs are a 'cold' contribution, as illustrated by intelligence advisers[64] and by specialized advisers, such as in economics and in science.[65] Specialized advisers can also guide decision-making as a whole by applying their way of thinking.[66]

Efforts to 'educate' the world pictures of rulers and, even more important, their ways of thinking, are more difficult and ambitious and depend largely on relations between the adviser and the ruler.[67] But suitable interaction processes can also help; thus, regular sessions between advisers and rulers where major issues are discussed at leisure can serve as important 'learning' opportunities for rulers. Similarly, weekends devoted to discussion of issues and regular briefing sessions, as well as suitably structured tours, can be used not only to convey information but to 'educate' rulers.

A special form of 'teaching' rulers is to provide them with records and information on relevant historical experiences, with the advisory system serving as an 'institutional memory' for rulers. This leads into interesting technical issues of data storage and data retrieval, both human and mechanized. Quite new vistas may be opening with modern computer systems, but as yet offices of rulers are a long way from utilizing the full potential of man–machine systems.[68]

A related issue is the continuity of advisers. Unless advisers serve for many years, an essential dimension of institutional memory and of learning from experience is missing; but many advisers must be changed with a change of ruler, to preserve confidential relations between advisers and rulers. Also, having advisers serve too long a term may reduce innovativeness. Countries differ in how they handle this, which is in part related to the issue of the mix between civil servants and special appointees in an advisory system.

Another, quite different major function of advisers is to manage the decision-making process, including agenda setting, organizing preparation of the decision by relevant departments, processing material for decision-making, recording decisions, monitoring implementation and, sometimes, dealing with feedback and learning following a decision. Decision process management is a major task of cabinet offices (however called).[69] It raises a number of serious problems, including dangers of routinization and paper overload, which increase with every refinement and formalization of working processes. Thus, in one country distinguished by its highly developed and formalized decision process management system, I found that all really important decisions were handled outside the formal process, which was much too cumbersome, and that the amount of staff papers produced by the process assured that most of them could not be taken into account in actual decision-making.

Substantive inputs into decision-making are another major task of advisers, discussed in more detail in the following sections. The mix between serving as a mentory decision process managing and making substantive decision inputs constitutes a major dilemma for advisers to rulers, a dilemma that is further aggravated by the various modes and types of substantive decision inputs, which in turn influence possibilities of serving as mentors to rulers and handling decision process management.

Contradictory Dimensions of Substantive Decision Inputs

Substantive decision inputs constitute the central contribution of advisers to rulers. Therefore, the contradictory dimensions of such inputs pose major problems to advisers. Some of these main contradictions include:

Idea Generation v. Option Evaluation v. Follow-up and Policy Learning. Idea generation involves invention and development of new proposals by advisers themselves and encouragement by them of policy inventiveness in organizations working for them. Option analysis deals with evaluation of proposals originating elsewhere. Follow-up and policy learning involve monitoring decision results and assuring feedback, including reconsideration and revision of decisions. All these decision inputs are needed and advisory systems engage to some extent in a mixture of all them. But these different dimensions not only compete for scarce resources, especially the limited time and attention of advisers and rulers alike, but require different knowledge, interests, structures and 'organizational cultures'.

Current and Pressing v. Critical and Basic. Many advisory systems are set up to handle critical issues and basic problems, but end up dealing with current matters and pressing agenda items. This is not surprising, taking into account external pressures to handle immediate problems first and the preoccupation of many rulers with what is visible and painful. This tendency is augmented by a taste often developed by advisers for the sense of sharing power which comes from handling current matters, as opposed to the 'egg-head' nature of thinking on long-term matters. My survey has led to the conclusion that advisory systems tend to focus on current and pressing issues and neglect basic as well as critical ones, unless the latter are very visible and thus become pressing. This is a serious weakness of rulers' advisory systems which may well constitute an inbuilt defect of its own, requiring institutional countermeasures, such as separate think-tanks to study important but non-pressing issues.

Two additional problems related to this particular dilemma are the role of the advisory system in crisis management and the balance between responsiveness and entrepreneurship in agenda-setting and advice-giving.

Crisis management is an important decision mode in many Western democracies and may become more critical because of escalating terrorism, disaster possibilities in sensitive physical facilities and so on. As rulers usually fulfil important roles in crisis management, it is very important that they are adequately prepared to take part in crisis decision-making. Therefore, in principle, advisers to rulers should prepare for and actively participate in crisis decision-making. But this often is not the case, for a variety of reasons, such as the monopolization of crisis management by other agencies of government; a tendency to regard crises as so unusual as not to require special preparation; and plain neglect because of overload of advisers with current 'normal' decisions. The political sensitivity of many types of crises, such as general strikes, also makes advance preparation politically difficult if leaks are expected, as they often are in democracies.

The unwillingness of rulers to participate in crisis games, which are a key method of preparing and 'running-in' crisis management systems, adds to the difficulties. This unwillingness illustrates a wider obstacle to upgrading the performance of rulers, namely rulers' dislike of situations in which they are subjected to testing and evaluation. The unacceptability of such situations constrains quite a number of possible means by which advisers could be of help.

Another serious dilemma for advisers involves on the one hand the balance between advisers responding to issue agendas imposed on them by the ruler, with his own preoccupations and external pressures, and on the other hand advisers engaging in issue-search and entrepreneurial initiative in putting on the agenda objectively important issues. My own empirical findings show that advisory systems tend to become mainly responsive, even if their organizational ideology and self-image pose issue identification and problem-search as major tasks.

Superficial Analysis v. In-depth Analysis. A fundamental dilemma facing advisers to rulers is posed by the issue of the depth of their work and, related to this, its quality. Improvement of rulers' performance requires in-depth analysis of issues, but pressures of work and limitations on resources all too often result in superficial analysis. The speedy turnover of issues on a ruler's agenda adds to the factors making any deep analysis nearly impossible in most advisory systems.

Two main solutions to the problem are to delegate in-depth analysis to the regular machinery of government, such as in the Policy Analysis and Review (PAR) attempts in the United Kingdom,[70] and/or to sub-contract deep analysis to academic research institutes, private consultants, party research organizations[71] or special think-tanks. But such outside bodies cannot fully compensate for the shallowness of work within the ruler's advisory system itself; most outside bodies are unable to engage in relevant and timely policy research and development and think-tanks too are not easy to integrate into the processes of advising rulers.

Discrete Decisions v. a Strategic Approach. Another syndrome of contradicting dimensions is posed by the conflict between focusing work on specific, delimited and discrete decisions, as against a strategic approach with emphasis on coherence between different decisions and their integration into overall grand policies.[72] While advisory systems to rulers often try to promote coherence and a strategic approach, this is quite impossible unless the ruler himself is strongly interested in it. This can happen when rulers are committed to an overriding grand design or ideology, but then the danger of becoming dogmatic surfaces. In the absence of a unifying grand concept on the part of the ruler himself, separate handling of issues as they come tends to dominate the advisers too.

Counter-attempts include efforts to use budgeting as an instrument to promote a strategic approach,[73] and endeavours to crystallize strategic thinking by cabinets and rulers, such as by using weekend retreats. Despite some achievements, success tends to be very limited.

Iconoclasm and Radicalism v. Incrementalism. The last dimension of decision input to be mentioned here is the tension between iconoclasm and radical innovation on one hand, and incrementalism with muddling through on the other. There is no scope here to discuss the debate on the need for iconoclasm and radical innovation so as to permit policy adaptation to rapidly changing conditions as against the stubborn support and intellectual justification of incrementalism;[74]

suffice it to say it is difficult to have much iconoclasm and radicalism among the advisory staff of a ruler beyond the ideology which the ruler himself is committed to.

If the ruler is committed to an ideology, his closer advisers will engage in iconoclasm and radicalism against former policies and civil service inertia,[75] but usually not in respect of the ideology or the 'pet ideas' of the ruler himself. If the ruler is more pragmatic, then only accidental inclusion of iconoclastic persons in his advisory system will result in a meaningful critique of accepted policy paradigms and radical innovation by the advisory system. The civil service components are often quite incremental in their modes of thinking and their decision inputs to rulers.

The conclusion emerging from this examination of just some of the contradictions prevailing in the main areas of decision input by advisers to rulers is that the very location of the advisory system near the heart of rulership with all its pressures cannot but promote rather one-sided contributions. Option evaluation, current and pressing issues, superficial analysis, discrete issues and limited innovativeness necessarily characterize most advisory systems.

The most radical effort to overcome these limitations is the idea of think-tanks, in the sense of policy research and development organizations isolated from current pressures but closely integrated into policy-making on the strategic level.[76] This solution has been tried out in only a few countries and its success in augmenting the performance of rulers and their staffs has been quite limited until now. The reasons for this in the main go beyond the scope of this discussion,[77] but include the characteristics of the advisory systems themselves which in fact make in-depth analysis and innovative policy options etc. quite unwelcome inputs, despite declarations to the contrary.

Knowledge Bases and Methods

The formidable problems surrounding advisers' decision inputs to rulers make all the more pressing the need for adequate knowledge bases. In principle, quite a varied range of knowledge is needed, including as a minimum:

1 experience and knowledge of government and its practices, as a whole and in main policy areas;
2 experience and knowledge of politics;
3 knowledge in disciplines dealing with main policy areas and policy issues;
4 knowledge in decision disciplines and interdisciplines, such as systems analysis, simulation, policy analysis etc.

The need for such types of knowledge is shaped by and in turn determines the methods used in advising rulers. For instance, simulations, games and structured decision analysis can be used for advising rulers; and man–machine systems have great potential for presenting complex information and analyses to rulers in a comprehensible form. But the uses of such knowledge, methods and equipment depend on an awareness of both their potential and their pitfalls, a desire to use them and the availability of suitable professionals on the advisory staff.

In fact, none of the advisory systems I have studied used such methods and very few systems included professionals qualified to use such methods and evaluate their usefulness. In this regard, the survey identified a vicious circle: present advisory staffs to rulers, whether civil servants or outsiders, including professionals in traditional disciplines such as economics, are often not aware of more advanced and modern methods for policy analysis etc. and therefore do not use them; they usually do not like them and downgrade their potential usefulness. Accordingly, professionals in the relevant relatively new disciplines are seldom included in the staffs of rulers, which in turn perpetuates ignorance and rejection of potentially useful knowledge by those staffs; and so on.[78]

The appropriate balance on advisory staffs between different kinds of personnel with diverse types of knowledge, and the tensions between them, pose many problems, as also happens when advanced methods and their professionals are ignored. Getting the mixture right between civil servants and political appointees in advisory units for rulers poses many difficulties, with most countries tending to one or the other extreme.[79]

'Islands of Excellence' or a Large Department?

The multiplicity of functions performed by advisory systems for rulers and the varied knowledge required leads to a need for substantive advisory organizations. If the ruler wants to monitor activities in the main ministries with the help of 'mirror' units in the ruler's office, each paralleling one of the main departments, then a large 'ruler's department' is needed. Such departments exist in a number of countries, quite unrelated to parliamentary–cabinet or presidential constitutional regimes.

However, whenever a large ruler's office exists, most of it does not advise the ruler in any meaningful sense of that term, more than is done by other main departments. Building up a large office of the prime minister or president may strengthen the ruler's control over the administration, for instance when the budgeting function is in his office, and may build up his political power (as debated in the United Kingdom when the idea of setting up a Prime Minister's Department was in vogue), but the real advisory units cannot become too large, otherwise they lose essential contact with the ruler and his inner circle.[80]

On the other hand, too small a unit can in no way fulfil the minimum essential functions of advisers to rulers. In fact, in the large majority of countries I surveyed, the size of the office of the ruler was much too small to meet urgent needs; advisory staffs were rudimentary and no compensatory mechanism could be identified.

Divided Loyalties

The loyalty of advisers is pulled in five main directions: loyalty to the ruler; loyalty to the civil service and various departments, or some interest group to which one belongs; loyalty to some ideology or other images of 'the public interest' and *raison d'etat*; loyalty to some professional frame of reference; and loyalty to oneself. Conflicts of interest between these loyalties cause major problems in advising rulers.

Some of the main problems can be summed up as follows:

1   If the staff of the advisory system comes from the regular civil service and is destined to return to the departments, unavoidable socialization and incentives combine to result in dominating loyalty to the civil service and the departments.

2   Members of the staff who are close to the ruler will usually be loyal to him personally.

3   Professionals may have overriding loyalties to their reference groups.

4   Depending on the political and social culture, advancement of personal interest can be subdued or quite blatant. Thus, use of advisory positions to prepare private jobs after a short term in office is widespread in some countries.

5   Ideologues, civil servants, intellectuals etc. will have a strong commitment to the 'public good' seen through their own looking-glass. This commitment may result in leaks, resignations, whistle-blowing and similar reactions to behaviour and decisions which they regard as anathema to their commitments.

The most acute conflict of loyalty among advisory staffs to rulers is probably that between loyalty to the civil service and its ideas on the one hand, and loyalty to the ruler and his conception of the public interest on the other. Here, an additional theoretical perspective opens, with advisers to rulers constituting a possible third group complicating the relationship between civil servants and politicians,[81] while perhaps solving some dilemmas that cannot be adequately handled within a dichotomous view of civil servants and politicians as the only components of the 'central minds of governments'.

The whole problem takes different forms in countries that permit political activity by senior civil servants and countries that strive for a non-political senior civil service. In all cases, a mix between civil servants and advisers committed to the ruler is needed.

My own survey has shown that adequate mixes are unusual. In most advisory units civil servants over-dominate within the staff; in a few there is a preponderance of political appointees.

Institutionalization, Mutability and Transience

The last dilemma facing advisers to rulers to be discussed here serves well to bring out the problematic nature of advisory units to rulers as a whole. Advisers to rulers depend on the rulers for their effectiveness, their positions and the very survival of the advisory units. But, advisers to rulers must not limit themselves to sycophancy and to merely making the ruler 'feel good'. This means, therefore, that adequate advice-giving depends on the ruler wishing to get advice, even when it is very unwelcome and disturbing.[82]

Ulysses and the Sirens serves as an appropriate metaphor:[83] the ruler must be willing to bind himself with the advice he receives. This difficult demand can be aided by the institutionalization of the advisory system, so as to protect it against sudden whims of rulers. But a ruler who does not want certain types of advice will eventually dispose of it, as is illustrated by the demise of the Central Policy Review Staff in the United Kingdom.

While requiring protection against less enlightened and non-self-managing rulers, advisory systems must also not be too rigid, because tailor-making advice to the habits, ways of thinking and preferences of specific rulers is essential for the effectiveness of that advice. Therefore, the single perhaps most difficult inherent dilemma for advisers is how to fulfil their functions and yet still adjust to specific rulers with all their personality features, likes and dislikes, Over-adjustment undermines the necessary functions of advisers to rulers, while under-adjustment diminishes the impact of advice and may bring about the destruction of the advisory structure as a whole, or its takeover by compliant servants of power. Institutionalization can help, but it is hard to strike a correct balance between too much and too little of it.

Principles for Redesign

The analysis presented in this paper is theoretical, but its orientation is applied. Diagnosis of the dialectic contradictions in rulership itself and identification of major areas of conflict within advisory systems permit penetration beyond the manifest symptoms and surface phenomena to the very roots of the problems of advising rulers. This in turn should permit the development of redesign principles for advisory systems, leading to operational proposals after application of those principles to conditions in specific countries.

These tasks are beyond the scope of this paper, but five such principles for redesign of advice systems can be derived from this discussion[84] and presented briefly, as a summary. These principles can also be viewed as a set of considerations for evaluating actual advisory systems, as discussed in the various contributions to this volume. They can also be seen as a continuation of the ideas presented in this present paper and as preliminary prescriptive conjectures in need of study, development, refutation tests and application.

Advisory Systems for Rulers are Necessarily Complex

It is impossible to handle the dialectic tensions built into rulership and the various contradictions of the advisory function with simple structures. Complexity is essential for handling complex issues. Therefore, the search for simple advisory structures for rulers is a chimera. A good advisory system will not only be complex, but loaded with internal pluralism and redundancy, inconsistencies, tensions and contradictions. These are not an unavoidable evil, but necessary features of preferable advisory systems for rulers.[85]

No Unitary Structure can Meet All Needs

It is impossible to meet main needs and contain strong conflicts of interest within a single unitary advisory structure. Therefore, a range of units is needed, constituting a partly integrated network. Thus, the minimum requirements of a preferable advisory system include: a close group of advisers, which fulfils emotional support functions, supplies political and personal power inputs, looks after ideology etc. and also gives policy advice; an outer group of advisers, which mainly handles 'cold' advice functions, decision process management, institutional memory tasks etc.; external units for in-depth analysis, iconoclasm etc., which should take a think-tank form, suitably adjusted to meet the needs of top-level decision-making. In addition, a variety of formal and informal brains trusts, personal networks inside and outside the machinery of government and politics, and additional supportive structures and circuits are needed.

There will be unavoidable friction between all these units and personnel but, if well managed, this will be a low price to pay for meeting the multiple requirements of advising rulers and coping with the main areas of conflict by dividing tasks and creating some 'distance' between different conflicting functions.

Critical Size and Composition Requirements

Given a division of labour between various advisory units, the core units must still achieve a critical size and include staff with the minimum necessary diversity of experience, skills and disciplines. It is hard to imagine an inner advisory group of less than, say, 10–15 persons and an outer advisory group of less than 20–30 persons which can meet minimum needs. This includes only the advisory staff to the ruler and not auxiliary personnel, such as those responsible for management of his routine, those performing cabinet office functions etc.

Advanced Work Methods and Self-monitoring are Essential

The complexities of the tasks facing advisers to rulers require advanced work methods. Also, constant self-monitoring and self-improvement are essential. These, in turn, require the location of some kind of 'advice on advice' function[86] in or near the advisory system. To underpin the application of advanced work methods, much innovative knowledge is needed; novel methods have to be developed and new types of policy professionals have to be trained.

The Broader Context of Improving Rulers

Advisory systems are but one institution that can be employed to upgrade the performance of rulers. Therefore, the improvement and redesign of advisory systems should, if possible, be undertaken in conjunction with broader efforts to improve the performance of rulers, such as consideration of their constitutional authority, political power and selection, side by side with suitable changes in countervailing units, such as legislatures. This is all the more important as improving the advice to rulers augments the power and authority of those rulers, and should, therefore, be considered within an overall reconsideration of the democratic capacity to govern.

These are but some of the improvement implications arising from the analysis presented here, which I hope bear out the underlying assumption that theoretical inquiry is essential for the effective improvement of practice.

Notes

1 Ludwig Wittgenstein, *Philosophic Investigations*, section 94. I am indebted to my son Itiel Dror for drawing my attention to this statement.

2 In an interesting attempt to identify all rulers since the emergence of 'governance' as historically known to us, their number has been estimated at about 13,000. See R. F. Tapsell, *Monarchs, Rulers, Dynasties and Kingdoms of the World: an Encyclopedic Guide to more than 13,000 Rulers and 1,000 Dynasties from 3,000 B.C. to the Twentieth Century* (Thames and Hudson, London, 1983). For discussions of contemporary rulers, see Jean Blondel, *World Leaders: Heads of Government in the Postwar Period* (Sage Publications, London, 1980); and, for some second level 'rulers', Jean Blondel, *Government Ministers in the Contemporary World* (Sage Publications, London, 1985).

3 See, for example, Gordon Donaldson and Jay W. Lorsch, *Decision Making at the Top: The Shaping of Strategic Direction* (Basic Books, New York, 1983).

4 Historic settings are essential for understanding particular arrangements for advising rulers in specific countries, as evolving with time. Thus, the situation in the UK must be studied in a historical perspective, as provided for the more recent period by John Turner, *Lloyd George's Secretariat* (Cambridge University Press, Cambridge, 1980); and John F. Naylor, *A Man and an Institution: Sir Maurice Hankey, the Cabinet Secretariat and the Custody of Cabinet Secrecy* (Cambridge University Press, Cambridge, 1984). But all set-ups of advisers to rulers share fundamental features and problems. These serve as the subject for the present paper, on a nomographic level.

5 Ethnographic studies of rulers and advisers in their natural habitat are essential for knowledge and understanding of their behaviour and problems and as a reliable foundation for designs for improvement. Such studies are very scarce, understandably so. For an appropriate methodology, on which the present paper is in part based, see David M. Hayano, *Poker Faces: The Life and Work of Professional Card Players* (University of California Press, Berkeley, Ca., 1982), Appendix A. I have changed his term of 'authentic adviser cum ethnograph', to express the bona fide advisory functions fulfilled, with ethnographic knowledge serving as a side-benefit but not the purpose for which the advisory positions were undertaken.

6 For some preliminary findings, see Yehezkel Dror, 'Policy analysis for advising rulers', in Rolfe Tomlinson and Istvan Kiss (eds), *Rethinking the Process of Operational Research and Systems Analysis* (Pergamon Press, Oxford, 1984), ch. 6. The results of the study as a whole will be presented in a book *Advising Rulers*, in preparation.

7 See Herbert Goldhamer, *The Adviser* (Elsevier, New York, 1978). For historic illustrations, see for instance Silas H. L. Wu, *Communication and Imperial Control in China: Evolution of the Palace Memorial System, 1693–1735* (Harvard University Press, Cambridge, Mass., 1970), passim, to be studied in conjunction with Herrlee G. Creel, *Shen Pu-Hai: A Chinese Political Philosopher of the Fourth Century B.C.* (University of Chicago Press, Chicago, Ill., 1974), especially chs 6 and 7; and John Crook, *Consilium Principis: Imperial Councils and Counsellors from Augustus to Diocletian* (Cambridge University Press, Cambridge, 1955), especially ch. III, to be read in conjunction with Miriam T. Griffin, *Seneca: A Philosopher in Politics* (Oxford University Press, Oxford, 1976), especially ch. 3, and Fergus Millar, *The Emperor in the Roman World (31 B.C.–A.D. 337)* (Duckworth, London, 1977), especially ch. III, sec. 7.

8 Contemporary comparative studies of advisory staffs to rulers are well illustrated by Colin Campbell, *Governments Under Stress: Political Executives and Key Bureaucrats in Washington, London, and Ottawa* (University of Toronto Press, Toronto, 1983), pt 1. Good monographic studies of particular advisory structures are illustrated by Jonathan G. Boston, *High Level Advisory Groups in Central Government: A Comparative Study of the Origins, Structure and Activities of the Australian Priorities Review Staff and the New Zealand Prime Minister's Advisory Group* (University of Canterbury, NZ, Master's thesis, 1980); and by Peter Hennessy, Susan Morrison and Richard Townsend, *Routine Punctuated by Orgies: The Central Policy Review Staff, 1970–83*

(University of Strathclyde, Department of Politics, Glasgow, 1984), Strathclyde Papers on Government and Politics No. 31. Attempts at constructing a theory are illustrated by Michael J. Prince, *Policy Advice and Organizational Survival* (Gower, Aldershot, 1983). Much relevant information is dispersed in biographies, diaries, autobiographies, historical studies, government reports etc., as well as in official documents, usually classified.

9 It is interesting to speculate on evolutionary explanations of basic features embedded in presently known forms of governance, which are quite limited in their main patterns, despite their apparent variance. Some relevant ideas can be found in Charles J. Lumsden and Edward O. Wilson, *Genes, Mind and Culture: The Coevolutionary Process* (Harvard University Press, Cambridge, Mass., 1981); and in its popular version, Charles J. Lumsden and Edward O. Wilson, *Promethean Fire: Reflections on the Origin of Mind* (Harvard University Press, Cambridge, Mass., 1983). For some different salient ideas, see Herbert A. Simon, *Reason in Human Affairs* (Standford University Press, Stanford, Ca., 1983), especially ch. 2. It is stimulating to apply to governance institutions, such as advisory systems to rulers, the evolutionary approach applied to growth in knowledge in Peter Munz, *Our Knowledge of the Growth of Knowledge: Popper or Wittgenstein?* (Routledge & Kegan Paul, London, 1985), but this is a separate endeavour.

10 Some of the theoretical constructs and redesign approaches applied in this paper to advising rulers are developed within a broader context in Yehezkel Dror, *Policymaking under Adversity* (Transaction Books, New Brunswick, NJ, 1986), especially, chs 6 and 9.

11 In the sense proposed in Sir Geoffrey Vickers, *The Art of Judgement: a Theory of Policymaking* (Chapman and Hall, London, 1984), ch. 4.

12 See, for example, Sidney Hook, *The Hero in History: a Study in Limitations and Possibilities* (John Day, New York, 1983).

13 To illustrate relevant studies, let me mention two of the better ones, which adopt quite different methods, but lead to similar conclusions: Valerie Bunce, *Do New Leaders Make a Difference: Executive Succession and Public Policy Under Capitalism and Socialism* (Princeton University Press, Princeton, NJ, 1981); and Patrick Weller, *First Among Equals: Prime Ministers in Westminster Systems* (Allen & Unwin, London, 1985).

14 Mass psychology is an unpopular subject in Anglo-American political science, but an essential one for understanding political leadership. A minimum mass psychological function of rulers includes maintaining the collective identity, as discussed in Erik H. Erikson, *Life History and the Historical Moment: Diverse Presentations* (Norton, New York, 1975), p. 22. Socioeconomic dislocations and accelerated structural change, together with widespread anxiety and accompanied by the potential of the mass media, may well produce new forms of 'mass-behaviour' in modern Western democracies, with critical functions to be fulfilled by rulers in meeting mass psychological needs and directing mass psychological processes into desirable 'enlighted' directions. Compare, for instance, Patrick Brantlinger, *Bread and Circuses: Theories of Mass Culture as Social Decay* (Cornell University Press, Ithaca, NY, 1983); Serge Moscovici, *The Age of the Crowd: a historic Treatise on Mass Psychology* (Cambridge University Press, Cambridge, 1985); and George F. Will, *Statecraft as*

Soulcraft: What Government Does (Simon and Schuster, New York, 1983). I belabour this point because, while obvious to anyone with historical perspectives, it is ignored in most discussions of political leadership in democracies. The mass psychological dimensions make rulers all the more important and thus add an ominous dimension to the inherent defects of rulers, as discussed in the text.

15 For a perceptive preview of such trends, see Richard Crossman, *Inside View: Three Lectures on Prime Ministerial Government* (Cape, London, 1972).

16 See Dror, *Policymaking under Adversity*, especially pp. 184–8.

17 This important concept, which fully applies to present and forseeable conditions in most Western democracies, was first developed in Joseph Schumpeter, *Capitalism, Socialism and Democracy* (Allen & Unwin, London, 1952), ch. 7.

18 In line with the papers is this volume as a whole, I discuss only Western democracies. In many developing countries the problem is much harder, because strong rulers are essential for societal architecture, while they are very susceptible to serious defects, to the point of total corruption, as illustrated in a literary way in Augusto Roa Bastos, *I The Supreme* (Alfred A. Knopf, New York, 1986). See also n. 43, below.

19 Classical thought was well aware of inherent defects of rulership. Plato first tried to overcome them through careful selection and education of rulers in *The Republic*, and later despaired of the possibility of improving rulers in *The Laws*. Tacitus clearly recognized the tendency of rulers to suffer from 'Cesars-craze', a concept well known and used in German literature. See, for example, Johannes Scherr, *Bluecher: Seine Zeit und Sein Leben* (Hesse & Becker, Leipzig, 1914), pt. 7, ch. 1, discussing the 'Kaiserwahnsinn' of Napoleon Bonaparte since about 1810. Modern literature on political leadership tends to neglect realistic analysis of such fundamental features of rulership. One of the exceptions is Bruce Buchanan, *The Presidential Experience: What the Office Does to the Man* (Prentice-Hall, Englewood Cliffs, NJ, 1978).

20 I leave aside quasi-medical approaches, as presented in Hugh L'Etang, *The Pathology of Leadership* (Heinemann Medical, London, 1968) and further developed in Hugh L'Etang, *Fit to Lead?* (Heinemann Medical, London, 1980). While stimulating and including many valuable insights, I think these books are unduly morbid in their conclusions. My own observation of some rulers identifies opposite tendencies towards what can be called 'psychosomatic health', the exhilarations of rulership serving to preserve health and stamina and constituting an antidote to fatigue and disease. Inbuilt tendencies of the 'language-game' of medicine to concentrate more on pathology than on immunities require care in applying medical concepts to political phenomena, despite their fascination and potential as illustrated by Brian W. Hogwood and B. Guy Peters, *The Pathology of Public Policy* (Clarendon Press, Oxford, 1985). This caveat should be kept in mind when medical terminology is sometimes borrowed in this paper.

21 On the general effects of strain and stress on decision-making quality, see Irving L. Janis and Leon Mann, *Decision Making: a Psychological Analysis of Conflict, Choice and Commitment* (Free Press, New York, 1977). For the concepts of maze policy behaviour and policy convulsions and additional impacts of pressure and adversity on decision quality, see Dror, *Policymaking under Adversity*, e.g., pp. 51–9.

22 Margaret G. Hermann, 'Indicators of stress in policymakers during foreign policy crises', *Political Psychology*, 1 (Spring, 1979), pp. 27–46. A striking case study is

Michael R. Beschloss, *Mayday: Eisenhower, Krushchev and the U–2 Affair* (Harper and Row, New York, 1986).

23 Nearly unavoidable defects during nuclear conflict decision-making raise some of the most serious spectres of fatal consequences of rulers in action. For some relevant discussions, see: Paul Bracker, *The Command and Control of Nuclear Forces* (Yale University Press, New Haven, Conn., 1983); Desmond Ball, *Can Nuclear War be Controlled?* (International Institute for Strategic Studies, London, 1981), Adelphi Paper 169; Gerhard W. Hopple et al. (eds), *National Security Crisis Forecasting and Management* (Westview Press, Boulder, Colo., 1983); and Daniel Ford, *The Button: the Pentagon's Strategic Command and Control* (Simon and Schuster, New York, 1985). Implications for strategic innovations, such as the Strategic Defense Initiative, require separate treatment. See Yehezkel Dror, 'Gambling with history, however unpleasant, is normal to the human condition', *Technological Forecasting and Social Change*, vol. 29, no. 1 (February 1986), pp. 76–81.

24 The author had an opportunity to survey the work schedule of a few rulers. In those cases very few free 'thinking hours' were available to the rulers, who were overburdened with activities many of which were not important in any objective, including political, sense. I have no basis for judging whether these findings are typical or exceptional, but my hypothesis is that this situation is quite common.

25 See, for example, Jerrold M. Packard, *American Monarchy: a Social Guide to the Presidency* (Delacorte Press, New York, 1983).

26 See Irving L. Janis, *Groupthink* (Houghton Mifflin, Boston, 1982).

27 See David Pears, *Motivated Irrationality* (Oxford University Press, Oxford, 1984), especially ch. 2.

28 On the concept, see 'Risk and policy analysis under conditions of uncertainty', *Options* (December 1985) p. 3 (published by the International Institute of Applied Systems Analysis).

29 For a controversial 'case study', see David A. Stockman, *The Triumph of Politics: Why the Reagan Revolution Failed* (Harper and Row, New York, 1986).

30 In the sense of Milton Rokeach, *Open and Closed Mind* (Basic Books, New York, 1960).

31 Cf. Lloyd S. Eltheredge, *Can Governments Learn? American Foreign Policy and Central American Revolutions* (Pergamon Press, New York, 1985), especially ch. 4.

32 See Richard Nisbett and Lee Ross, *Human Inference: Strategies and Shortcomings of Social Judgment* (Prentice-Hall, Englewood Cliffs, NJ, 1980); and Miles Hewstone (ed.), *Attribution Theory: Social and Functional Extensions* (Blackwell, Oxford, 1983).

33 See Robert Axelrod (ed.), *Structure of Decision: the Cognitive Maps of Political Elites* (Princeton University Press, Princeton, NJ, 1976).

34 See Alexander L. George, 'The causal nexus between cognitive beliefs and decision-making behavior: the "operational code" belief system', in Lawrence S. Falkowski (ed.), *Psychological Models in International Politics* (Westview Press, Boulder, Col., 1979), ch. 5.

35 Daniel Kahneman, Paul Slovic and Amos Tversky, *Judgement under Uncertainty: Heuristics and Biases* (Cambridge University Press, Cambridge, 1982); and, somewhat different, Dietrich Doerner et al. (eds), *Lohhausen: Vom Umgang mit Unbestimmtheit und Komplexitaet* (Hans Huber, Berne, 1983).

36 See Dror, *Policymaking under Adversity*, especially pp. 16–74.

37 Some of the dangers of 'historic thinking' are already discussed in Friedrich Nietzsche, *The Use and Abuse of History* (1873) (Bobbs-Merrill, Indianapolis, NY, 1949), especially pp. 3–22. The dependence of political discourse and thinking on historic metaphors is well discussed in Alexander Demandt, *Metaphern fuer Geschichte: Sprachbilder und Gleichnisse im Historisch-Politischen Denken* (Beck, Munich, 1979). Misleading effects of historic metaphors on rulers are illustrated in Ernest R. May, *'Lessons' of the Past: the Uses and Misuses of History in American Foreign Policy* (Oxford University Press, Oxford, 1972), to be contrasted with the recommendations developed in Richard E. Neustadt and Ernest R. May, *Thinking in Time: the Uses of History for Decision-Makers* (Free Press, New York, 1986).

38 See, for example, James D. Barber, *The Presidential Character: Predicting Performance in the White House* (Prentice-Hall, Englewood Cliffs, NJ, 1972), as contrasted with revised views of who was a successful ruler, as illustrated by Fred I. Greenstein, *The Hidden-Hand President: Eisenhower as Leader* (Basic Books, New York, 1982).

39 For example, James MacGregor Burns, *Leadership* (Harper & Row, New York, 1978).

40 A striking case is provided by William Mackenzie King, for many years a successful prime minister of Canada, but posthumously revealed as mentally marginal, to put it conservatively. See Joy E. Esberey, *Knights of the Holy Spirit: a Study of William Lyon Mackenzie King* (University of Toronto Press, Toronto, 1980).

41 See Wilhelm Lange-Eichbaum and Wolfram Kurth, *Genie Irrsinn und Ruhm: Genie-Mythus und Pathographie des Genies*, 6th ed. (Ernest Reinhardt, Munich 1979); and Dean Keith Simonton, *Genius Creativity and Leadership: Historiometric Inquiries* (Harvard University Press, Cambridge, Mass., 1984).

42 See, for example, Ann Ruth Willner, *The Spellbinders: Charismatic Political Leadership* (Yale University Press. New Haven, Conn., 1984).

43 As mentioned in n. 18 above, in many Third World countries quite different types of leaders emerge, and are needed, than in Western countries. See, for example, Robert H. Jackson and Carl G. Rosberg, *Personal Rule in Black Africa: Prophet, Tyrant* (University of California Press, Berkeley, Ca., 1982); and Mustafa Rehai with Kay Phillips, *Leaders in Revolutions* (Sage Publications, London, 1979). In some Third World countries, rulers are much more prone to 'rulers-craze' than even the worst rulers in Western democracies. For example, in addition to the literary portrait provided in Roa Bastos, *I The Supreme*, see Ryszard Kapuscinski, *The Emperor: Downfall of an Autocrat* (Harcourt Brace Jovanovich, New York, 1983); and Mansour Khalid, *Nimeiri and the Revolution of Dis-May* (KPI, London, 1985).

44 I am here tentatively applying the theory put forward in Henry Fayol, *General and Industrial Management* (Pitman, London, 1949, first published in French in 1916), that when a person moves up a hierarchy his advance depends on success on the lower level, which demonstrates capacities that often do not fit the higher level. This idea has been popularized in the so-called 'Peter Principle'. See Laurence J. Peter and Raymond Hull, *Peter Principle: Why Things Always Go Wrong* (Morrow, New York, 1969).

45 The question cannot be avoided whether some hypothetical non-democratic regimes may not acquire advantages over democracies by better selection of rulers. At

present this is not the case, ruler selection in Communist countries suffering from weaknesses of its own. See, for example, George W. Breslauer, *Khrushchev and Breshnev as Leaders: Building Authority in Soviet Politics* (Allen & Unwin, London, 1982). Still, it is conceiveable that some future 'meritocratic' regime may adopt a neo-Platonic mode of selection and preparation of rulers. But see Michael Young, *The Rise of the Meritocracy 1870–2033* (Thames and Hudson, London, 1958). Working out such a model may serve to sensitize democracies to try to improve rulership selection and preparation, within the paradigms of democracy.

46 As the reader has surely already noticed, I am using a Popperian approach to try to advance knowledge on the subject of this paper. See Karl R. Popper, *Conjectures and Refutations: the Growth of Scientific Knowledge* (Routledge and Kegan Paul, London, 1963), as discussed and further developed in Munz, *Our Knowledge of the Growth of Knowledge*.

47 Hayano, *Poker Faces*, is illuminating here.

48 The Crossman diaries are still a unique document in this respect – Richard Crossman, *The Diaries of a Cabinet Minister*, 3 vols (Hamilton, London, 1975–7) – as are, in a different way, the personal diaries of Moshe Sharett, see Moshe Sharett, *Personal Diary*, 8 vols (in Hebrew) (Maariv Library, Tel-Aviv, 1978).

49 I borrow this term from a classical 'mirror-of-princes' written by Claude de Seyssel in 1515. See Claude de Seyssel, *The Monarchy of France* (Yale University Press, New Haven, Conn., 1981), pt I, chs 8–11.

50 Additional innovations are necessary for upgrading the performance of rulers. Thus, learning opportunities for candidates for rulership, in the form of National Policy Colleges, should be considered. See Dror, *Policymaking Under Adversity*, pp. 293–4. Urgently needed is a modern version of a mirror-of-princes, the lack of books written for senior politicians being all the more amazing in comparison with the multitude of texts directed at business executives. I hope to try my hand at such a book, tentatively entitled *Policy-Mirror for Rulers*.

51 That more ambitious task is in part taken up in Dror, *Policymaking Under Adversity*, especially chs 6–10. It will be further developed in Yehezkel Dror, *Retrofitting Governance: Selective-Radical Reforms Versus Incapacities to Govern*, in preparation.

52 Some relevant questions are posed in an unpublished paper by Stephen J. Wayne. Aldous Huxley has some good insights in *Grey Eminence: a Study in Religion and Politics* (Harper, New York, 1941). Some aspects of rulership and advisers to rulers are well perceived in literary works, which add important dimensions to presently available scholarly studies from the outside. Good illustrations are the novels of C. P. Snow. Unavoidable realities of advisory staffs often neglected in textbooks are revealed by Christopher Buckley in *The White House Mess* (Knopf, New York, 1986), based on his personal experience.

53 Good literary insight into loneliness as an important feature of rulership is provided by some of Shakespeare's dramas focusing on rulers, not least *Hamlet*. Marguerite Yourcenar, *Memoirs of Hadrian* (Farrar, Straus & Giroux, New York, 1954), is thought-provoking.

54 See Alexander L. George and Juliette L. George, *Woodrow Wilson and Colonel House: a Personality Study* (Dover, New York, 1964); and Michael Medved, *The Shadow*

212   SYSTEMS OF ADVICE

Presidents: the Secret History of the Chief Executives and Their Top Aids (Times Books, New York, 1979).

55 Additional interesting 'adviser types' missing nowadays are: 'court Jews', see Stelma Stern, *The Court Jew: a Contribution to the History of the Period of Absolutism in Central Europe* (The Jewish Publication Society of America, Philadelphia, 1950); court artists, traces of whom survive in some countries as poets laureate, see Martin Warnke, *Hofkuenstler: Vorgeschichte des modernen Kuenstler* (DuMont, Cologne, 1985); and court historians, a role nowadays sometimes fulfilled by appointing suitably qualified 'advisers' who are expected to write about their experiences, as illustrated by Arthur M. Schlesinger Jnr in John F. Kennedy's White House.

56 For some aspects of this problem, see Randell B. Ripley, *Policy Research and the Clinical Relationship* (Mershon Center, Colombus, Oh. 1977), Position Papers in the Policy Sciences, No. 1, January.

57 It should be kept in mind that in most languages no separate words exist for 'politics' and 'policy'. See Arnold J. Heidenheimer, 'Politics, policy and police as concepts in the Western languages or: 'Why are the "Kontis" deprived?', Paper presented at the annual meeting of the American Political Science Association, Chicago, 1983.

58 It is interesting to ponder the importance of the mass media in the minds of rulers and of politicians in general. Ideally, one would like the mass media to serve as an important antidote to the defects of rulership, such as by reducing their ego-inflating tendency – somewhat comparable to the Roman slave who accompanied emperors during their Triumph parades, whispering all the time into their ears that they were only mortals. But it seems more likely that rulers are interested in the mass media 'coldly' as instruments of influence, and 'hotly' as a mirror on the wall, with negative feedback by the mass media being more often rejected as 'unreasonable hostility' than accepted as a serious input.

59 See, for example, Michael Baruch Grossman and Martha Joynt Jumar, *Portraying the President: the White House and the News Media* (Johns Hopkins University Press, Baltimore, Md, 1981).

60 As described, for instance, in Marcia Williams, *Inside Number 10* (Weidenfeld & Nicolson, London, 1972), ch. 9.

61 Relevant here is 'Philosophy comes down from the clouds', *The Economist*, 299, (26 April 1986), pp. 101–5. See also, Christopher Hodgkinson, *The Philosophy of Leadership* (Blackwell, Oxford, 1983).

62 Equivalent institutionalized functions in other cultures are illustrated by the 'Censorate' at the court of Chinese emperors and court prophets in biblical Israel.

63 On that concept in an applicable context, see Harry G. Frankfurt, 'Freedom of the will and the concept of a person', *Journal of Philosophy*, 68 (1971), pp. 5–20.

64 Interfaces between security intelligence and rulers demonstrate all the defects of rulership and all the contradictions within advising rulers, often in an extreme form. Taking into account the long and persistent history of intelligence failures and the unlimited resources devoted in vain in many countries to overcoming them, the difficulties of intelligence for rulers strongly support conjectures on the inherent nature of defects of rulership and expose the inadequacy of presently known ways of coping with them. Illuminating illustrations abound, for instance, in the outstanding volumes of F. H. Hinsley et al., *British Intelligence in the Second World War: Its*

Influence on Strategy and Operations (HMSO, London, vol. 1 (1979), vol. 2 (1981), vol. 3, pt 1 (1984).

65 See, for example, Roger B. Porter, *Presidential Decision Making: the Economic Policy Board* (Cambridge University Press, Cambridge, 1980). The diaries of a White House science adviser clearly bring out his 'teaching' functions, see George B. Kistiakowsky, *A Scientist at the White House* (Harvard University Press, Cambridge Mass., 1970).

66 Sir Solly Zuckerman dramatically illustrates this possibility.

67 Lord Rothschild is an example of a senior adviser who tried to 'educate' his masters and apparently enjoyed some successes, thanks to his special qualifications and his relationship with the ruler.

68 None of the offices of rulers I surveyed used available computer systems adequtely. In particular, in none of the cases where the matter could be checked did the ruler himself work with an interactive system in more than a perfunctory way. It should be added that a preliminary survey of mine failed to identify any serious attempts to design suitable 'work stations' for rulers, neither by governments nor by private computer and software manufacturers and developers. Security intelligence in some countries is advanced in some uses of computers for information storages and processes, but as far as I could find out not in modes meeting the particular needs of decision-making at the top level. Some crisis decision-making command and control systems are relatively advanced, but still lack essential elements, such as adequate handling of uncertainty.

69 The 'Cabinet Paper System' of the Canadian Privy Council Office well illustrates a sophisticated decision process management system.

70 See Andrew Gray and Bill Jenkins, 'Policy analysis in British central government: the experience of PAR', *Public Administration*, 60 (1982), pp. 429–50.

71 See, for example, John Ramson, *The Making of Conservative Party Policy: the Conservative Research Department since 1929* (Longman, London, 1980). Another illustration is supplied by the work of the Heritage Foundation in Washington DC and its impact on the first years of the Reagan administration. See Charles L. Heatherly (ed.), *Mandate for Leadership* (The Heritage Foundation, Washington, DC, 1981).

72 For attempts to expound a strategic approach for rulers, see Ben W. Heineman, Jnr and Curtis A. Hessler, *Memorandum for the President: a Strategic Approach to Domestic Affairs in the 1980s* (Random House, New York, 1980).

73 The Canadian PEMS illustrates a major effort in that direction. See Privy Council Office, *The Policy and Expenditure Management System* (Privy Council Office, Ottawa, 1981).

74 See Yehezkel Dror, *Public Policymaking Re-examined* (Transaction Books, New Brunswick, 1983), pp. 143–7; and Dror, *Policymaking Under Adversity*, especially pp. 144–7, 155–8.

75 In this connection it is interesting to note a multi-country field study which indicates that politicians are more important as innovators in contemporary Western democracies than civil servants. See Joel D. Aberbach et al., *Bureaucrats and Politicians in Western Democracies* (Harvard University Press, Cambridge, Mass., 1981).

76 See Yehezkel Dror, 'Think tanks: a new invention in government', in Carol H. Weiss and Allen H. Barton (eds), *Making Bureaucracy Work* (Sage, London, 1980).

77 See Yehezkel Dror, 'Required breakthroughs in think tanks', *Policy Sciences*, 16 (1984), pp. 199–225.

78 In most Western democracies no adequate university programmes exist for training professionals in knowledge urgently needed for upgrading advisory systems for top decision-making and similar staff functions. Public Policy Schools in the USA too need some major changes to meet the needs of top decision-making. See Yehezkel Dror, 'New advances in public policy teaching', *Journal of Policy Analysis and Management*, 2 (1983), pp. 449–54. In this connection, the whole notion of 'professional' advisers to top decision-makers needs reconsideration. It is stimulating here to apply Donald A. Schon, *The Reflective Practitioner: How Professionals Think In Action* (Basic Books, New York, 1983).

79 See, for example, Walter Williams, *Strangers and Brothers: the Dilemma of Organizing and Staffing the American Presidency* (Institute of Governmental Research, University of Washington, Seattle, 1981).

80 For a relevant case study, see Larry Berman, *The Office of Management and Budget and the Presidency, 1921–1979* (Princeton University Press, Princeton, NJ, 1979).

81 See, for example, Ezra N. Suleiman (ed.), *Bureaucrats and Policy Making*, Holmes & Meier, New York, 1984).

82 Another related need is for a code of ethics appropriate for advisers to rulers. For some relevant ideas, see Hugh J. Miser and Edward S. Quade (eds), *Handbook of Systems Analysis: Overview of Uses, Procedures, Applications, and Practice* (North-Holland, New York, 1985). pp. 316–25. In this connection the temptation for advisers to usurp the prerogatives of rulers and act in their stead without proper authorization should be mentioned. Goethe, himself a minister and adviser to a ruler, expressed this temptation well in a letter of 1789: 'Whoever devotes himself to government without being himself the Ruler, must be a philistine, or a cheat, or a fool' (free translation of the German).

83 See Jon Elster, *Ulysses and the Sirens: Studies in Rationality and Irrationality* (Cambridge University Press, Cambridge, 1979), pt II; and Thomas C. Schelling, *Choice and Consequence: Perspectives of an Errant Economist* (Harvard University Press, Cambridge, Mass., 1984), chs 2, 3.

84 To supplement the error-reducing, 'debugging' approach adopted in the main by this present paper, and as an alternative basis for the redesign of advisory systems to rulers, appropriate models of 'ultra-rationality' which fit the tasks and conditions of rulership are needed. See Dror, *Public Policymaking Re-examined*, pt IV; and Dror, *Policymaking under Adversity*, especially ch. 7. These need further advancement, on lines in part illustrated in n. 85 below.

85 Metaphorically, complex notions of 'intelligence' and 'mind structure' can serve as parts of relevant models, as presented, for instance, in Douglas R. Hofstadter, *Goedel, Escher, Bach: an Eternal Golden Braid* (Basic Books, New York, 1979); and Douglas R. Hofstadter, *Metamagical Themas: Questing for the Essence of Mind and Patter* (Basic Books, New York, 1985). In the absence of relevant models, which are both advanced and relevant to reality, even outstanding books proposing designs for advisory systems to rulers lean towards simplistic notions and ignore unavoidable

features of the environment of rulers. See, for example, Alexander George, *Presidential Decisionmaking in Foreign Policy: the Effective Use of Information and Advice* (Westview, Boulder, Colo., 1980).

86 In line with the broader requirement of 'meta-policy-making', that is policy-making on policy-making. See Dror, *Public Policymaking Re-examined*, especially pp. 160–1, 172–3.

Index